Albert Shaw of the *Review of Reviews*

Albert Shaw

of the *Review of Reviews*

* * * * *

An Intellectual Biography

Lloyd J. Graybar

The University Press of Kentucky

ISBN: 0-8131-1300-8

Library of Congress Catalog Card Number: 73-80464

Copyright © 1974 by The University Press of Kentucky

A statewide cooperative scholarly publishing agency
serving Berea College, Centre College of Kentucky,
Eastern Kentucky University, Georgetown College,
Kentucky Historical Society, Kentucky State University,
Morehead State University, Murray State University,
Northern Kentucky State College, Transylvania University,
University of Kentucky, University of Louisville, and
Western Kentucky University.

Editorial and Sales Offices: Lexington, Kentucky 40506

To the memory of M and M

Contents

Acknowledgments

In the course of this work, which has taken the better part of a decade, many archivists and librarians have aided me, but my thanks go particularly to the now retired Robert W. Hill and his colleagues in the Manuscripts Division of the New York Public Library and to the many helpful members on the staff of the John Grant Crabbe Library at Eastern Kentucky University. Mr. Dale B. Terry, formerly the registrar at Grinnell College, and various members of the staff of Grinnell's Burling Library have answered numerous letters requesting information about Albert Shaw's undergraduate achievements at Iowa College. Almost invariably they have been able to supply the information I sought, and then some.

Intellectually I wish to thank Professor Eric L. McKitrick and the late Professor Richard Hofstadter of Columbia University who encouraged me to initiate this study as a doctoral dissertation and to keep at it even when I had my doubts about it. In one stage of revision after another many friends were of invaluable assistance. Whether reading all or portions of the manuscript each had thoughtful suggestions to offer. Among these friends are: Professors James M. Banner, Jr., of Princeton University, Joseph O. Baylen of Georgia State University, Daniel Leab of Columbia University, Gerald W. McFarland of the University of Massachusetts, and Glen Kleine, Bert M. Mutersbaugh, and Doris Sutton, all of Eastern Kentucky University.

A singularly large debt is due Mr. Albert Shaw, Jr., who without trying to influence my opinions on these matters shared with me on numerous occasions recollections of his father and of his own considerable role in the management of the *Review of Reviews* during its final two decades. His loan of a full set of the *Review of Reviews* greatly facilitated my research. Pictures and other memorabilia were provided by Mr. Shaw and by Mrs. Jonnie Robinson of Shandon, Ohio. Dean Theodore Peterson of the College of Communications of the University of Illinois, Professor Bruce H. Westley of the School of Journalism at the University of Kentucky, and Professor Herbert Shapiro of the University of Cincinnati clarified some of the intricacies of the periodical publishing industry for me. Professor Arthur S. Link, editor of the Papers of Woodrow Wilson, took a continuing interest in this project and was of much help on several occasions.

For financial assistance I am indebted to the American Philosophical Society, which granted me the funds needed to begin the final stages of this study, and to Eastern Kentucky University, which was consistently generous in its backing. Of the many university officials whose support was needed to secure this aid, Dean Frederic Ogden of the College of Arts and Sciences deserves a special note of thanks.

The following editors have been obliging in permitting me to reprint in revised form materials first published as articles: Professor William D. Metz, for "Albert Shaw's Search for the Ideal City," *The Historian,* XXXIV (May 1972), 421-35; Professor Guido H. Stempel III, for "Albert Shaw and the Founding of the *Review of Reviews,* 1891-97," *Journalism Quarterly,* XLIX (Winter 1972), 692-97, 716; and Mrs. Helen M. Thurston, for "Albert Shaw's Ohio Youth," *Ohio History,* LXXIV (Winter 1965), 29-34.

I also wish to thank the women who did most of the typing and who perforce showed great patience in deciphering my handwriting: Mrs. Cynthia B. Napoleon and Mrs. Shirley Wheeler of Bellows Falls, Vermont, and Miss Elsanna Fisel and Mrs. Pauletta Perkins, of Richmond, Kentucky.

In my dedication I have expressed my gratitude and devotion to the two people who in their own special ways contributed the most to the successful completion of this work. For whatever merits it has I am indebted to the people named above as well as to the many others who furnished their assistance at different times during the past several years. For the faults that remain I am solely responsible.

Preface

The contributions of Albert Shaw (1857-1947) to the progressive movement were substantial and dated from its very beginnings. Armed with a doctorate in history and political economy from the Johns Hopkins University and motivated by a desire to put his expertise to socially productive use, he became involved in the municipal reform movement of the 1880s and 1890s. Through his influential writings he helped shift the focus of reform away from the prevailing laissez faire liberalism and toward the activism of Bull Moose progressivism.

For a generation thereafter, Shaw was deeply involved in reform, taking as much of a personal role in it as his busy career in journalism would permit, keeping in close touch with its political spokesmen like Theodore Roosevelt and Albert Beveridge, championing their efforts in his periodical, the *Review of Reviews*. In it and in the several books he wrote, he asked many of the questions that troubled thoughtful Americans in the years that surrounded the turn of the century. How could the difficulties that attended the amazing growth of cities be overcome? What did the eclipse of privately owned industries by gigantic trusts and holding companies mean? Did labor have a right to organize? Should an attempt be made to preserve rural culture? What was America's mission to the world? Should politics be responsive to the people or to those who sought special favors?

In answering such questions Shaw was influenced by humanitarian feelings, by his associations as a student at Iowa College and the Johns Hopkins University with such scholars as Jesse Macy and Richard T. Ely, and by the public point of view his ownership of a nationally circulated magazine gave him. His fealty—until 1912 and after 1916—to the national Republican party also ought to be considered as an element in his thought. Particularly noticeable, however, in his responses is a concern with the health of the nation. Its soundness required the well-being of the people, the subordination of selfish interests to the general good, the preservation of America's traditional values in a time of flux. To attain these ends he was willing to see concepts of property sharply revised and the federal balance altered at the expense of the states.

Progressivism, of course, was a heterogenous movement, and in his thinking Shaw was most characteristic of that small group of reformers whose ranks included Theodore Roosevelt, Albert Beveridge, and Herbert Croly, all of whom have become known as New Nationalists. But he was representative of a much larger number of progressives in that he recurrently posed the question of what the industrialization of America meant.

Until 1916 Shaw did not have to choose between reform and nationalism; previously they had reenforced each other. But when faced with a choice between supporting Woodrow Wilson, who seemed stronger on domestic issues, or Charles Evans Hughes, who appeared to have the sounder ideas on foreign policy, Shaw decided, as did Roosevelt and Beveridge, to rejoin the Republican party and back Hughes. Unlike his two close friends, who died in 1919 and 1927 respectively, Shaw lived a full generation beyond the heyday of progressivism. Throughout the 1920s Shaw still thought of himself as a progressive and continued to support certain reform measures, but he grew increasingly estranged from the urban liberalism that emerged as the dominant trend in reform after World War I. Largely for the sake of national unity he upheld the program of the New Deal for an entire year, but by early 1934 he decided that he could no longer support the administration of Franklin Roosevelt. The New Deal, he declared, was corrupt and in turn was corrupting millions of Americans. The people were being coddled as well as bribed. Unions and other lobbies were advancing their selfish aims, heedless of the general good. However he expressed them, Shaw's jeremiads were but variations on a theme: Americans had forsaken the ways of their forefathers and, unless they re-

dedicated themselves to the ancestral verities, they faced a
future blighted not only by economic depression but by
spiritual bankruptcy.

Shaw the reformer and nationalist cannot be separated from
Shaw the editor. In any event his editorial career merits study
on its own. I have paid much attention to it, trying to show
both his standing in journalism and the ways in which his
professional concerns interacted with his attitude toward
public issues. But I have emphasized the latter. He believed
that his profession carried with it the obligation to stand for
the right things. Accordingly I have tried to show why he
supported the causes he did to the exclusion of others that
were perhaps more worthy than he realized.

1

Buckeye and Hawkeye, 1857-1881

An Ohioan by birth, Albert Shaw remained conscious of his western background throughout his life. The theme of the West held a recurrent fascination for him. Although he recognized that the settlement of the West had been marred by the thoughtless exploitation of the environment, and cogently insisted that such waste could not be tolerated in the America of his day, he was even more impressed by the positive legacy of the pioneers and judged his contemporaries by their standards of energy, patriotism, and resourcefulness.

Shaw acquired his abiding respect for the pioneers during his youth in Paddy's Run, Ohio. Born in 1857, he was old enough to have had a personal acquaintance with some of the men who had pioneered Ohio two generations before. Like several members of his own family, they had come to Ohio from the older states to the east and had made it the focus of what he called a "more perfectly blended Americanism."[1]

Albert's grandfather, Hezekiah Shaw, was a typically adventuresome frontiersman. Born in Pennsylvania in 1783 of Ulster-Scot derivation, he moved to Kentucky with his parents in 1795, then as a young man rode circuit for the Methodist church in Louisiana, Tennessee, and Mississippi at a time when much of these areas was still wilderness, and finally settled down near Paddy's Run in 1811 to combine farming with the itinerant preaching that remained his calling. Later that year he married Rebecca Halstead, a petite young woman who with her parents and brother Griffin had moved to Ohio from North Carolina in 1804. The log cabin in which Hezekiah and Rebecca Shaw lived during the first years of their marriage was a reminder both of their modest circumstances and of the area's recent settlement.[2]

Four children, a daughter and three sons, came of their marriage. Griffin, the youngest son, studied medicine in Ohio, settled in Indiana, and in 1843, at the age of twenty-six, married a Susan Colburn by whom he had two children, Griffin, Jr., and Lucy. After his wife died, Doctor Shaw was married again, in 1852, to Susan Fisher of Chester, Vermont. Of old New England stock, Susan Fisher had been reared in the Congregational tradition and educated near home before contracting to go west to teach. The family of four moved to Ohio in 1854 in order to escape a malaria epidemic which had already infected Shaw's two older children and claimed the life of the first born of his second marriage. Two children were born to the Shaws in Paddy's Run: Mary and—on July 23, 1857—the baby of the family, Albert.[3]

The community in which Albert Shaw was born and raised was a crossroads village, situated in Butler County in southwestern Ohio six miles from the Indiana line and twenty-two miles from Cincinnati. It had once carried the exotic nickname of Bagdad and would receive the mundane name of Shandon

[1] Most of the information on Shaw's youth comes from his unpublished autobiographical study, "Ohio as I Remember" (1941, hereafter referred to as the "Ohio MS"). Prior to depositing it in the New York Public Library (which already had possession of the extensive Albert Shaw Manuscripts), Albert Shaw, Jr., made a copy of it available to me. I have numbered the pages consecutively within each chapter and shall refer to them in that way. For the life of Hezekiah Shaw see Shaw, "Ohio MS," ch. 4, pp. 14-26.

[2] William Leon Halstead, *The Story of the Halsteads of the United States* (Ann Arbor, Mich.: privately published, 1934), pp. 84, 97. Rebecca's maiden name was actually Holstead, a variant spelling that had been used for generations. The earlier spelling, Halstead, was resumed by the Ohio branch of the family. Ibid., pp. 53, 70-79, 97-101.

[3] Shaw, "Ohio MS," ch. 7, pp. 2-9, 17-20; Shaw, "Preface to Life of Murat Halstead" (unpublished typescript, 1941), p. 8, Shaw MSS. For a study of Susan Fisher Shaw's ancestry see Philip Fisher, *The Fisher Genealogy: Record of the Descendants of Joshua, Anthony and Cornelius Fisher of Dedham, Mass., 1636-1640* (Everett, Mass.: Massachusetts Publishing Co., 1898), pp. 6-10, 18-21, 32-33, 51-52, 75, 112-13, 188-89, 287, 378. Anthony Fisher arrived at Boston on the ship *Rose* in 1637 and settled at Dedham. Halsteads had also stopped at Dedham, but only briefly before they moved to Concord, Mass. (Shaw, "Ohio MS," ch. 1, p. 12; W. L. Halstead, *Story of the Halsteads*, pp. 85, 97).

in 1893, but the Paddy's Run of Albert Shaw's boyhood was a title both quaint and descriptive. The creek of that name rippled by on its way to the Great Miami River, its banks shaded with the foliage of the pawpaw, persimmon, maple, and oak. Prosperous farms extended back into the surrounding countryside. Even in the village it was possible to raise vegetables and keep livestock, as the Shaws themselves did. The interests of Albert's father were in fact quite diversified, for besides being a doctor and a farmer of sorts, Griffin Shaw owned a store, speculated in real estate, and mixed in politics. In Indiana he had once served in the state legislature. His brick home in the center of Paddy's Run served as a focal point for political rallies.[4]

Among the earliest of Albert's memories were those relating to the Civil War. Most of the settlers in and around Paddy's Run were Union-loving, but a considerable number of southerners had migrated to the area, and there seems to have been a certain amount of "Butternut" sympathy as well.[5] Griffin Shaw himself was a former Douglas Democrat who transferred his allegiance to the Republicans with the outbreak of the secession crisis. He thus joined the party that his abolitionist father had undoubtedly preferred and to which his wife was already devoted. As a reward for his new loyalties, Doctor Shaw received an appointment to the Butler County conscription board in 1863. The additional burden of his new duties soon undermined his health. When he was afflicted later that year with a stomach ailment, probably appendicitis, complications set in, and in his weakened condition he soon died. He

[4] *A History and Biographical Cyclopaedia of Butler County, Ohio* (Cincinnati: Western Biographical Publishing Co., 1882), pp. 428-31, map facing p. 642; *Tenth Census of the United States: 1880. Population* (Washington: Government Printing Office, 1883), p. 301; Stephen Riggs Williams, *The Saga of the Paddy's Run* (Oxford, Ohio: n.p., 1945), pp. 15-20, 83-88; Shaw, "Ohio MS," ch. 6, p. 4, ch. 12, pp. 4-6, ch. 13, pp. 13-14, 38-39, 42-44. Also see Murat Halstead's "Paddy's Run Papers," which appeared weekly in the *Cincinnati Commercial-Gazette* from May 4 to August 16, 1895, for a charming description of Paddy's Run in a previous generation.

[5] James E. Campbell, *Butler County in the Civil War* (Hamilton, Ohio: n.p., 1915), pp. 6-7; Shaw, "Ohio MS," ch. 13, pp. 42-43.

had given his life for his country, the Shaws liked to think.[6]

The loss of his father (just three years after the death of Hezekiah Shaw) affected Albert deeply. "I was only six years old when my father died," he recalled, "and nobody will ever know how bereft and forlorn I felt as I grew older and realized the need of a father's direction and general backing."[7]

To compensate, he turned elsewhere for guidance: to Roger Williams, an older friend who became in effect a father-surrogate, and to his devoted mother with whom he developed an extremely close relationship. Albert also spent much time with various Halstead relatives. He saw a good deal of his granduncle, Colonel Griffin Halstead, and came to respect both him and his brilliant son, Murat. By the time Albert was born, the latter had left home and was already gaining recognition as a shrewd young newspaperman. Destined to achieve national recognition in the 1870s as a spokesman for the Liberal Republican cause and as editor of the *Cincinnati Commercial,* he furnished his young kinsman with an excellent example. Although Albert did not have the opportunity to see his cousin as much as he would have liked, he nevertheless admired him for his principled Republicanism no less than for his high professional standards.[8]

In their everyday routines Albert and the others in the family were able to adjust themselves to Griffin Shaw's death. The children got along well with each other and with their mother. Money caused no substantial problems: a house, a farm, several parcels of land, and the store, the last of which Susan Shaw soon sold—all had been left by Doctor Shaw. These

[6] W. L. Halstead, *The Story of the Halsteads,* p. 97; Shaw, "Preface to Life of Murat Halstead," pp. 8-9; Shaw to Mrs. Elaine Jones Fitton, Jan. 8, 1924, Shaw MSS.

[7] Shaw to Murat Halstead, Feb. 18, 1901, Shaw MSS.

[8] Shaw, "Ohio MS," ch. 15, pp. 13-19. For a brief description of Halstead's distinguished career see Albert Shaw, "Murat Halstead, Journalist," *Review of Reviews* (Amer. ed.), XIII (1896), 439-43. Until 1929 the *Review of Reviews* was paginated consecutively throughout each volume. Thereafter each issue was separately paginated. For the sake of brevity references to the *Review* will therefore use only volume number, year of publication, and the appropriate page numbers. Starting with the January 1929 issue of the *Review* months will also be given.

were worth at least $10,000, and there was always enough for pleasant trips to Cincinnati for the theatre, for concerts, or shopping, even lengthy visits to maternal relatives in Vermont and Iowa. In the 1860s and 1870s these were experiences far beyond the ken of the average boy of rural upbringing.[9]

Paddy's Run was a predominantly Welsh community, and the tenor of the place, in Shaw's words, was one "of intelligence promoted by good schools, and of social conduct influenced by churches."[10] Albert attended a two-room frame elementary school where, as he remembered, he had the special privilege of carrying the water buckets from the pump. His teachers were methodical, stressing spelling, the "3 R's," and memorization of selections from McGuffey's Readers. Thus were emphasized the values of sobriety, morality, piety, and industry that were his heritage from his mother who reared her children in her own tradition of Congregationalism. As the years passed, Greek and Latin, algebra and geometry, English stylistics, readings in Story's *Commentaries on the Constitution,* and various works of history formed the ascending levels of his education. In leisure hours he read *Robinson Crusoe, Tom Brown's School Days,* Scott, Dickens, Twain, the seafaring tales of Elisha Kent Kane, and the biographies of Jared Sparks.[11]

Yet Albert Shaw, while a conscientious and exceptionally able student, was hardly a bookworm and found ample time to participate in the various activities of a rural life. A share of his spare time he spent in play. Swimming, skating, singing, snowball fighting, and baseball were all great favorites. Young Shaw also found occupation on neighbors' farms, where he

9 Shaw, "Ohio MS," ch. 8, p. 1; ch. 13, pp. 13-14, 27-37, 53; interview with Albert Shaw, Jr., May 10, 1962; property inventory recorded in the Butler County Courthouse, Hamilton, Ohio, SS #02661.

10 The town's spirit was one of morality rather than of bitter sectarianism. All major Protestant denominations were readily accepted into the local Congregational church. Shaw, "Shandon Centennial," *Ohio Archaeological and Historical Quarterly,* XIV (Jan. 1905), 6-7; Shaw, "Ohio MS," ch. 14, pp. 12-15; interview with Albert Shaw, Jr., May 10, 1962. On McGuffey's Readers see Richard D. Mosier, *Making the American Mind: Social and Moral Ideas in the McGuffey Readers* (New York: King's Crown Press, 1947).

11 Shaw, "Ohio MS," ch. 9, pp. 30, 44-48, ch. 11, pp. 39-45, ch. 12, pp. 14-27, ch. 14, p. 7.

worked on some weekends and during the summer. Moral censure was attached to the idler.[12]

The moral nature of the Shaw household and of the community was made evident in other ways. In 1874 a temperance crusade swept Paddy's Run. Mrs. Shaw and most Republicans—members of the "God-and-Morality Party"—embraced the cause. Albert observed the movement closely, attending several temperance meetings himself and taking a keen interest in his mother's activities as a picket at various local saloons. Too gentle really to enjoy picketing, she regarded commitment to such an admirable cause as a moral obligation and kept at it until temperance triumphed. Joy reigned in Paddy's Run when the most conspicuous "saloonatic" capitulated.[13]

Politics engendered similar enthusiasm among the townspeople. As a small boy Albert had been exposed to the new Republican ardor of his father and the more settled faith of his mother, and impressions have a way of becoming durable. At first his political credo (if such it may be called) was summed up in the notion that to be a Republican was a good thing—and fun. His active experience in politics dated from the age of seven when he first banged his drum in behalf of Abe Lincoln and the Union; four years later he was a regular participant in torchlight parades.[14]

Shaw had drawn even closer to his mother in these years, for his small circle of intimates had been suddenly and shockingly reduced. Griff, his half brother, died; Roger Williams, his closest friend, passed away shortly thereafter in 1873. Actually the loss of a brother was the lesser tragedy, for Griff had been away from home during most of the decade prior to his death. But the passing of Williams—able in scholarship, strong of character, and warm of personality—had

12 Ibid., ch. 11, p. 19, ch. 12, pp. 5-14, ch. 13, pp. 5-7; Shaw diary (Jan. 1 to Apr. 28, 1874), Jan. 1, 2, 17, Feb. 13, Shaw MSS.

13 The prohibition episode can be followed in the "Ohio MS," ch. 8, pp. 40-45, ch. 13, p. 48, and in Lloyd J. Graybar, ed., "The Whiskey War at Paddy's Run: Excerpts from a Diary of Albert Shaw," *Ohio History*, LXXV (Winter 1966), 48-54, 72-74.

14 The activities of the young Republican drummer are related in Shaw, "Ohio MS," ch. 13, pp. 49-50, 55.

brought profound grief. It was Williams who had shown Albert the happy times of a good baseball game; he had also given his young friend much good advice, along with a personal example which had a lot to do with Shaw's going into journalism. Williams (whose brother-in-law was Albert's teacher) had even planned the program of education that Shaw should follow in high school. The study of English, with the practical thought of a journalistic career evidently in Williams's mind, was to be stressed. Williams himself, while still attending Miami University in nearby Oxford, had purchased in 1870 the *Citizen,* the weekly newspaper of that college community. There Albert, to his delight, had every chance to observe the operation of the presses and the many activities of a newspaper. The example of Shaw's famous cousin, Murat Halstead, was not uninspiring. But this more tangible contact with an actual newspaper, and with an editor whom he worshipped, impressed him profoundly. Williams's death grieved people all over the county, and no one felt it more than Shaw.[15]

In 1874 Susan Shaw decided there was nothing to hold her in Paddy's Run: Lucy was now married to a lawyer, Richard R. Stephenson, and living in Indiana;[16] and Albert was approaching the close of his high school days. Mrs. Shaw's intention was to move to Grinnell, Iowa, where she had numerous relatives (most of whom lived on farms in the vicinity) and where Albert could attend Iowa College. After a delay of some months during which time he received tutoring in the subjects Iowa College freshmen were taking, the Shaws moved to Grinnell in the spring of 1875.[17]

In appearance Grinnell presented a sharp contrast to Paddy's Run, for it lacked the rural facade of the Ohio village. Its population was some twenty-four hundred, about eight times that of Paddy's Run, and it impressed Shaw as a small city "in

15 Ibid., ch. 10, pp. 1-46. Shaw, it is interesting to note, devoted entire chapters to his father and to Williams.

16 Shaw's admiration for Stephenson, an able lawyer and later a judge and an implacable foe of corrupt courthouse rings in Indiana, is mentioned in ibid., ch. 9, pp. 41-46.

17 Ibid., ch. 12, pp. 1-2, 20; Shaw diary, Jan. 16, 1874.

which the typical family did not keep cows; did not feed pigs; did not make and mend chicken-coops; did not prune trees, or gather a variety of fruits in season."[18]

But the transition to life in Iowa was not as difficult as it might have seemed, for Grinnell had certain characteristics which were bound to appeal to the Shaws. Located in Poweshiek County in east central Iowa, a bit over one-fourth of the way between Des Moines and the Mississippi River town of Davenport, it had been founded in 1854 by Josiah Grinnell, the young man to whom Horace Greeley supposedly said "Go West" and who, as Stewart Holbrook puts it, had "arrived in Iowa with a complete stock of carefully tended Yankee notions of the intellectual sort." Thus tradition gave it a pleasing moral tone. The "most typical New England community that has grown up west of the Mississippi River" was Shaw's apt description of it. Local pundits simply called it "Saint's Rest."[19]

Iowa College, renamed Grinnell in 1909, stemmed from the same traditions. Opened in 1848 in Davenport by Calvinist missionaries from Andover, the college was moved to Grinnell a decade later. Legend has it that orthodoxy reached its pinnacle under the presidency of George Magoun, who ruled from 1865 to 1884 over the college's two large buildings and one hundred students (give or take half the number in some years). The lore attached to his name is impressive. Leonine in manner (with a beard to match), Magoun held his students to an imposing set of regulations. One commandment, redolent of New England traditions, stipulated attendance at religious observances every morning and evening and twice again on Sundays. The prohibitions were numerous and resembled the rules of seventeenth-century Harvard.[20] When, for example,

[18] Shaw, "Ohio MS," ch. 12, pp. 4-5.

[19] Josiah Grinnell, *Men and Events of Forty Years: Autobiographical Reminiscences of an Active Career from 1850 to 1890* (Boston: D. Lothrop Co., 1891), pp. 86-87, 220; Stewart Holbrook, *The Yankee Exodus: An Account of Migration from New England* (New York: Macmillan, 1950), p. 138; Leonard Fletcher Parker, *History of Poweshiek County, Iowa,* 2 vols. (Chicago: S. J. Clarke Publishing Co., 1911), I, 75-80, 355-57, 362-74; Susan Shaw to Shaw, July 23, 1877, Shaw to William Dean Howells, May 31, 1899, both in Shaw MSS.

one professor was asked how he managed without the opera and theatre, he replied sardonically, "You forget that we have the church and the sewing society."[21]

But perhaps life was not that sterile. The smallness of the school and the cordiality of the personal relationships that generally prevailed among the few dozen students and eight or ten faculty members did much to offset the barrenness of the code. Shaw, for one, had no complaints about it. Although he undoubtedly missed the chance to attend the theatre, as he had previously been able to do, he was able to keep himself profitably and enjoyably occupied without joining the sewing society.[22]

A handsome and personable youth six feet in height, Shaw fitted well into life at Iowa College. He participated in the available extracurricular activities; he sang, debated, served on the editorial board of the college monthly—the *News Letter*—played on the struggling baseball team (and according to gossip charmed the ladies as well). He excelled as a student. His schedule which would lead to the A.B. degree was weighted with Latin and Greek, Bible and Scriptural history, and assorted science courses but also included scatterings in belles lettres, philosophy, logic, rhetoric, modern languages, the Constitution of the United States, and Magoun's formidable "pets" based on Noah Porter's *Human Intellect* and Mark Hopkins's *Evidences of Christianity*.[23]

20 John Scholte Nollen, *Grinnell College* (Iowa City: State Historical Society of Iowa, 1953), pp. 43-50, 70-72.

21 Ibid., p. 72.

22 Ibid., pp. 92-95; Harry Downer, "Speaking of Old Grinnell" (unpublished typescript in Grinnell College Library, 1937), pp. 2, 3, 17, 18, 23, 26, 29; Shaw, Foreword to Katherine Macy Noyes, ed., *Jesse Macy: An Autobiography* (Springfield, Ill. and Baltimore: C. C. Thomas, 1933), pp. xi-xii; Helen Whitcomb to Shaw, Sept. 4, 1877, Shaw MSS.

23 Nollen, *Grinnell College*, pp. 70-71; Downer, "Speaking of Old Grinnell," pp. 9, 43-44; Forrest Chapman, "Albert Shaw," *Verse and Fiction*, III (1921), 31; Maurice Friedland, "Albert Shaw, Grinnellian," *Grinnell Magazine*, I (Apr. 1917), 195-98; W. G. Ray, "History of Baseball," *Grinnell Review*, XII (Dec. 1916), 50-55; *Grinnell Herald*, Nov. 23, 1880; transcript of Shaw's record, 1875-79; Whitcomb to Shaw, Sept. 4, 25, 1877, Mary Shaw Fisher to Shaw, July 9, 1880, Annie Merrill to Shaw, July 9, 1880, Sam Merrill to Shaw, Jan. 28, 1882, Sept. 16, 1883, all in Shaw MSS.

The chief academic impress that Shaw received was not from his formal classwork but through his relationship with one faculty member, Jesse Macy. Macy would one day win professional acclaim as a pioneering political scientist, but when Shaw first met him he was bogged down in administrative work and in teaching whatever had to be taught. Nevertheless, a reputation as a fine teacher and human being was already his. The solicitude that he tendered Shaw was characteristic. It seems that Shaw, having arrived in Grinnell in April 1875, wished to join the freshman class which had already completed two of the year's three terms. His request was irregular, but he would be admitted provided he could pass a series of special examinations. Macy was to examine him in English and American history. Shaw was worried, having already decided that "he wouldn't be thought anything of in Grinnell." Macy suggested they go for a walk and on returning to town informed Shaw that he had passed the examination. Macy "had so directed the conversation," Shaw recalled, "as to take me off my guard and draw me out upon a variety of matters having to do with the significance of historical occurrences and situations, rather than with mere facts or dates. It was his object to find out whether, in my eighteenth year, I had learned to think." It was the start of an enduring and cordial relationship in which Macy shared with his new protégé the enthusiasm he was then developing for historical and governmental studies.[24]

Albert Shaw normally would have been graduated in 1878, but during the spring of 1877 he had left college temporarily. Shaw and his mother had decided that some time spent at travel and different types of work would give him a broader outlook on life than he had been able to gain in his sheltered existence in Paddy's Run and Grinnell. He spent several months at a variety of pursuits: touring the urban East (the previous year he had visited the Dakota frontier), undertaking

[24] Mary Shaw Fisher to Shaw, Apr. 8, 1882, Shaw MSS; Shaw, Foreword to Noyes, ed., *Jesse Macy*, p. xii. For the fullest discussion of Macy see John Park Coleman, "In Pursuit of Harmony: A Study of the Thought of Jesse Macy" (Diss., State University of Iowa, 1968).

independent study, teaching in a one-room Iowa school, even selling farm machinery and observing farm life. During this time, Shaw much later concluded, he had "adjusted [his] points of view, accepted the universe with cheerful but sober optimism, and adopted creeds of life that have never been seriously changed."[25]

Following his graduation in the summer of 1879, Shaw made another lengthy trip east, going first to New England by way of Chicago and Montreal. At Boston, as at several other places, he visited a printing establishment, in this case the Riverside Press. The museums and the standard historical scenes also held their share of interest, the grave of Charles Sumner moving him to make the lengthiest jottings in his diary.[26]

Shaw next visited New York where he found much to do. He met Whitelaw Reid probably to reminisce about Butler County (where Reid had attended college) and to observe the operation of Reid's great paper, the *Tribune;* he attended concerts; and he acted like a tourist and rode on the "el."[27] One Sunday he went to Jerry McAuley's prayer meeting for derelicts. The sight of the good being done at this Water Street Mission moved him to note: "I never was so impressed with a sense of Christ's power in the world and the sure ultimate triumph of his cause."[28]

On his return home in mid-November Shaw acquired a half-interest in the *Grinnell Herald.* Samuel A. Cravath, who had owned the paper since 1872, more than once offered partnerships to qualified Iowa College men, probably from the desire to have an industrious and responsible associate. Nor-

[25] Shaw, "Iowa Speech" (address at Grinnell, June 1934); Charles Sumner Little to Shaw, July 9, Aug. 2, 1876, Mary Shaw to Shaw, July 20, Aug. 19, 1876, Whitcomb to Shaw, July 15, Aug. 30, Sept. 4, 1877, all in Shaw MSS. The contemporary evidence, as far as it goes, coincides with Shaw's recollection in this 1934 speech of what he did during his time off. However, he mentions that his leave lasted an entire year, while his college transcript indicates that he divided this free time into periods of several months each.

[26] *Grinnell Herald,* July 4, 1879; Shaw diary (Aug. 25 to Nov. 10, 1879), Shaw MSS; the Boston visit is covered by the entries of Sept. 17, 18, 20.

[27] Ibid., Oct. 2-4.

[28] Ibid., Oct. 5.

mally he charged only a modest price; and if one man left him, the next graduating class might have a replacement at hand.[29] The opportunity was just what Shaw needed. A few months earlier he had written his cousin, Murat Halstead, about a job on the *Cincinnati Commercial*. Instead he received the advice: "If you want to be a journalist learn as fast as possible all things that you can master. Select a country paper and write for it. Keep on writing whether your articles are published or not. Do not ask pay. Describe events. Discuss questions. Familiarize yourself with the details. Seek an acquaintance with the editor." Joining the *Herald* as junior editor thus allowed Shaw to learn the newspaper business from Cravath as well as to continue his studies with Jesse Macy (whch led to the awarding of a master's degree in 1882).[30] The visits he had made to newspapers and printing plants on his recent trip enabled him to bring some knowledge of the latest methods to the job.

The *Herald,* a biweekly Republican paper, was representative for its time and place. Its four pages were filled largely with local news and advertising, but there was room for some discussion of state, national, and foreign developments. Most of the writing, recalled printer Bill Day, was done by Shaw.[31] Editorially the *Herald* carried weight during an election campaign. As one of the larger centers between Des Moines and the Mississippi River towns, Grinnell was politically strategic,

29 Downer, "Memories of Old Grinnell," pp. 34, 37; *Grinnell Herald,* Nov. 18, 1879; S. A. Cravath, "The *Herald:* Its History, Appliances, Owners, Abodes, Associate Publications, etc.," ibid., Apr. 1, 1900; W. H. Day, "Albert Shaw as a Fellow Printer, Knew Him from '75-'85," ibid., June 1, 1934. Family tradition has it that Shaw purchased his share of the paper with a legacy from his father. Interview with Albert Shaw, Jr., Feb. 10, 1965.

30 Halstead to Shaw, May 4, 1879, copy in the possession of Albert Shaw, Jr.; Shaw to Halstead, Oct. 24, 1899, Shaw to Lucy Shaw Stephenson, Aug. 6, 1912, both in Shaw MSS; K. M. Noyes, ed., *Jesse Macy,* p. 86.

31 Cravath, "The *Herald*"; Day, "Shaw as a Fellow Printer"; Shaw notebook (only a few scattered pages from an undated book of editorial notes for use in the *Herald*), Shaw MSS. The *Herald* for these years is available on microfilm at the Stewart Public Library, Grinnell. Helpful in obtaining a perspective of the various Iowa newspapers is William J. Petersen, *The Pageant of the Press: A Survey of 125 Years of Iowa Journalism, 1836-1961* (Iowa City: State Historical Society of Iowa, 1962).

and the presence there of numerous merchants, a branch of the Farmers' Alliance, a Grange store, and a WCTU chapter made for several shadings of opinion. The *Herald* as a moderate Republican paper had to deal with opponents on all flanks. The Democracy was easy for Shaw to score: he had only to wave the bloody shirt of Civil War memories. The Greenbackers posed considerable difficulty, for Grinnell was located in the Congressional bailiwick of their popular spokesman, General James Weaver, and they were temporarily able to capture the support of town patriarch Josiah Grinnell. But Shaw believed that the principal Greenback doctrine of monetary inflation was wrong and said so, either criticizing it himself or occasionally turning the chore over to the more informed Jesse Macy.[32]

The *Herald* also had to contend with Republicans of the spoils-minded Stalwart faction—and with zealous prohibitionists. An advocate of honest government and civil service reform, Shaw was too much of a reformer to please Republican spoilsmen and too discriminating in his approach to the liquor question to suit rabid prohibitionists.[33] Still a teetotaler himself, Shaw explained his position on it this way: "Under local option, Grinnell had always been a temperance town. Most of our fellow-citizens were total abstainers. Some of us did not believe, however, that State-wide prohibition could be enforced in the beer-drinking towns, largely German, lying along the Mississippi and Missouri Rivers. Neither," he continued, "did we believe that a police regulation like prohibition ought to be forced into the Constitution. . . . Mr. Macy held the same view; and I as a young editor wrote articles on this subject that made me temporarily unpopular with the militant prohibition leaders."[34]

In November 1881 Shaw announced that he would take a

[32] For the political situation see *Grinnell Herald,* Nov. 5, 1878, June 25, Nov. 11, 1880, Sept. 30, Nov. 8, 1881; Parker, *History of Poweshiek County,* I, 150-52, 352-53.

[33] *Grinnell Herald,* June 11, Aug. 6, 31, Sept. 3, 17, Oct. 28, 1880; Susan Shaw to Shaw, Sept. 8, 1883, Shaw MSS.

[34] Shaw, Foreword to Noyes, ed., *Jesse Macy,* pp. xiv-xv.

leave of absence from the *Herald* to enter graduate work at the Johns Hopkins University. What prompted his decision to undertake advanced education at this time is not clear, but something may be inferred from Shaw's personal and business situation. Never a robust person, Shaw had given much of himself during his two years on the *Herald*. His position not only required that he write editorials and other copy but also that he gather news, keep accounts, solicit advertising, and assist with a job press. Tired of this sort of work, which he was finding intellectually stifling and losing faith in his ability to keep up with the routine, Shaw must have been receptive to change. The decision to pursue advanced scholarship followed easily. Although a spacious range of professional alternatives from the ministry to law and even politics were his, his commitment to journalism was too firm to be abandoned altogether. A graduate education would furnish a needed change and some answers to editorial questions having to do with political and economic matters that had been puzzling Shaw. There was also the example of Roger Williams, who had gone from the *Citizen* in Oxford, Ohio, to Göttingen University on his way, he had hoped, to the higher ranks of the newspaper profession.[35] Shaw wrote Herbert Baxter Adams, the head of historical and political studies at Johns Hopkins, to explain his position: that he was a young editor who wished to attend some lecture courses which might help him to understand better the issues of the day. Adams warned Shaw that his students did not pursue such limited aims, but were undertaking "original research" and advised him not to come. Shaw claimed to have been frightened by the mention of research, but he decided to go anyhow.[36]

---

[35] *Grinnell Herald*, Nov. 28, 1881; Shaw, "Woodrow Wilson—Memories and Reflections" (unpublished typescript, 1944-45, hereafter referred to as the "Wilson MS"), ch. 5, pp. 2-4, Shaw MSS; Mary Chapman to Shaw, Mar. 21, 1879, Mary Shaw to Shaw, Mar. 14, 1879, Richard Stephenson to Shaw, July 7, 1883, all in Shaw MSS. Shaw related that he had been offered the chance to run against James Weaver in a Congressional election. Interview with Albert Shaw, Jr., June 20, 1964.

[36] Shaw, "Education for Journalism" (address to State Editorial Association, Madison, Wis., 1891), p. 6 of typescript, Shaw MSS; Shaw to Adams, Feb. 7, 1901, Herbert Baxter Adams MSS, Johns Hopkins University Library.

Except for brief returns to Grinnell, Shaw's life in small-town America was over. Like countless others of his generation he now turned to the city for advancement: to Baltimore for a higher education, to Minneapolis for professional opportunity, and ultimately to New York where he achieved a nationwide editorial reputation.

But the years spent at Paddy's Run and Grinnell left their impression on Shaw. They gave him a vocation, a political faith, a sturdy patriotism, and standards by which to measure his country's development. There was a time in his life later when he appeared to have reconciled himself intellectually and emotionally to the thought that urban life was inevitable and could be made satisfying, but he retained an enduring affection (punctuated by moments of rebellion) for the America he had known in his youth. The passage of time made the small-town style of life seem all the more noble. To Albert Shaw the townspeople and, even more so, the small husbandmen of the Midwest were the ideal Americans, the embodiment of democratic individualism and self-reliance. America's greatness, he believed, depended on the perpetuation of values like these.

2

At the Johns Hopkins and Elsewhere, 1882-1884

The entries in Shaw's diary under January 5, 1882, are sparse and do nothing to indicate the anticipation with which he had looked forward to this day or the significance it would have for his career. He merely listed his activities: unable to attend the trial of Charles Guiteau, instead did some sightseeing in Washington, arrived in Baltimore in the afternoon, met Will Noyes (an Iowa College classmate with whom he intended to room), together hunted for a boardinghouse.[1]

If Shaw glimpsed the university at all that day, he did not think it worth mentioning. In truth there was nothing much to it, for there was a marked disparity between its glittering reputation and its unpretentious appearance. Its buildings were few and fitted blandly into the surrounding neighborhood of aging brick homes that had been converted to roominghouses in which many of the early Johns Hopkins students lived. Conditions, however, had much to recommend them. Living expenses were reasonable, and all but the least pecunious students found their quarters adequate or better and the board anywhere from good to excellent.[2] Since tuition was only forty dollars a term, there is no reason to think that an instructor exaggerated when he commented that "in Baltimore a student can live on the fat of the land for $500 a year."[3]

But the substance of the Johns Hopkins was in its superb intellectual atmosphere. Chartered in 1874, it had already made an international reputation for its program which emphasized graduate studies. Under the presidency of Daniel Coit Gilman, Hopkins had attracted several veteran scholars of wide renown, at least as many more highly promising younger ones, and a correspondingly alert and ambitious group of graduate students.[4]

Shaw enrolled in the Department of History and Political Science. Political economy, which he expected might answer some of his editorial queries, was administered as part of the department as well, for the social sciences had not yet been separated into their several current divisions. The ranking historian, Herbert Baxter Adams, had once taught an economics course, and the economist, Richard T. Ely, knew much history. Adams and Ely were young (respectively only thirty-one and twenty-seven years of age), and both held doctorates from the great German university at Heidelberg. Neither had yet achieved the professional eminence that others on the faculty possessed, but they were rapidly climbing in status through imaginative teaching and frequent publications.[5]

Adams was developing a new style of historical research with which the terms *seminar, monograph,* and *germ theory* are coupled. None of these originated with him, but he added refinements and used them in combination with insight and success.

The historical seminar (or seminary, as it was then often called) was a weekly meeting at which professors and students

1 Shaw diary (Dec. 30, 1881, to Apr. 20, 1882), Jan. 5, 1882, Shaw MSS.

2 *Johns Hopkins University Circulars,* I (1879-1882), 189; John C. French, *A History of the University Founded by Johns Hopkins* (Baltimore: Johns Hopkins Press, 1946), pp. 75-77; Hugh Hawkins, *Pioneer: A History of the Johns Hopkins University, 1874-1889* (Ithaca, N.Y.: Cornell University Press, 1960), p. 273.

3 Quoted in ibid., p. 272.

4 Ibid., pp. 38-62, 269-72.

5 Ibid., pp. 169-78; *J. H. Circulars,* I, 189; Richard T. Ely, *Ground Under Our Feet: An Autobiography* (New York: Macmillan, 1938), pp. 5, 104-5; Benjamin G. Rader, *The Academic Mind and Reform: The Influence of Richard T. Ely in American Life* ([Lexington]: University of Kentucky Press, 1966), pp. 16-22; John Martin Vincent, "Herbert B. Adams: Tributes of Friends. With a Bibliography of the Department of History, Politics and Economics of the Johns Hopkins University, 1876-1901," in J. M. Vincent, J. H. Hollander, and W. W. Willoughby, eds., *Johns Hopkins University Studies in Historical and Political Science,* ser. XXIII, extra no. (Baltimore: Johns Hopkins Press, 1902), p. 9; Shaw, "Recollections of President Gilman" (1943), pp. 2-7 of copy of typescript, Shaw MSS.

gathered to read and discuss papers resulting, it was hoped, in a more enriching intellectual experience than could be gotten from listening to an instructor's monologue.[6] Adams explained, perhaps with undue optimism, that it was "merely the development of the old scholastic method of advancing philosophical inquiry by the defence of original theses. The seminary is still a training-school for doctors of philosophy; but it has evolved from a nursery of dogma into a laboratory of scientific truth."[7]

The monograph, a study which was to be the product of research on some historical problem, was similarly inspired by German scholars pursuing the scientific ideal. Adams wished his students to study some aspect of American economic or institutional history. His special interest was in the origins of the institutions of government, for he felt that there was an identifiable continuity between the primitive governmental arrangements of Saxon England and the Teutonic tribes of a still earlier day and the mature democracy of nineteenth-century America.[8]

This was the germ theory of history. Although some of his ablest students found the approach stultifying, it was on the whole attractive to the Hopkins scholars of the 1880s. Thanks to its use of evolutionary metaphors the germ theory shared the scientific aura that was in vogue at the time and thus allowed the individual researcher to feel that his own project, however modest, was part of a larger whole. The possibility of having one's findings published in the *Johns Hopkins University Studies in Historical and Political Science,* a monograph series that Adams began editing in 1882, provided additional impetus for research.[9]

6 Hawkins, *Pioneer,* pp. 224-29; Herbert B. Adams, "Methods of Historical Study," in Herbert B. Adams, ed., *J. H. Studies,* ser. II, nos. 1-2 (Baltimore: N. Murray, Publication Agent, 1884), pp. 67-88, 103; H. B. Adams, "The Germanic Origins of New England Towns. With Notes on Cooperation in University Work," in Adams, ed., *J. H. Studies,* ser. I, no. 2 (Baltimore: N. Murray, Publication Agent, 1882), pp. 39-57.

7 Adams, "Methods of Historical Study," p. 64.

8 Jurgen Herbst, *The German Historical School in American Scholarship: A Study in the Transfer of Culture* (Ithaca, N.Y.: Cornell University Press, 1965), is pertinent.

Ely, also influenced by German thought, repudiated the views of the classical English economists and particularly those of the Manchester school with its dogmatic acceptance of free trade and free competition. He renounced such "laws" for the belief that political economy should be studied as a mutable doctrine whose lessons when infused with a sense of ethics could be applied to the problems of one's own age. From this relativist perspective he included such novel topics as the labor movement, social communities, and municipal administration within the field of political economy.[10] His interests were timely and his attitude toward them such that his biographer has described him as "a missionary and an evangelist to the American public."[11]

The previous decade had seen the ideas of social Darwinism reach a floodtide. This famous complex of beliefs made it clear that man should be left free to rise or fall in society through the application of whatever native talent he possessed. The "fittest" would rise to the top and perhaps become a Captain of Industry. The burgeoning city slums testified to the abilities of many of the others. Throughout this process government was to keep hands off—laissez faire—and allow the results to be worked out in natural fashion.[12]

But an intellectual counterattack in which the Johns Hopkins scholars were to play a conspicuous role was soon undertaken. Adams, for example, felt that laissez faire was an erroneous concept and that government must intervene in the

---

9 Adams, "Methods of Historical Study," pp. 67-88, 103; Richard Hofstadter, *The Progressive Historians: Turner, Beard, Parrington* (New York: Knopf, 1968), pp. 38-41, 65-68, 77, offers interesting but rather caustic comments on Adams's role in the development of historical scholarship in the U.S.

10 Richard T. Ely, "The Past and the Present of Political Economy," in H. B. Adams, ed., *J. H. Studies,* ser. II, no. 3 (Baltimore: N. Murray, Publication Agent, 1884), pp. 143-202; Rader, *The Academic Mind and Reform,* pp. 28-53.

11 Ibid., p. 2.

12 Among the several good works pertaining to this subject are: Richard Hofstadter, *Social Darwinism in American Thought, 1860-1915,* rev. ed. (Boston: The Beacon Press, 1955); Eric Goldman, *Rendevous with Destiny: A History of Modern American Reform,* rev. ed. abr. (New York: Vintage Books, 1958), pp. 66-161; and Henry Steele Commager, *The American Mind: An Interpretation of American Thought and Character Since the 1880's* (New Haven: Yale University Press, 1959), pp. 11-55, 199-246.

social process, while Ely with his deep feeling for human brotherhood struck forcefully at social Darwinism in advocating the new presentation of political economy. More than any economist of the era he helped undermine the intellectual props of the laissez faire credo; his Christian idealism inspired others to commit themselves to the cause of reform.[13]

Johns Hopkins was in the process of becoming one of the great centers of reform thought, yet the daily routine of its faculty and students had to be shaped by scholarly tasks. Many hours were needed for class and preparation and even more for individual research in what Shaw, in a striking frontier metaphor, called "the Hopkins atmosphere of calm study, where each man was bravely and resolutely digging away in the subject matter that he had staked out for his own claim."[14] Shaw understandably complained to his mother that the new regimen was difficult, but despite his fears the problem of adjustment was neither persistent nor critical. The first lecture he attended was one in a series of ten by the psychologist G. Stanley Hall. Afterward he heard Ely discuss modern communism.[15]

Ely's class completed, Shaw was free for his first weekend in Baltimore. On Friday evening he went with Noyes to see the Italian tragedian Ernesto Rossi perform in the play *Edmund Kean*. Some reading on communism on Saturday and attendance at three churches on Sunday—Congregational, high Episcopal, and Presbyterian—filled the remainder of his leisure. On other occasions he enjoyed a walk or perusing a novel, though his mother reminded him to "read something better on Sundays."[16]

The new week saw Shaw spending many hours in class

---

13 Hawkins, *Pioneer*, pp. 305-7; Sidney Fine, "Richard T. Ely, Forerunner of Progressivism, 1880-1901," *Mississippi Valley Historical Review*, XXXVII (March 1951), 599-624. Shaw's former mentor, Jesse Macy, was also something of a reformer. See Nollen, *Grinnell College*, pp. 92-100; Coleman, "In Pursuit of Harmony," pp. 84-104.

14 Shaw, "Wilson MS," ch. 5, p. 19.

15 Shaw diary, Jan. 5, 6, 1882; Shaw to Susan Shaw, Jan. 11, 1882, Shaw MSS.

16 Shaw diary, Jan. 6, 7, 8, 29, Feb. 12, Mar. 8, 1882, Shaw MSS; Susan Shaw to Shaw, Apr. 15, 1882, in possession of Albert Shaw, Jr.

or else in reading. Adams's talk tracing the office of constable to the old Saxon tithing-man was of "intense interest," Shaw felt,[17] but what most absorbed him was visiting lecturer Austin Scott's course on constitutional history. For it Shaw spent about five hours a day reading various works on the Constitutional Convention, undertook an intensive study of Marshall's Supreme Court decisions, and passed several early morning hours at Scott's apartment discussing constitutional questions while the professor was shaving and dressing. The culmination of the class came with an appropriately informal examination on which Shaw received Scott's compliments.[18]

Following a short visit to Washington in February to see his mother who was staying there with daughter Mary (now the wife of Dr. John C. Fisher), Shaw began his first full semester. He took Ely's political economy course and three classes with Adams. One course, international law, drew much of Shaw's attention. Faithful to the germ theory, Adams traced all law to patriarchal institutions of ancient times, this historical approach making the course partly a survey of European diplomacy. The reading was arduous but varied. Hearn's *Aryan Household* proved interesting to Shaw. Other assignments were in Maine's *Village-Communities,* Fustel's *Ancient City,* Spencer's *Principles of Sociology,* and Freeman's *Historical Geography of Europe.*[19]

In addition to the three lecture courses Shaw also was enrolled in Adams's Friday evening seminary in institutional history, the class which more than any other epitomized the Johns Hopkins approach to historical scholarship. The roster of scholars was typically brilliant during Shaw's first term at Hopkins. Both Adams and Ely were present. J. Franklin Jameson occupied a student's position for the time being, though by the fall he was a member of the academic staff. He became one of Shaw's closest friends. Charles Levermore, Edward Bemis, and Elgin Gould were other able seminar

17 Shaw diary, Jan. 11, 1882, Shaw MSS.
18 Ibid., Jan. 10-Feb. 3, 1882; Shaw, "Recollections of Gilman," p. 8, Shaw MSS.
19 Shaw diary, Feb. 6-9, 13-18, Mar. 1-15, Apr. 19, 1882, Shaw MSS; *J. H. Circulars,* I, 190.

students whom Shaw got to know well. All achieved considerable professional success: the first as president of Adelphi College and as a student of internationalism, the others as experts in municipal administration.[20]

Shaw soon received an assignment. James Bryce, Regius professor of civil law at Oxford, had indicated to Adams that papers on American government could be of use in the preparation of a study that would turn out to be the *American Commonwealth*. Adams asked his students to write some. Gould chose Pennsylvania; Shaw, Illinois. Immediately Shaw began reading pertinent chapters of Tocqueville and numerous pamphlets on township government, supplementing this with research in the Peabody and Baltimore Bar libraries and at the Library of Congress. Although he spent considerable time on his other courses, on German, and some at his favorite diversions, Shaw managed to finish the paper in less than three weeks and to report on it to the seminary. It was good enough for Jameson, who often complained to his diary, to interrupt commentary such as "unspeakably stupid," "wretched," and "intolerably tedious" with the notation that Shaw's work was "excellent and interesting."[21]

The core of the paper dealt with the origins and forms of governmental institutions in Illinois, but Shaw tried to keep the taint of antiquarianism from it by viewing his data within a broad conceptual framework. According to him, early settlers brought with them to Illinois the institutions of government

20 Vincent, ed., "Adams: Tributes of Friends," pp. 25, 60, 80, 88, of bibliography section; Elizabeth Donnan and Leo F. Stock, eds., *An Historian's World: Selections from the Correspondence of John Franklin Jameson*, Memoirs of the American Philosophical Society, vol. XLII (Philadelphia: American Philosophical Society, 1956), pp. 1-2; George McAneny, "Serving the City," and R. Fulton Cutting and Joseph S. Auerbach, "The City and Suburban Homes Company," in *Elgin Ralston Lovell Gould: A Memorial* (New York: privately published, 1916), pp. 45-46, 53-58 respectively; Richard Hofstadter and Walter Metzger, *The Development of Academic Freedom in the United States* (New York: Columbia University Press, 1955), pp. 432-35.

21 Edmund Ions, *James Bryce and American Democracy, 1870-1922* (New York: Humanities Press, 1970), pp. 120-21; *J. H. Circulars*, I, 206-7; Shaw, "Recollections of Gilman," pp. 7-8; Shaw diary, Feb. 11, 24, Mar. 3, 1882, both in Shaw MSS; J. Franklin Jameson diary, Jan. 27, Feb. 24, Mar. 3, 1882, J. Franklin Jameson MSS, Library of Congress.

that they already knew. Settled largely by people of Yankee background, the northern half of the state derived its early system of government from the New England town (and beyond that the Teutonic forest). In the lower half of Illinois feudalistic models of government borrowed from the South were at first established. When adapted to the new environment, the admirable New England institutions gradually spread over most of the state.[22]

Shaw completed one more paper, "The Growth of Internationalism," before the close of the school year. Once more genuflecting before the germ theory, he used evolutionary insights to forecast the growth of an international order. The growth of jurisprudence, the development of a law-abiding spirit, the unspoken agreement that war had come to be an "instrument of law" rather than an act of plunder or revenge all indicated a trend to internationalism. Although the optimum stage might not be reached for generations, only one conclusion was possible: "that the world is making strong and tangible progress toward union, law, and perpetual peace."[23]

Both papers were well received, for they were a happy combination of lucid and succinct writing, original research, and the type of scholarly insight that was then fashionable. Shaw's on Illinois was a particular success. Adams liked the paper very much, Shaw was pleased to hear, and sent it and Gould's to Bryce. "Both are valuable," commented Bryce—"that on Illinois has greatly struck me by its clearness, precision, conciseness, and especially by the philosophical spirit which runs through it." And Adams could later add the fillip that it would be published in the *Fortnightly Review*, a prominent Liberal journal in England.[24]

22 H. B. Adams, "The Germanic Origins of New England Towns. With Notes on Co-operation," p. 50; Shaw, "Local Government in Illinois," in Adams, ed., *J. H. Studies*, ser. I, no. 3 (Baltimore: Johns Hopkins University, 1883), pp. 5-19, also available as "Local Government in America," *Fortnightly Review,* n.s. XXXII (Oct. 1, 1882), 485-95.

23 *J. H. Circulars*, I, 239; Shaw, "The Growth of Internationalism," *International Review*, XIV (Apr. 1883), 267-83.

24 Shaw diary, Feb. 24, 1882; Adams to Shaw (with enclosure Bryce to Adams), Mar. 25, Sept. 4, 1882, all in Shaw MSS.

Adams told Shaw this was "a big feather in your cap." Any scholar would have hoped to make the dual publication of an article in the *Review* and in the *Johns Hopkins Studies* the start of a productive career, and it proved to be such, albeit in a circuitous manner. But at the time it marked only a hiatus in Shaw's career. The press of business forced him to return to Grinnell after having completed only five months at the Johns Hopkins. But the experience had been rewarding, recalled Shaw. "I found friends, encouragement, the right direction as to my reading, and the most stimulating atmosphere of study. I learned more and accomplished more," he claimed, "than in any preceding two years of my life."[25]

Albert Shaw returned to the *Herald* with a new but short-lived "zest." Sheer exhaustion soon robbed him of it, for he had to handle the duties of the ailing Cravath in addition to his regular ones. Discontent returned, and Shaw came to feel that being in Grinnell—which he now derided as a "bleak prairie"—was akin to exile, half a continent distant, he complained to Jameson, from the hub of American scholarship. He decided to quit the *Herald* at the first opportunity and sold his interest in it to Cravath on February 1, 1883, in time for him to return to Baltimore that winter, he hoped. But Adams disappointed him by advising that he stay home and do research and other preparation for the next academic year. Shaw also sounded out Jameson about the situation there. As usual his friend spotted some ills but, in hopes of promoting Shaw's prompt return, mentioned that it was "perhaps a good place to work in." Jameson, however, soon had to note in his diary that "my statements of facts upon which *I* should have decided to come to Baltimore, have decided him not to."[26]

Learning that Shaw had decided to accept his suggestion, Adams urged him to "keep in good health and keep your eyes

[25] Adams to Shaw, Sept. 4, 1882, Shaw MSS; Shaw, "Education for Journalism," p. 6.

[26] Ibid., pp. 6-7; *Grinnell Herald*, Feb. 2, 1883; Adams to Shaw, Feb. 19, 1883, Jameson to Shaw, Feb. 27, 1883, both in Shaw MSS; Shaw to Jameson, Jan. 18, Feb. 23, Mar. 12, 1883; Jameson diary, Mar. 15, 1883, all in Jameson MSS.

open for pioneer work in the institutional and economic fields. I am satisfied that we shall gain more by striking Northwest and Southwest than by hanging around Plymouth Rock, or courting the favor of New England antiquaries."[27] Ely also had a request, asking Shaw to secure information for him on a community of Icarian socialists in Iowa. Ely needed it for a few pages of a book he was doing. Shaw's reply that he would visit the project led Ely to suggest that the Iowan make a seminar report on the Icarians. Shaw was also thinking of studying Chicago's government.[28]

In spite of his dissatisfaction with his recent experience on the *Herald,* Shaw hoped to continue in the newspaper business and through a friend, Newton Hawley who lived in Minneapolis, contacted General Alvred Bayard Nettleton, owner of that city's *Tribune,* to apply for a job. In June, Nettleton invited Shaw for an interview at which he asked Shaw to write a trial column on German socialism, a subject of current interest: coincidentally Shaw had studied it under Ely. The results so impressed Nettleton that he published the column and on generous terms offered Shaw a job as his principal editorial assistant.[29] He was to begin work the first of September and until the following June, wrote Nettleton, stay "in Baltimore and Washington mainly carrying on such studies and investigations, as will in your judgment tend most to fit you for permanent work of a high grade in the field of journalism." For mailing in editorials to be written in his spare time, Shaw would receive $10 weekly salary. After

27 Adams to Shaw, Apr. 21, 1883, Shaw MSS. The advice Adams gave Shaw encourages speculation about the former's relationship with Frederick Jackson Turner. Ray Allen Billington, *Frederick Jackson Turner: Historian, Scholar, Teacher* (New York: Oxford University Press, 1973), pp. 60-75, offers the fullest discussion of this subject.

28 Adams, *Germanic Origins,* p. 50: Shaw to Jameson, Feb. 23, 1883, Jameson MSS; Ely to Shaw, Apr. 15, 21, 23, 1883, Shaw MSS.

29 "A Western Man of Letters," *Northwest Illustrated Monthly Magazine,* XI (Oct. 1893), 5-6; Ely, *Ground Under Our Feet,* p. 105; Hawley to Shaw, Jan. 3, June 5, 27, 1883: Nettleton to Shaw, June 8, 1883, Shaw MSS. Ely proudly recalled Shaw's practice article on German socialism but wrongly dated it in the summer of 1884. The one in question would seem to be "German State Socialism" in the *Tribune* of June 17, 1883.

commencing full-time work his pay would be doubled with the promise that within four or five years it would climb as high as $2,500 annually, a sum which compared favorably with what his professors were earning at Hopkins.[30]

Shaw quickly accepted this offer which gave him the opportunity to return to school and yet to remain active professionally. As a favor to Nettleton he postponed his trip east for a month in order to cover a promotional junket to Yellowstone Park and then to fill in at the *Tribune* office for awhile, only arriving in Baltimore in the middle of October.[31]

Shaw found new quarters with Charles Levermore and enrolled again in his former department which was now staffed by Adams, Ely, and Jameson. Scott was not back, but Bryce and John Shaw Billings, who spoke on Roman law and municipal hygiene respectively, were exciting visiting lecturers. Adams was very enthusiastic about the students presently registered. Bemis, Gould, Levermore, Burr Ramage, and Lewis Wilhelm were all old acquaintances of Shaw. Notable additions were Charles Shinn of California (not Chinese, Adams pointed out), Davis Dewey from Vermont, and his brother John, whose main interest, however, lay in philosophy. It was at this time that Shaw met Woodrow Wilson, who became a companion in the new Hopkins glee club and a close friend. Shaw was to spend many hours with Wilson going over chapters from the latter's *Congressional Government*.[32]

Despite his late start Shaw hoped to receive the doctorate that academic year. Adams had called it a possibility, by stipulating that Shaw would first have to pass a good examination.[33] His health might have been an obstacle, for the high-

[30] Hawkins, *Pioneer,* p. 173; Nettleton to Shaw, June 20, 1883, Shaw MSS.

[31] Ibid., June 26, July 12, 20, 1883; Shaw to Jameson, July 18, 1883; Jameson diary, Oct. 8, 16, 1883, Jameson MSS.

[32] Ions, *Bryce and American Democracy,* pp. 118-22; Jerome Nathanson, *John Dewey: The Reconstruction of the Democratic Life* (New York: Scribners, 1951), p. 2; *J. H. Circulars,* III (1883-1884), 16-20; Shaw, "Wilson MS," ch. 5, pp. 13, 17, 20-22, 32, 36; Jameson diary, Oct. 16, 1883, Mar. 21, 1884, Jameson MSS; Adams to Shaw, Nov. 14, 1882, Feb. 19, 1883, Shaw to W. F. Melton, June 26, 1913, all in Shaw MSS.

[33] Adams to Shaw, Aug. 1, 1883, Shaw MSS.

strung Shaw suffered from what he called nervous backaches, as well as a weight deficiency, and proneness to colds. But fortunately the university had a new physical education officer who prescribed special exercises which helped build Shaw's frame to an unusual degree of robustness.[34]

The academic obstacles to his hopes were the oral examination and a dissertation that he wanted to complete by early April. Shaw applied for a degree in November and chose for his thesis the topic of Icarian life that he had corresponded about with Ely; he enlarged the scope to include a discussion of the intellectual origins of this communistic group.[35]

Evidently Shaw had done considerable research on the Icarians during the spring and summer, for he reported on them to the first seminar he attended on his return. Jameson was impressed enough after talking with him to jot down that Shaw was "just mighty bright. I wish I had his literary gifts."[36] To expedite his progress Shaw quit writing for the *Tribune* in March. He finished on time and achieved his customary success in having his work published. *Icaria* was the title. Editions were printed in America, England, and two years later in Germany, where the work appears to have been most successful.[37] The purpose of the study, in Shaw's words, was to "picture [the community's] inner life as a miniature social and political organism, to show what are, in actual experience, the difficulties which a communistic society encounters, and to show, by a series of pen-portraits, what manner of men the enterprise has enlisted."[38] Shaw traced the Icarian ideal to Etienne Cabet's book, *Voyage en Icarie*, written in 1840, which urged man to forsake an exploitative social and economic life

---

34 Interview with Albert Shaw, Jr., Mar. 20, 1965; Shaw to Jameson, July 20, 1884, Jameson MSS; Shaw memorandum of information from the *J. H. Circulars, 1883-84*, Feb. 18, 1943, Shaw MSS.

35 Shaw's application for Ph.D. degree, Nov. 7, 1883, copy in possession of Albert Shaw, Jr.

36 Jameson diary, Oct. 19, 1883, Jameson MSS.

37 Shaw, "Wilson MS," ch. 7, p. 11; Nettleton to Shaw, Mar. 28, 1884, Shaw MSS.

38 Shaw, *Icaria: A Chapter in the History of Communism* (New York & London: G. P. Putnam's Sons, 1884), pp. v-vi.

for a rational, communal society—or what scholars call Utopian socialism. Shaw then described the actual settlements made in America by the French followers of Cabet and demonstrated that poor planning and factionalism had recurrently impeded the success of the various Icarian communities since the founding of the first one in Texas in 1848. Shaw based his work on the considerable amount of Icarian literature and pamphlets he had read, interviews, and observations of the colony near Corning, Iowa, that he had visited.[39]

The most interesting thing about the monograph is not the story of the Icarians themselves but Shaw's selection of the topic and his handling of it.[40] A member of America's first generation of trained social scientists, Shaw intended to employ his knowledge in socially relevant areas and, starting with his study of the Icarians, investigated a series of topics, any one of which might have been taken from a primer of the new political economy. Over the next decade he undertook in succession research into laissez faire, cooperative modes of labor, the protective tariff, and municipal government. Most of these subjects were potentially controversial, for they dealt with the relationships between capital and labor and especially between capital and government. Although he sometimes reached conclusions that were unsettling to conservatives, Shaw was careful to make his findings as palatable as possible to them. His style was not that of the doctrinaire but of the scholar judiciously marshalling the facts in support of his thesis.

His dissertation completed, he still had to worry about the oral examinations that were scheduled for May. Predictably Shaw felt apprehensive about his prospects. Although he was strongly prepared in the areas on which Adams and Ely were likely to examine him, he would also have to face Basil Gilder-

[39] Ibid., pp. 9-16, 29-44, 47-136. The dissertation title was "Etienne Cabet and the Icarian Community." Several cartons of the source materials are in the Shaw MSS.

[40] For a contrasting analysis of Cabet and the Icarian idea see Christopher H. Johnson, "Communism and the Working Class before Marx: The Icarian Experience," *American Historical Review*, LXXVI (June 1971), 642-89.

sleeve and Paul Haupt, specialists in Greek and Semitic languages respectively. Shaw's recollection was that they were "likely to discover my comparative ignorance of historical times that preceded William the Conqueror." Jameson, who asked Shaw a question or two, was disappointed in his friend's performance on the test. He thought Shaw had only done well. Nevertheless Shaw's overall record at the Johns Hopkins was impressive enough for him to receive the degree with very high honors, and he returned to Minneapolis the scholarly editor.[41]

41 Hawkins, *Pioneer,* pp. 51, 159; *J. H. Circulars,* II, 120; Jameson diary, May 23, 27, 28, 1884, Jameson MSS; Shaw memo of information from *J. H. Circulars;* Adams to Shaw (with enclosed letter of reference), July 8, 1884, Jameson to Shaw (with enclosed letter of reference), July 12, 1884, all in Shaw MSS.

3

In Minneapolis and Abroad, 1884-1890

When Shaw arrived in Minneapolis in the summer of 1884 to resume his journalistic career, the city was in the midst of a phenomenal expansion that saw its population climb past 160,000 by the end of the decade, better than three times what it had been in 1880. Spotlighted by the completion of the Northern Pacific Railroad to the West Coast in 1883 and by the continued growth of her grain trade, Minneapolis moved into the top twenty cities. Moreover, to the discomfort of many jealous Minneapolitans, neighboring St. Paul was developing in an equally impressive manner.[1]

Although the *Minneapolis Tribune* had been founded in 1867, its major growth did not begin until 1880 when General A. B. Nettleton, the new owner, purchased a morning franchise for the services of the Associated Press and started the moribund paper on its way to success. Under Nettleton and Alden Blethen (who succeeded him in 1884) circulation climbed from a low of 2,100 in 1880 to 16,000 a decade later.[2]

The *Tribune* was a morning daily, Republican in politics, normally printing an eight-page edition on weekdays, sometimes a longer one on Fridays or Saturdays, one of twelve to twenty-four pages on Sundays, and a farmer's weekly. The paper boasted of having the latest printing equipment and a speedy telegraphic news service. Facilities of the Associated and Western Associated Presses, and the employment of agents in Milwaukee, Chicago, Washington, and New York, as well as four hundred special correspondents in northwestern communities from Wisconsin to Oregon gave the *Tribune* quick access to the latest developments. The staff, unlike that on the *Grinnell Herald*, was that of a typical metropolitan paper,

with several dozen men in various specialized departments.[3]
A. B. Nettleton was an intriguing personality. A onetime
Oberlin student, he had had a spectacular Civil War career,
rising from private in the Ohio Volunteer Cavalry to the brevet
rank of brigadier general. After the war he was associated
with newspapers in Sandusky, Ohio, and Chicago. He then
worked for the firm of Jay Cooke as a securities publicist before
returning to journalism in Philadelphia. Next he operated
the *Tribune* for four years, selling it in 1884 to Alden Blethen,
formerly a teacher and lawyer in Maine, and more recently
with the *Kansas City Journal*. William Haskell, of the family
which owned the *Boston Herald*, was associated with him, but
of the two Blethen was the key figure. One of his first acts
was to bring in personnel—referred to in the trade as the Kansas
City "cowboys"—from his old paper. Shaw, however, impressed
him sufficiently to hold the important role of chief editorial
writer and associate editor.[4]

Reporting for work in 1884, Shaw inevitably devoted much
of his attention to the political campaign. It was the year of
the mugwump bolt from the Republican presidential candidate, James G. Blaine, to Democrat Grover Cleveland. Many
of Shaw's friends, for instance Walter Scaife in Baltimore, and
even Ed Howell in Grinnell, favored this movement for civil

[1] R. I. Holcombe and William H. Bingham, eds., *Compendium of History
and Biography of Minneapolis and Hennepin County, Minnesota* (Chicago: H.
Taylor & Co., 1914), pp. 140-44; Horace B. Hudson, ed., *A Half Century of
Minneapolis* (Minneapolis: Hudson Publishing Co., 1898), pp. 60-61, 348.

[2] A brief history of the *Tribune* can be found in Isaac Atwater, "The Press
of Minneapolis," in Isaac Atwater, ed., *History of the City of Minneapolis,
Minnesota*, 2 pts. (New York and Chicago: Munsell & Co., 1893), I, 361-66.
Average daily circulation statistics for the *Tribune* in these years are reported
in the *American Newspaper Annual* (Philadelphia: N. W. Ayer & Son, 1880ff.).
The figures given are from the 1880 volume, p. 226, and the 1890 edition, p.
367.

[3] *Minneapolis Tribune*, Apr. 12, Aug. 5, 1884 (annual number), Jan. 1, 1890;
Souvenir of the Press Club of Minneapolis (Minneapolis: n.p., 1904), pp. 100-104,
126-27.

[4] Lester B. Shippee, "Alvred Bayard Nettleton," *Dictionary of American
Biography*, 2d ed.; "Alden Joseph Blethen," *National Cyclopaedia of American
Biography*, 40 vols. (New York: James T. White and Co., 1897-1955), XVII,
364-65; Hudson, ed., *A Half Century*, pp. 219, 223-34; Blethen to J. T. Thurman,
Feb. 11, 1893, Shaw to Haskell (not sent), Dec. 1, 1899, both in Shaw MSS.

service reform, honesty and economy in government, and a lower tariff. They were particularly numerous at Johns Hopkins where Scaife reported his acquaintances "mugwumps to a man," and Jameson counted eleven mugwumps, but two Blaine men, one old-line Democrat, and one doodlebug—or waverer.[5] Shaw's political standards were much like theirs, but situated in Minneapolis he viewed things differently from them. Mugwumps were scarce there, and Shaw who felt that the movement was peculiarly eastern remained a Republican. He confessed some misgivings about Blaine but by and large was satisfied with him.[6]

Blaine's candidacy actually had much to recommend it. Although his long political career had been spotted by involvement in a dubious railroad bond deal and by association with the maligned spoils system, sins which the mugwumps could not forgive him, he was the most able and farsighted Republican leader of the 1880s. His economic nationalism, embodied in a program that emphasized the protective tariff and a dynamic foreign policy, had wide appeal among rank-and-file Republicans.[7]

Shaw thus had material with which to formulate soundly constructed editorials, but too often he relied on banalities and sweeping generalizations. Blaine, for instance, was to be admired for such qualities as his "magnetism" and made more fit to be president, it seemed, because an English periodical had slighted him. Cleveland, on the other hand, represented a vague series of potential calamities: the revenge of the South, the degradation of the Negro, and the conceit of the East all appeared to be connected with him.[8] Shaw once charged:

[5] Jameson to John Jameson, Nov. 2, 1884, in Donnan and Stock, eds., *An Historian's World*, p. 37; Howell to Shaw, Nov. 25, 1884, Scaife to Shaw, Dec. 1, 1884, Charles Levermore to Shaw, Aug. 10, 1885, all in Shaw MSS.

[6] *Tribune* (local columns), June 26, Aug. 10, 14, 21, Sept. 18, Oct. 23, Nov. 6, 1884; Shaw to James Bryce, Feb. 9, 1888, Bryce MSS, U.S.A. 18, Bodleian Library, Oxford University.

[7] Allan Nevins, *Grover Cleveland: A Study in Courage* (New York: Dodd, Mead, 1932), pp. 156-87, is the standard source on the 1884 election. For a favorable view of Blaine, see H. Wayne Morgan, *From Hayes to McKinley: National Party Politics, 1877-1896* (Syracuse: Syracuse University Press, 1969), pp. 152-56, 202-3, 439.

"Above all it is impossible for them [certain select circles in the East] to comprehend the Mississippi Valley and these great regions which have become dominant in national affairs. They really regard the earnest, enthusiastic people of states like Iowa and Kansas as 'rowdies,' 'rabble,' 'riff-raff,' etc.," he continued. "Blaine and the Iowa people, bless their simple souls, think this is the best country in the world, and they are proud of it, and have a whole-souled belief in the things which have made it what it is."[9]

The "select circles" frequently received more specific indictment as mugwumps. Shaw congratulated young Theodore Roosevelt for refusing to join their movement, but for the actual bolters he reserved the most abrasive language. He belittled the significance of their movement and noted their alienation from the mass of the people, their twisted logic, and their general peevishness.[10]

Shaw seems to have recognized that his editorials fell short of the standards he had set for himself. Evidently regretting some of the things he had said about Cleveland, he wrote Woodrow Wilson after the election: "I have given you all Jesse—for $35 a week and promise of an advance. Now I will turn me to less harassing themes. . . . Again, let me say, I'm glad it's over." But what was he to do? Even Nettleton whose "serious and conservative" attitude toward journalism he later praised had reprimanded him for writing "too exhaustively." "Popularize and simplify," he admonished Shaw, "the average daily food of our constituency must be of a lighter sort in the form of short, crisp, idiomatic editorial utterances."[11]

---

8 Thanks to Albert Shaw, Jr., who gave the author scrapbooks of his father's editorial writings, a fairly complete inventory is available of what Albert Shaw wrote for the *Minneapolis Tribune*. Very often he wrote a minimum of three editorials per day. This would comprise a column and a half, or better than fifteen hundred words daily. On Blaine see the *Tribune*: July 31, Aug. 16, 21, 24, Sept. 25, Oct. 26, 1884. On Cleveland see ibid.: July 19, 26, Aug. 6, 9, 26, Sept. 19, Oct. 16, Nov. 5, 1884.

9 Ibid., Aug. 16, 1884.

10 Ibid., July 17, 23, 24, Aug. 10, 18, Oct. 14, 1884.

11 Shaw to Wilson, Nov. 16, 1884, Woodrow Wilson MSS, Library of Congress; Shaw, "Address at Minnesota Society Dinner" (New York, 1902), pp. 11-12 of typescript, Shaw MSS; Nettleton to Shaw, Mar. 28, 1884, Shaw MSS.

Working for a partisan newspaper, Shaw had to be partisan. Democrats existed in season and out, and particularly when they governed the nation could often be upbraided for some misdeed. When they were not especially noticeable, the city of St. Paul—or one of its papers—furnished a convenient substitute for editorial ire. Shaw accused St. Paul of everything from being jealous of and unfair to Minneapolis to being Democratic which was just as bad.[12]

Not everything he wrote was so trite. His comments on foreign affairs, for instance, followed the general Blaine policy of advocating a large navy, commercial expansion in Latin America, and a strong regard for American interests everywhere, but they were generally well done.[13] Unlike some of his harsher editorials on political issues, these dealt with matters with which Shaw was in wholehearted agreement.

His statements on the need for a Central American canal are particularly revealing. In 1884 there was considerable discussion about the prospects of constructing such a canal, for Ferdinand de Lesseps of Suez fame headed a foreign venture to build a waterway across Panama, and the United States itself negotiated for canal rights across the territory of Nicaragua. Shaw felt that it was unfortunate that French interests should have gained prior rights in Panama but did not believe war with France should be risked in an effort to drive them out. Instead the United States should forge ahead with the Nicaraguan project which was to be jointly controlled by Nicaragua and the United States, the preponderant voice to belong to this country. Great Britain, however, protested that the U.S. had no right to undertake such a

---

12 For national politics one can consult the *Tribune:* May 29, Aug. 6, Sept. 4, Dec. 4, 1885, Mar. 5, July 17, 1886, June 26, Sept. 20, 1887. On the rivalry with St. Paul see ibid.: Nov. 25, 1884, Sept. 7, Oct. 19, 1886, June 30, July 29, 1887, Feb. 5, 1888.

13 The traditional monograph on Republican foreign policy in the 1880s is Alice Felt Tyler, *The Foreign Policy of James G. Blaine* (Minneapolis: University of Minnesota Press, 1927). A most informative recent study is Walter LeFeber, *The New Empire: An Interpretation of American Expansion, 1860-1898* (Ithaca, N.Y.: Cornell University Press for the American Historical Association, 1963), pp. 102-49. For the diplomatic goals Shaw favored, see the *Tribune:* Sept. 18, 1886, June 1, Aug. 24, 1887, Jan. 31, Feb. 13, 1888.

commitment, for in the Clayton-Bulwer Treaty of 1850 England and the United States had pledged to act together in any Central American canal venture. Shaw disregarded history to claim that the agreement had been ill-advised to begin with. It should now be ignored, he concluded; it was a "disgrace to the country" and "utterly incompatible with the wider applications of the Monroe Doctrine."[14]

Shaw also retorted to other European powers which held that the projected canal should be neutralized under international control. He rejected their contentions, saying that the waterway would be open on liberal terms to world commerce but that in case of war it must be a "part of our coast line" politically. He predicted that great commercial gain would follow its completion and criticized the eastern press for failing to uphold America's side of the debate with England. The following year the new Cleveland administration yielded to British protests and withdrew the still pending Nicaraguan treaty from further consideration.[15] When a canal treaty was finally secured almost two decades later, it was with Panama.

There were other editorials that must have gratified Shaw. He regarded his newspaper work as a chance to do good, to stand for the right things; and there were few areas where more needed to be done than in the field of municipal government. Even in a young city like Minneapolis matters such as slums, sanitation, mass transportation, and political corruption demanded attention. They were problems that he was uniquely prepared to understand and interpret. His study *Icaria* had required the sort of detailed analysis of the functioning of a community which could now be useful, and his contact with the Hopkins scholars—especially Richard Ely—helped Shaw become an incisive critic of laissez faire. To advocate a policy of "let alone" as the solution for the problems of a rapidly growing city would have been folly.

He insisted that three things be done—that corruption (already present in the form of a ring headed by Albert "Doc"

14 Ibid., Dec. 4, 20, 1884.
15 Ibid., Jan. 25, 1885, Mar. 2, 1886.

Ames) be driven out of Minneapolis government, that the city introduce and maintain the latest techniques in sanitation, and that an enlightened policy to govern the granting of franchises be formulated. Shaw was no gas-and-water socialist, but neither was he averse to municipal ownership of selected utilities. His main concern, however, was that franchises be awarded only after close study. Minneapolis, for instance, should not hastily give away a lucrative route to a streetcar company and then bemoan the ill use made of the privilage. Local traction service had been good, but Minneapolis as a general rule should only make such a grant after exacting certain conditions which would ensure a substantial revenue to the city and/or economical rates to the customer, as well as decent service.[16]

Shaw also revealed in other ways his recent and continuing contacts with the Johns Hopkins community. He became a charter member of the new American Economic Association, gave Ely's studies favorable reviews when he had the opportunity, and did scholarly work of his own. Shaw's most substantial effort, "Cooperation in the Northwest," appeared as part of a volume planned by Ely and entitled *History of Cooperation in the United States*.[17] Shaw and other disciples of Ely each discussed the cooperative movement in one region. It was a timely topic, and Shaw's treatment of it indicated a willingness on his part to be sympathetic to labor—especially when the workers behaved in a fashion becoming the middle class.

16 Shaw recalled with pride his advocacy of a good public health service. Shaw to John Kingsbury, May 2, 1935, Shaw MSS. On the sanitation problem see the *Tribune:* Nov. 9, 1883, Dec. 21, 1884, Mar. 7, 20, Oct. 7, 1886, Feb. 1, Apr. 10, 1888. On franchises see ibid.: Nov. 15, 1884, Jan. 30, 1886, June 7, 8, Aug. 23, 1887, Mar. 6, 1888. On local politics see ibid.: Feb. 7, Oct. 17, 1886; Shaw to Bryce, Feb. 9, 1888, Bryce MSS. Ames who acceded to the mayoralty in 1886 was the principal, almost twenty years later, of one of Lincoln Steffens's most famous muckraking articles.

17 *Tribune*, Nov. 18, 1883, Feb. 1, May 3, Aug. 23, 1885; Shaw, "Cooperation in the Northwest," in Herbert Baxter Adams, ed., *History of Cooperation in the United States, J. H. Studies*, ser. VI, nos. 4-6 (Baltimore: N. Murray, 1888); Ely to Shaw, Sept. 16, 1885, Jan. 27, Feb. 22, 1886, all in Shaw MSS; Shaw to Ely, Dec. 18, 1887, Richard T. Ely MSS, State Historical Society of Wisconsin.

His attitude toward labor is clearly limned in a lengthy section of the monograph dealing with the coopers of Minneapolis. The need for flour barrels made their trade a necessary adjunct of the rising Minneapolis milling industry and afforded them auspicious circumstances in which to test the cooperative mode of labor. Some coopers established a cooperative shop in 1868 only to have success denied them when one of their number converted the enterprise into a business for himself and bought out his erstwhile associates. A second try in 1874 brought better results when Charles Pillsbury, who was himself only getting started, granted a group of cooperative coopers a contract to supply one of his mills with barrels. Their success led others to follow. Shaw was much impressed by the strength of character the participants seemed to derive from their semientrepreneurial status. The majority were home-owning married men who possessed the admirable virtues of thrift, sobriety, and everything that has always smacked of old New England.[18] "Their sympathies," he observed, "are with law and order and public morality. They are Knights of Labor, with few exceptions, but are always opposed to violent or unreasonable methods; and their influence upon the whole body of Minneapolis Knights, which is very large, is strong and salutary."[19]

Earlier Shaw had done a forthright article on laissez faire. On its completion he sent it to Bryce who arranged for its publication in the *Contemporary Review* as "The American State and the American Man." Its thesis was that laissez faire was neither practical nor practiced. The state was actively concerned with the lives of its citizens, he argued. It created legislation on the school system and supported a state university (most of the examples Shaw used came from Minnesota and the surrounding area), passed fish and game statutes, regulated railroads and grain elevators, and operated in the public sphere in several other ways. In a lengthy concluding statement Shaw listed his ideals. He called for complete "emancipation from

18 Shaw, "Cooperation in the Northwest," pp. 199-242.
19 Ibid., p. 238.

the laissez-faire bugbear"; its replacement by the acknowledge-
ment that "it is within the legitimate province of the State
to do anything and everything"; and the tempering of this
legislative power by the use of "statistical and comparative
study" as a preliminary to law-making. "The theories of a
Herbert Spencer," he added with a flourish, "could afford
little practical aid, and neither could the theories of a Henry
George; for the *laissez-faire* doctrine of government is as
foreign to the true genius of social and political life in the
Western States as is the ultra-Socialistic doctrine."[20]

Shaw had additional publications. Some articles for the
Chautauquan, reviews for the *Dial,* and editorship of a collection of essays, *The National Revenues,* were among these. The
last is worth notice. It was a highly prestigious association for
him, the roster of contributors reading like a "Who's Who"
of the academic world, or at least of the AEA. Included
among the authors were Ely, Woodrow Wilson, John Bates
Clark, Edwin R. A. Seligman, and J. Laurence Laughlin.[21]

Despite his considerable success as an editor and a scholar,
Shaw grew dissatisfied with his lot. On the surface his personal
affairs seemed satisfactory. He shared a home with his mother,
had a decent salary, and made congenial friends among the
professional people of Minneapolis. Two unhappy experiences—one a broken engagement, the other a dispute with his
employer—mar the record, but he had become disillusioned
well before either occurrence.[22]

His attitude, it seems, developed much as it had in Grinnell.
Newspaper work was not exactly what he wanted. It was, he

20 Shaw, "The American State and the American Man," *Contemporary Review,*
LI (May 1887), 695-711; Shaw to Bryce, Nov. 27, 1885, Feb. 2, 1886, both in
Bryce MSS; Bryce to Shaw, Jan. 3, 1886, Percy Bunting to Shaw, Jan. 17, 1887,
both in Shaw MSS.

21 Shaw, ed., *The National Revenues: A Collection of Papers by American
Economists* (Chicago: A. C. McClurg & Co., 1888). A chronological listing of
Albert Shaw's publications is available in the bibliography.

22 Shaw to H. B. Adams, Jan. 9, 1887, Adams MSS; Shaw to Jameson, July
18, 1883, Feb. 18, 1888, both in Jameson MSS; Elgin R. L. Gould to Shaw, Aug.
19, 1884, Mary Shaw Fisher to Shaw, July 7, 1886, W. H. Burke to Shaw, Oct.
24, 1887, Charles Pillsbury to Shaw, July 20, 1891, Stewart Anderson to Shaw,
Oct. 17, 1899, all in Shaw MSS.

lamented to Wilson, "a pretty tiresome grind," which placed him, he had complained earlier, "in the constant condition of a man who is running to catch a train."[23] And despite an opportunity to do some good in his editorials, he could not always reach in Minneapolis the type of audience he desired nor consistently write in the learned manner he preferred. In 1886 Shaw had had a chance to teach at Indiana University but rejected the offer to remain at his job.[24] Within the next two years, however, he decided that he had to get away from the editorial routine.

Matters moved swiftly in 1888. Shaw narrowly missed receiving a bid to teach at Cornell but did get an offer from Wesleyan, which he declined. (The post was accepted by Wilson.) Instead he decided to travel to Europe with a brief stop on the way east to lecture before the Cornell Political Science Association. He had considered such a trip for some time but perhaps because of its expense had postponed making it. When he finally decided to go he had three purposes: relaxation, sightseeing, and research. For several years he had wished to study foreign municipal institutions and now saw the chance to do so.

The suggestion from Jesse Macy, who was then touring Great Britain, that Shaw join him to "go through the country notebook in hand and take a sort of photograph of the present political and social conditions of England" was surely an inducement for Shaw to journey abroad at this time. In any event he had nothing to lose. His old job in Minneapolis would probably remain available to him; if not, he would be well rested and even better prepared for the academic career that was his whenever he wanted it. In fact the possibility remained that Cornell might yet offer him a position.[25]

23 Shaw to Wilson, May 23, 1887, Wilson MSS; Shaw to Jameson, Nov. 2, 1884, Jameson MSS.
24 David Starr Jordan to Shaw, Apr. 14, 22, May 1, 10, 1886, all in Shaw MSS.
25 Ely to Shaw, Oct. 31, 1885, Oct. 9, 1886, Jan. 26, Apr. 23, 1888, Macy to Shaw, Sept. 21, 1887, all in Shaw MSS; Shaw to Jameson, Feb. 18, Mar. 14, Oct. 22, 1888, all in Jameson MSS; *Minneapolis Journal,* May 29, 1889.

Shaw sailed for England in the spring of 1888, planning
first to go to London for a visit with Bryce. The Englishman
was then finishing his *American Commonwealth* and was
anxious to have Shaw comment on it. Several informed
Americans contributed to the making of the *American Commonwealth,* but Shaw still took special pride in his role in the
preparation of this classic work since Bryce had first started
to consult him when he was still only a student. Bryce had
quoted extensively from his "Local Government in Illinois,"
had welcomed his opinions on laissez faire and on local politics
in Minneapolis, and now wished to have Shaw read the manuscript in order to see what revisions might be called for. Since
most of Bryce's closest American contacts were with eastern
intellectuals, it seems likely that he expected Shaw to offer
certain insights which otherwise might not be made available
to him. Shaw was a primary source of information on the
upper Midwest. Shaw's influence was again felt: Bryce accepted his advice that he modify some disparaging remarks on
American colleges and universities, the western ones in particular.[26]

In the course of their discussions about the *American
Commonwealth* and other matters, Shaw was at Bryce's home
for dinner several times. He met there such luminaries as
William Gladstone and Lord Acton and in general received
entrée to the British Liberal establishment. Among those
persons he met through Bryce was the editor of the *Pall Mall
Gazette,* William T. Stead. This acquaintanceship resulted
quickly in the chance to do some writing for the newspaper.
In the long run it had profound consequences, steering Shaw
to the post he would hold for almost half a century, the
editorship of the American *Review of Reviews.*[27]

26 Shaw to Jameson, Feb. 18, 1888, Jan. 10, 1889, both in Jameson MSS; Bryce
to Shaw, Nov. 27, 1884, Mar. 24, June 21, 25, Aug. 12, Sept. 30, 1888, Susan
Shaw to Shaw, Oct. 2, 1888, all in Shaw MSS; Ions, *Bryce and American
Democracy,* pp. 128-41, 300-301; James Bryce, *American Commonwealth,* 2 vols.
(London and New York: Macmillan, 1888), I, vii, 572-76, II, 90-92, 410, 525-53;
Shaw, "James Bryce, As We Knew Him in America," *American Review of
Reviews,* LXV (1922), 281.
27 Ibid.; William T. Stead to Shaw, Feb. 1, 1889, Shaw MSS.

There were other highlights to Shaw's trip: enjoyable and profitable visits to Birmingham, Edinburgh, and especially Glasgow, which was carrying on some unusually interesting municipal activities. He also made a rewarding stop at Bath where he attended the annual meeting of the British Association for the Advancement of Science and presented a paper in which he analyzed trends in American tariff politics.[28] The conclusion he reached was that the United States had been and would remain essentially protectionist but that in the future specific rates should be framed by an impartial commission of experts rather than in the partisan atmosphere of Congress.[29]

Shaw hated to leave Great Britain. Nevertheless a visit to the Continent had been part of his plans, and Shaw finally journeyed to France late in 1888. After three months in Paris Shaw toured several German cities before joining Will Noyes and his wife for a trip through Italy. From Italy Shaw proceeded alone to Egypt and then to Beirut for a visit with his ailing mother and with the Fishers (with whom she was staying). Dr. Fisher was practicing there at the Protestant College. Traveling next to Tripoli, Athens, and Constantinople, he concluded his trip by returning overland to England via Belgrade and Paris.[30]

After returning home he submitted to the *Chautauquan* some superficial sketches of the various nations he had visited, while for the *Century Magazine* he began a series of articles (completed only after he had moved to New York) in which he analyzed municipal government in detail. Throughout the

[28] Bryce to Shaw, Sept. 11, 30, 1888, Susan Shaw to Shaw, Sept. 1, 1888, Shaw to Hollis Godfrey, Apr. 7, 1926, all in Shaw MSS; Shaw to Jameson, Oct. 22, 1888, Jameson MSS; British Association for the Advancement of Science, "Journal of Sectional Proceedings" (1888), no. 4, pp. 11-12, no. 5, pp. 12-13; Shaw, "Wilson MS," ch. 7, p. 34.

[29] The published version of the paper is cited here. Shaw, "The American Tariff," *Contemporary Review*, LIV (Nov. 1888), 683-94.

[30] W. L. Halstead, *Story of the Halsteads*, p. 100; Susan Shaw to Shaw, Feb. 18, 1889, William C. Gates to Shaw, Mar. 5, 1889, William W. Folwell to Shaw, Apr. 25, 1889, all in Shaw MSS; Shaw to Susan Shaw, June 8, 18, 23, July 9, 12, 24, 27, 1889, all in the possession of Albert Shaw, Jr.; Shaw to Jameson, Jan. 10, 1889, Jameson MSS.

series Shaw was again most concerned with the problems of sanitation, the functioning of utilities, and the effectiveness of administration. As a rule he found British cities impressive in the quality of their officials and in the operaton of their services. Public health precautions were satisfactory, and the utilities were well managed. If they remained under private ownership, excellent service was ensured by sensible regulations. On the Continent as well he found much that he admired. Even Budapest displayed an intelligent attitude toward these problems and maintained a surprisingly good record in sanitation considering its proximity to the backward Ottoman Empire. In short he was highly pleased with municipal life in Europe and felt that American communities could profit by studying it.[31]

The trip to Europe was of vital importance to Shaw. Not only did it bring him into contact with Stead, but also it gave him the opportunity to develop systematically his thinking about urban problems. Even before he began the series of articles on municipal government, Shaw's progressivism was clearly prefigured. His faith in his country's future, his belief in the constructive politics of a Blaine, his intellectual commitment to the study of social and economic questions, and his rejection of the laissez-faire dogma all pointed the way to his emergence as an important progressive thinker. Yet the chance to study at first hand the cities of Europe proved indispensable, for it enabled Shaw to draw together his ideas, to publish a group of articles that attracted much favorable attention, and to prepare the way for the publication of additional works that brought him to the forefront of the emerging progressive movement of the 1890s.

In the immediate sense, though, the trip was a failure, for the year's break did not serve to dispel his discontent with the

---

[31] R. O. Beard to Shaw, Sept. 29, 1888, Shaw to George A. Gates, Nov. 7, 1896, Shaw to John Kingsbury, May 2, 1935, Shaw to Nellie Hall, Apr. 24, 1936, all in Shaw MSS; Shaw to Adams, July 17, 1890, Adams MSS; Shaw, "Glasgow: A Municipal Study," *Century Magazine*, n.s. XVII (Mar. 1890), 721-36; "How London is Governed," ibid., n.s. XIX (Nov. 1890), 132-47; "Budapest: The Rise of a New Metropolis," ibid., n.s. XXII (June 1892), 163-79.

grind of newspaper journalism. From the time of his return to Minneapolis in the summer of 1889 Shaw seemed prepared to move, refusing Blethen's suggestion to purchase a share in the *Tribune* or even to sign a long-term contract.[32] He remained dissatisfied with his job and must also have been influenced in his desire to leave Minneapolis by his mother's continued illness. Afflicted with a lung ailment, Mrs. Shaw had returned to the United States with the Fishers and remained with them when they settled in Dr. Fisher's home town of Warsaw, New York. She would die there in 1892. A job in the East would thus have appealed to Shaw.[33]

Although he claimed that he could have had a minor position in the government or diplomatic service, Shaw finally seemed about to begin an academic career. Another leave of absence from the *Tribune* in the late fall of 1889 gave him the chance to lecture on European urban conditions at Cornell, Johns Hopkins, and Michigan universities. He taught the same course commendably at all three schools and succeeded in bolstering his already impressive scholarly credentials.[34] Several job possibilities now loomed. Herbert Baxter Adams submitted his name for the presidency of the University of Kansas, where there was a "grand opening for a man with your eastern training and western experience," he advised. Nothing resulted of this, but Wesleyan offered him the chair he had once refused. Wilson had resigned it to go to Princeton. Shaw again declined it but, he reported to Adams, found himself tempted to join Wilson, whose new position required him to teach both political science and political economy. Although Wilson was knowledgable in the latter discipline, he did not

32 Shaw to Adams, Aug. 8, 27, 1889, both in Adams MSS; Shaw to Susan Shaw, Aug. 19, 1889, Shaw MSS.

33 W. L. Halstead, *Story of the Halsteads,* p. 100; W. C. Gates to Shaw, Mar. 5, 1889, Susan Shaw to Shaw, Aug. 21, 1889, James E. Rhodes to Shaw, June 11, 1890, Shaw to Susan Shaw, July 16, Oct. 20, 1890, all in Shaw MSS.

34 Shaw, "Wilson MS," ch. 7, p. 30; Shaw to H. B. Adams, Aug. 27, 1889, Adams MSS; Shaw to Susan Shaw, Aug. 22, 1889, Frank Trissal to Shaw, Aug. 13, 1889, D. F. Emerson to Shaw, Nov. 17, 1889, Charles Kendall Adams to Shaw, Nov. 11, 1889, Andrew D. White to Shaw, Nov. 23, 1889, all in Shaw MSS; Shaw to Jameson, Oct. 29, 1889, Jameson MSS.

wish to teach it. He sought instead to have a separate chair of political economy established for Shaw.[35]

Wilson kept lobbying for him for over a year, but since the situation at Princeton remained indefinite Shaw decided to consider alternatives to it. He could at last have gone to Cornell, where two years before his appointment to a professorship in political economy had been blocked by the protests of some faculty members of free trade convictions. Their objections, so the story goes, were founded on the assumption that his employment by a Republican journal meant that he had to be an avid protectionist. Reluctance to see dissension created on the staff had caused the administration to table Shaw's nomination, but when the supposedly less sensitive professorship of political institutions and international law became vacant, faculty endorsement was forthcoming. Rumored since May, Shaw's appointment, which was to take effect with the 1891-92 academic year, was confirmed in October. Several papers even announced it. But just before news of it appeared in the press, Shaw had received a more intriguing offer: the chance to move to New York and manage an American edition of the recently established British periodical, the *Review of Reviews*.[36]

The offer came from his English acquaintance, William T. Stead, the founder and owner of the *Review*. On Stead's invitation Shaw went to London in November 1890 to discuss matters and secured what seemed a favorable agreement.[37] He would receive the $5,000 basic salary that Stead's proposition had mentioned (this was $2,000 more than he could earn at either Cornell or Minneapolis), half of the net profits of

35 Shaw, "Wilson MS," ch. 7, p. 27; Adams to Shaw, May 9, 1889, Shaw to Susan Shaw, June 9, 1890, both in Shaw MSS; Shaw to Adams, May 31, 1890, Adams MSS.
36 Shaw, "Wilson MS," ch. 7, pp. 32-36; Shaw to Susan Shaw, May 3, June 9, Oct. 20, 21, 28, 1890, C. K. Adams to Shaw, May 31, June 5, 1890, Stead to Shaw, Oct. 1, 4, 1890, Scaife to Shaw, Jan. 11, 1891, all in Shaw MSS; Shaw to Wilson, Nov. 6, 1890, in Arthur S. Link, ed., *The Papers of Woodrow Wilson, 1890-92* (Princeton: Princeton University Press, 1969), VII, 71-74.
37 *Minneapolis Tribune*, Nov. 17, 1890; Shaw to Susan Shaw, Oct. 20, Dec. 3, 12, 1890, all in Shaw MSS.

the American edition, and the promise of a year's severance pay in case of dismissal without notice. Editorially Shaw's discretion would be wide: "to leave out, put in, alter or cut about each successive number, so long as he conducts it [the magazine] in harmony with the broad general principles laid down in the first number, as interpreted by the issues of the first year." Control over all personnel and financial matters would rest with Shaw, who would be responsible only to Stead in London. He accepted the proposition while in England and returned to the United States just after Christmas to begin his new duties.[38]

The reasons why Shaw chose the editorship seem clear. In the short run money was not much of a factor. Although his financial resources were committed in unremunerative investments in real estate, the greater income that the *Review* offered was balanced by the uncertainty that attended its newness. More important was the chance to settle in New York, at the center of events. As Adams put it: "Cornell University is a lonely monastery compared with New York and the editorial bureau, such as you will establish in that metropolis." Another consideration was that the new job was in the nature of a compromise between the career alternatives that confronted him. Editing a monthly magazine, Shaw could reason, would allow him to analyze events more reflectively than had been possible in his work on the daily *Tribune*. He even hoped to have more time available for outside studies, perhaps to do some teaching.[39] And, after all, journalism had long been his chosen profession. It deserved at least one more try.

[38] William T. Stead and Albert Shaw, cosigners, Memorandum of Agreement as to the Publication of the American Edition of the Review of Reviews, Dec. 26, 1890, Shaw MSS.

[39] Shaw to Susan Shaw, July 16, Sept. 27, Oct. 10, 20, 21, Dec. 26, 1890, Adams to Shaw, Jan. 24, 1891, all in Shaw MSS.

4

Dr. Shaw and His *Review*, 1891-1920

The *Review of Reviews* had been founded in London by the brilliant and erratic William T. Stead. A veteran journalist as well as a crusader for social reform and the "white man's burden," Stead was likely to rise to a journalistic coup or to sink into the mire of a lost cause. In 1890, however, he was at the height of his journalistic career when he established a magazine which he expected would serve as a clearinghouse for other magazines, or as he entitled it, the *Review of Reviews*. Typically Stead, thinking that the periodical should have wide distribution, had first gone to Rome to try and interest the Pope in undertaking the project. When the Pope refused, Stead returned home, started the magazine himself, and took "Vatican, London" as his cable address.[1]

The first portion of the new *Review*, an eighty-four page small-quarto monthly, presented Stead's analysis of current events, "The Progress of the World," perhaps some mention of his aspirations for human betterment, and a character sketch of some prominent person. A selection of political cartoons, added at the end of the first year, gave another dimension to the *Review*'s presentation of what Stead liked to call "contemporary history." The substance of the periodical was contained in two sections that ran about twenty pages each. "Leading Articles in the Reviews" summarized the best in current periodical literature. "The Reviews Reviewed" surveyed the contents of the leading magazines, emphasizing English and American ones, and noticed publications from Western Europe and Russia as well as various specialized journals. In addition a major book review, a brief listing of other new books, and another listing of magazine articles plus an index to them served to keep the reader well informed.[2]

Its reception was encouraging, and Stead, who was devoted to promoting unity among the English-speaking peoples, decided to publish editions in the United States (and later Australia) in the hope of spreading common ideals in these lands. At first he only forwarded materials which enabled the Critic Company of New York to publish in the U.S. copies of the English prototype. Stead soon realized, however, that reissuing a periodical some weeks after it had appeared in London resulted in a stale and unimaginative magazine. Flexibility could be obtained only by producing fresh copy in America. To succeed, Stead needed in New York an editor of competence and reliability. Under the circumstances Albert Shaw had seemed a logical choice, for in addition to having a superb education and a decade's experience in journalism, Shaw was a known commodity.[3] Or so Stead believed.

Recruiting a staff was the most vexing of the many problems Shaw faced at the start of his editorship. He turned his attention to it even as he was settling his affairs in Minneapolis, for it was urgent that he begin building an organization. The *Review* would not do its own printing, so a large crew was not needed. Nevertheless difficulties arose and there was con-

1 Estelle Stead, *My Father: Personal and Spiritual Reminiscenses* (London: William Heinemann, 1913), pp. 95-104; Frederic Whyte, *The Life of W. T. Stead*, 2 vols. (New York and Boston: Houghton Mifflin Co., 1925), I, 100-101, 287-89, 310-12; Shaw, "William T. Stead," *American Review of Reviews*, XLV (1912), 689-95. In establishing the *Review of Reviews*, Stead had been associated with George Newnes, an imaginative and enterprising journalist, who nevertheless found it impossible to work with Stead and soon sold out to him. Raymond L. Schults, *Crusader in Babylon: W. T. Stead and the Pall Mall Gazette* (Lincoln: University of Nebraska Press, 1972), pp. 250-55. Professor Joseph O. Baylen, whose important biography of Stead will soon be available to scholars, has also done numerous articles on the Englishman. The ones which do most to show the development of Stead's thinking on journalism are "W. T. Stead and the 'New Journalism,'" *Emory University Quarterly*, XXI (Fall 1965), 196-206, and "The 'New Journalism' in Late Victorian Britain," *Australian Journal of Politics and History*, XVIII (Dec. 1972), 367-84.

2 Frank Luther Mott, *A History of American Magazines*, 5 vols. (Cambridge: Harvard University Press, 1930-68), IV, 657-58; see, for example, *Review of Reviews*, III (Jan. 1891). All subsequent references are to the American edition, the name of which was altered several times.

3 Whyte, *Life of Stead*, I, 313-23; Stead to Shaw, Oct. 1, 1890, The Critic Co. to Shaw, Nov. 6, 1890, both in Shaw MSS.

siderable employee turnover at the outset, especially in the key post of business manager. The position initially went to William C. Gates, formerly of the *Milwaukee Sentinel*. Hoping to free himself for editorial work and writing, Shaw expected that Gates, an old acquaintance of his, would accept full responsibility for all business affairs and on this assumption promised him a basic salary equal to his own and half of his share of the profits. Gates handled the important early details of locating an office in New York, hiring a printer, and purchasing paper; but in less than two years he had to be released for lack of initiative. What must have been the low point in a deteriorating relationship between the two came when Gates strode into Shaw's office, tossed some ledgers on his desk, and told him to look up the information he wanted in them himself. His successor did not receive the same terms. A replacement proved unsatisfactory, but Shaw ultimately found the type of man he wanted as business manager in Charles Lanier (son of the poet Sidney Lanier), who held the position almost forty years.[4]

No other post was quite so difficult to fill. Robert Finley did well in an editorial role until he left to become manager of S. S. McClure's syndicate operations. William B. Shaw, a Hopkins man, as were Lanier and Finley, joined the *Review* in 1894, having already contributed a good article. A former associate of Albert Shaw on the *Tribune* turned out poorly as an editor, but later additions such as Howard Florance, William Menkel, and George Pettengill proved able. A few men handled the minor positions, and four women in secretarial capacities completed the staff.[5]

[4] "Memorandum" between Albert Shaw and William C. Gates, Feb. 17, 1891, in "Supreme Court-Appellate Division—First Department, William C. Gates, Plaintiff-Respondent, against William T. Stead, Defendant-Appellant," Case on appeal (New York: Appeal Printing Company, 1900), pp. 7, 27-29, 66-68, 76-77; *Buffalo Courier*, Nov. 16, 1892, Scrapbooks, Shaw MSS; William T. Stead to Shaw, Aug. 5, 1893, Shaw to Stead, Apr. 4, 1892, Shaw to Newton Hawley, Apr. 7, 1892, Charles Lanier to Shaw, June 5, 1892, June 23, 1893, Stead to Shaw, Aug. 5, 1893, Shaw to Howard Florance, Aug. 16, 1934, all in Shaw MSS.
[5] Belinda, "Shaw's Work Shop," *Minneapolis Journal*, Feb. 6, 1892, Scrapbooks, Shaw MSS; *Review of Reviews* Weekly Pay Roll, Sept. 6, 1892, William B. Shaw to Florance, July 19, Oct. 19, 1937, W. B. Shaw to Shaw, Dec. 16, 1893, Feb. 25,

The first issue of the American *Review* appeared in April, 1891. It was much like the English edition in departmentalization; succeeding numbers remained so. The American *Review*, like its prototype, was designed for a middle-class audience. Nevertheless changes were evident from the start, for Shaw wished to enhance the *Review*'s appeal to Americans. He enlarged the magazine, adding to it more caricatures and a number of contributed articles and preparing a longer and usually more subdued "Progress" than Stead had been in the habit of doing. "Leading Articles" remained substantially the same, save that this department focused more on American material, while the "Reviews Reviewed" was shortened in order to provide space for other departments. Both sections were retitled. Technical changes were all for the better. The paper used was superior, and illustrations were more profuse and more sharply reproduced, making the *Review* a leader among contemporary publications in the use of visual materials.[6]

Despite the quality of the magazine it was unlikely to catch on and show a profit at once, and for that reason the first months or even years were crucial: could the *Review of Reviews* survive an initial deficit? Stead was not independently wealthy but felt he could maintain the *Review* and quickly advanced £2000 to Shaw. By the end of 1891 he had supplied an additional £3000, or almost $25,000 just in the abbreviated first year. But in the meanwhile Stead had fallen into financial difficulty in London and found it necessary to borrow. He mortgaged the *Review*, the American edition included. Friction between the two editors resulted, for the mortgage, which carried with it the threat of foreclosure and assumption of control by outsiders, made for tension between them.[7]

1894, W. W. Tryon to Shaw, Oct. 24, 1898, all in Shaw MSS; Shaw to Daniel Coit Gilman, Mar. 21, 1895, Daniel Coit Gilman MSS, Johns Hopkins University Library; Harold S. Wilson, *McClure's Magazine and the Muckrakers* (Princeton: Princeton University Press, 1970), p. 22.

6 Mott, *American Magazines*, IV, 657-59; see, for example, *Review of Reviews*, III (Jan. 1891) and (Amer. ed.), V (June 1892).

7 "Gates against Stead," pp. 10d, 35-36; Shaw to Stead, Jan. 8, 1893, Stead to Shaw, Sept. 16, 1891, Statement, W. T. Stead to the Review of Reviews Co.,

Even beforehand matters had not been altogether serene. Separated by the Atlantic Ocean, Shaw and Stead blamed each other for certain alleged errors. Most of the recriminations originated with Shaw, who felt that as the editor on the scene his judgments about the American *Review* had to be accepted. Temperament was deeply involved too. Whereas Stead was unpredictable in his behavior, Albert Shaw was a highly responsible and ambitious man. Viewed in this perspective, the events of the *Review*'s first half dozen years, which saw Shaw constantly enlarging his role, seemed almost inevitable.

The initial difficulty had come early. Shaw took alarm at reports that Stead was engaged in schemes which might divert the Englishman's attention from the business of establishing the *Review*. A misunderstanding as to the speed with which material could be forwarded to New York also irked Shaw. Stead sidestepped a confrontation. He simply pointed out to Shaw that "I am what I am" and noted that transatlantic quarreling would not resolve much.[8]

Shortly they were at it again when Shaw touchily refused to feature a sketch on the controversial theosophist Madame Blavatsky that had occupied a prominent place in the English *Review*. Although Stead had himself written an enthusiastic introduction to the article in question, he deferred to Shaw and merely remarked that "if it suits [you] better to leave out Madam Blavatsky, for Heaven's sake leave Madam Blavatsky out." As it turned out, Shaw did use the article, albeit in abbreviated form and in a less conspicuous place than it had originally held.[9]

Although minor in itself, the dispute was symptomatic of

1893, all in Shaw MSS. This statement lists Stead's advances between March and November 1891, as £4524 or $21,952.37. Shaw later stipulated total advances for 1891 as £5000 (Shaw to Stead, Jan. 9, 1893, Shaw MSS), so perhaps an entry is not listed. The dollar-pound exchange rate for each payment varied between 4.815 to 4.88. The average was $4.85 7/9 to £1 sterling.

[8] Stead to Shaw, Mar. 25, 1891, Shaw to Stead, Aug. 26, 1891, both in Shaw MSS.

[9] Shaw to Adams, May 28, June 9, 1891, both in Adams MSS; Stead to Shaw, June 10, 1891, Shaw MSS. The article Shaw objected to had appeared as a character sketch in the English *Review of Reviews*. See William T. Stead and A. P. Stinnett, "Madame Blavatsky," III (June 1891), 548-58.

the fundamental incompatibility of the relationship between Shaw and Stead. As such it involves an interesting story that had its background in Shaw's academic ambitions. At the time he assumed the editorship of the *Review of Reviews,* Shaw still entertained hopes of being called to Princeton. Wilson had informed him that the administration would not object if he continued to edit the *Review* while teaching there. Shaw unrealistically thought he could do both. But a group of Princeton trustees took exception to a pair of shrill and "flippant" articles in the initial issue of the American *Review.* Under pressure to meet the printer's deadline, Shaw had used them just as they had appeared in the London edition. The decision probably cost him the coveted chair, for the concerned trustees reasoned that Princeton could not afford, even so indirectly, to be associated with the controversial Stead and questioned the wisdom of hiring Shaw. Other candidates were looked at more favorably than before. Shaw hastened to assure Wilson of his sound judgment. He wrote that he admired Stead's moral earnestness but realized that his own constituency was conservative (the names of clerics and college presidents were prominent on its subscription list) and would act accordingly in deciding which of Stead's articles to use. Thus his decision to handle the Blavatsky piece with caution.[10]

The deflation of Shaw's Princeton bubble preceded by only a few months an internal crisis on the *Review;* together they forced him to abandon the idea of combining academic and editorial careers and to commit himself without reservation to the American *Review of Reviews.* The magazine's financial woes precipitated Shaw's decision. Shaw had underestimated possible deficits for the first year of operation, and Stead had supplied £1000 more than the £4000 Shaw had predicted necessary. That was all the hard-pressed Stead could spare, and the American *Review* was faced with a shortage of funds. Shaw sailed for London late in 1891 to discuss the

---

[10] Wilson to Shaw, Nov. 11, 1890, June 26, July 14, 1891; Shaw to Wilson, Nov. 6, 1890, July 1, 1891, all in Link, ed., *Papers of Wilson,* VII, 71-74, 75-76, 225-26, 229-32, 243-45.

situation with Stead, but his arrival only aggravated it; Stead simply ignored his presence to work on a book of ghost stories. Shaw finally had to demand an interview during which the two worked out a new business arrangement. Shaw, who had to borrow to do so, would cover additional deficits in return for an interest (tentatively set at 45 percent) in the American *Review*. After setting a cash value of about £2500 on this share, it was agreed that Shaw would pay directly to Stead whatever portion was not needed to cover operating losses. In return, Stead promised to have the mortgage on the American edition raised.[11]

The future of the enterprise, however, was still far from assured, and Shaw was in the process of working up a case of dyspepsia over it. But remaining sure of eventual success, he sought a larger stake in the American *Review of Reviews*. Stead lamented that Shaw seemed to think more of money than of the Anglo-Saxon race, but as usual the Englishman yielded and asked Shaw to propose definite terms.[12] Alarmed by Stead's tardiness in having the mortgage lifted, Shaw decisively set forth his views: he informed Stead that he wanted immediate acquisition of a half-interest plus the commitment of an additional 5 percent. "I know now," claimed Shaw, "that I can make the American Review a success as an *influence and a power*." Although he would have "the American edition carry as much as it safely can of your material," Shaw continued, "I must in justice to myself and to my American constituency have the magazine in such trim that if you died tomorrow, or if all the ships in the Atlantic were sunk, or if an earthquake swallowed up your island, the American Review could go right on without a break or an embarrassment."[13] Acceptance of the proposition would in effect reduce Stead to the honorary post of inspirational editor that Shaw had

11 "Gates against Stead," pp. 10e-10f, 35-41, 90-93, 103-4; undated Shaw Memorandum on the financial situation; David Eshbaugh to Shaw, Jan. 14, 1892, Stead to Shaw, Oct. 21, 1891, Jan. 16, 1892, Feb. 6, 1892, all in Shaw MSS.

12 Shaw to Hawley, Feb. 6, 1894, Stead to Shaw, Feb. 6, 1892, May 19, 1893, all in Shaw MSS.

13 Shaw to Stead, Apr. 4, 1892, Shaw MSS.

allotted him, but Stead acquiesced and the momentum in defining the relationship between the two editors was more clearly than ever with Shaw.[14]

This series of events culminated in the incorporation of the *American Review* at the end of 1892. The timing of this move was influenced by the filing of a law suit against Stead by the recently discharged William Gates, but it had been envisioned by Shaw for several months. Attorney Horace Deming handled the details of incorporation which was the logical means of operating the magazine as a legal entity separate from the English *Review*. The two men remained the principal owners, Shaw holding 55 percent of the stock.[15] He maintained, he assured Stead, his "own practically autocratic control of the American Review of Reviews quite as much for your sake as for my own."[16] Shaw and Stead assumed two of the directorships. The remaining places were filled by Shaw's banker, his brother-in-law John Fisher, and his financial adviser, or as Stead characterized the three, "men of straw."[17]

Six months prior to the incorporation, funds had been so short that the harassed financial manager had exclaimed: "In God we trust; all others cash."[18] Yet because the *Review* had succeeded in gaining a valued reputation and identity an upswing soon set in, and in 1893 Shaw's hopes were fulfilled. The first quarter of the year was profitable thanks to heavy subscription revenues. But that source of income quickly dwindled, and the financial ledger for April bordered on the red. About 85,000 copies of the *Review* were then being printed, but almost an eighth of that total accounted for no cash income, for many had to be distributed gratis to adver-

14 Shaw to Stead, Apr. 14, 1892, Shaw MSS.

15 William T. Stead and Albert Shaw to the Review of Reviews Company. Assignment valid Dec. 24, 1892; Stead to Shaw, Apr. 4, 14, Nov. 23, 1892, Shaw to Stead, Jan. 14, 27, Nov. 23, 1893, Jan. 11, 1894, all in Shaw MSS. Shaw had to borrow to cover this and investments in unproductive western properties. Hawley to Shaw, Nov. 23, 1891, Jan. 30, 1893, Shaw to Hawley, Feb. 6, 1894, all in Shaw MSS.

16 Shaw to Stead (extract copy), Jan. 14, 1893, Shaw MSS.

17 Stead to Shaw, Dec. 3, 1892, Shaw MSS.

18 Gates to Shaw, June 24, 1892, Shaw MSS.

tisers, as exchanges with other magazines, or else were returned to the office unsold. Yet revenue for the remainder of the year proved to be heartening. At year's end the books showed a surplus of almost $25,000, 60 percent of which could safely be distributed. Stead now received the final payment due him for the equity he had relinquished in the *Review*. The board voted Shaw a $5,000 salary increment and an equal amount as a bonus for his double work as manager and editor.[19]

The upturn in the *Review*'s fortunes came when it was most needed, for by early 1893 a combination of overwork, grief occasioned by his mother's passing the previous summer, and the stress of his continuing difficulties with Stead had brought Shaw to the point of collapse. Leaving Robert Finley in charge of the office, he took his first extended break, traveling, visiting relatives (he met his future wife while staying with sister Lucy in Noblesville, Indiana), and only settling down to editorial routine at the end of the year.[20]

On his return to the office he again found himself embarrassed by Stead. The trouble began when the irrepressible Englishman undertook a trip to Chicago in the fall of 1893. Stead soon began drawing much attention to his outspoken remarks about vice and poverty. After leaving the city briefly, he returned in December to deliver a shocking speech in which he accused society matrons of caring only for their comforts and of ignoring the abominations of the slums. Stead included in these impromptu remarks the charge that for this they were "the most disreputable women" in Chicago. The press, already alienated from Stead, thought the performance "insulting" and "offensive," with the alarmed Shaw privately agreeing from New York.[21]

19 Monthly statements of the Review of Reviews Co. for Months of Apr. through July 1893; Lanier to Shaw, Jan. 3, 1894, Shaw to Stead, Jan. 11, 1894, Stead to Shaw, Jan. 18, Feb. 4, Apr. 22, 1893, all in Shaw MSS.

20 Wilson, *McClure's Magazine and the Muckrackers*, p. 22; Shaw to Adams, Feb. 15, 1894, Adams MSS.

21 Joseph O. Baylen, "A Victorian's 'Crusade' in Chicago, 1893-1894," *Journal of American History*, LI (Dec. 1964), 421-29; Shaw to Hawley, Feb. 6, 1894, Shaw MSS.

The publication of Stead's *If Christ Came to Chicago* early the following year greatly aggravated matters. The book, which was intended to shock Chicagoans into reform, announced the presence of sin and corruption and specified their whereabouts, opening with a map of Chicago's tenderloin district. Many were not so sure of the results, however, and even feared that the revelations might increase sin by making it easier to find. Fearful that the uproar surrounding Stead would undermine the *Review*'s hard-earned reputation, Shaw dissociated himself as much as possible from Stead and refused to market *If Christ Came to Chicago* through the *Review*.[22]

There were other quarrels that directly concerned the *Review*. Stead still contributed articles and supplied information on, and copies of, the British and Continental periodicals necessary for such sections of the magazine as "Leading Articles." Delays in shipment of the various proofs, illustrations, and periodicals were understandably annoying. Another irritant was Stead's habit of advertising an English *Review* with subordinate American and Australian editions. That, of course, was not the case, for Shaw had established a distinctly American periodical, and he insisted that this be recognized.[23] The demarcation between the two periodicals was made clear in Shaw's editorials which diverged sharply from the original ideals of Stead. While Shaw over the years was a friend of Britain, he would not in a specific clash of national interests subscribe to the Anglo-Saxon sentimentality which captivated Stead. The boundary dispute of 1895 which aroused considerable American wrath at British efforts to secure territorial gains for a colony at the expense of Venezuela furnished occasion for a demonstration of this. The American *Review* stood forth as a paragon of patriotism to note the "reckless" or "evil" ways of British statesmen. And its editor privately observed to Stead: "I believe that Anglo-Saxon civilization

22 Baylen, "A Victorian's 'Crusade,'" pp. 430-32; Shaw to George A. Gates, Dec. 31, 1894, Shaw MSS.
23 Shaw to Stead, Dec. 30, 1893, Nov. 20, Dec. 1, 1894, July 22, 1895, Stead to Shaw, Dec. 14, 1894, all in Shaw MSS.

would have a better chance if England were a little less greedy for territory."[24]

The two at last argued heatedly in 1897 when Stead refused to reduce further his share in the American *Review of Reviews*. Lanier had petitioned for a share in the corporation, he and Shaw agreeing it should come from Stead's interest. Stead's reply that each should sell one hundred shares to Lanier threatened Shaw's control of the corporation, for Shaw would then hold only a minority of the stock. Stead had added gratuitously that Shaw was suspiciously secretive in his conduct of financial affairs. Mutual recriminations resulted.[25] Shaw reminded Stead that the Englishman had received handsome financial balm for his discomfort and in effect suggested that he had been as helpful to the *Review* as an appendix is to a man. Stead, in turn, accused Shaw of returning Anglo-American relations to the status of 1776 and pleaded for "auld lang syne." The *Review*, he charged, was to have been "a pulpit from which to preach the Anglo-American Alliance. I left you to keep the keys of my pulpit, and now you have shut me out of it."[26] A change in the magazine's title at about this time to the *American Monthly Review of Reviews*—"the emphasis just a little stronger on the two prefixed words," insisted Shaw— furnished a convenient summation of the divergence between the two men.[27]

This sharp exchange proved to be useful in clearing the atmosphere, and outwardly correct relations were resumed. Thereafter, until his death when the *Titanic* sank in 1912, Stead remained a contributor to the magazine as well as its second largest stockholder. Ironically it was the American *Review* that provided a large part of Stead's income during

24 *Review of Reviews* (Amer. ed.), XII (1895), 645, XIII (1896), 9, 137, XIV (1896), 647-49; Shaw to Stead, Nov. 27, 1895, Shaw MSS.

25 Shaw to Stead, Jan. 22, 1897, Stead to Shaw, Feb. 4, 1897, both in Shaw MSS. Lanier finally acquired this stock from Stead's widow in 1913, a year after Stead's death. Andrew Carnegie to Lanier, Nov. 26, 1913, Andrew Carnegie MSS, Library of Congress.

26 Shaw to Stead, Apr. 30, 1897, Stead to Shaw, July 14, 1897, both in Shaw MSS.

27 Shaw to Joseph Gilder, June 22, 1897, Shaw MSS.

this last period of his life, for his own English edition had languished since the Boer War.[28]

At the time of the quarrel the *Review of Reviews,* to use the name which has stuck, had been on the threshold of its most successful years. Although it was by then profitable, continued success was by no means assured, for the periodical industry in the 1890s was expanding and highly fluid. Readership was climbing, and enterprising journalists like Shaw and S. S. McClure were parlaying imaginative new editorial concepts into Alger-like success stories. But by the same token the fluidity of the business—which has been called "the freest of free enterprise"—narrowed the margins for error,[29] a situation which had much to do with Shaw's mistrust of Stead's connection with the American *Review.*

The main trend in the periodical industry was the popularization and growing relevancy of the contents of the general magazine and the contest for mass circulations and the lucrative advertising accounts that went with them. It was the latter that generally determined the profitability of a periodical. Among the new periodicals *Munsey's* and *McClure's* achieved fabulous success in sales at a dime an issue, while the *Review* was sold at the moderately high price of a quarter. The *Review of Reviews* could succeed at this price, because it offered something different from the great dime monthlies. While *McClure's* and several other ten-cent monthlies did offer features of social concern, especially in their muckraking articles of the early 1900s, the *Review*—with the exception of the *Literary Digest* and possibly of *World's Work* after its establishment in 1900—did more with the reporting and analysis of current events than any other magazine of the era.

[28] Emma Stead to Carnegie, Apr. 30, 1912, Oct. 18, 1913, Henry Stead to Carnegie, May 4, 1912, all in Carnegie MSS. Shaw later had a chance to purchase the faltering English edition but decided not to get involved with it. Daniel O'Connor to Shaw, Nov. 15, 1922, Shaw to Lanier, Nov. 17, 1922, both in Shaw MSS.

[29] Theodore Peterson, *Magazines in the Twentieth Century* (Urbana: University of Illinois Press, 1964), pp. 10-11, 66-68, 129. For the vicissitudes of editing another new magazine of the 1890s, see Wilson, *McClure's Magazine and the Muckrakers,* pp. 60-103.

Not only was Shaw's editorial section popular, but in an age when the number of magazines was proliferating—from 2,369 monthlies in 1900 to 2,977 in 1910—its digests of other periodicals and their featured articles seemed a very helpful guide and time-saver.[30] For a while the *Review* even took the slogan "The Busy Man's Magazine," but gentlemen of leisure wanted to read it too. A reader promised: "If perchance I were put on a desert island or banished, I would ask but one favor, and that would be to have [your] paper sent me."[31] Although guest Number 27571 at San Quentin also claimed to be a faithful reader, it "seems to have been welcomed," Shaw proudly commented, "in the families of professional men and thoughtful people quite generally." A friend of Shaw, the novelist Winston Churchill, claimed that of all the magazines, the best were "Scribner's for Fiction and the *Review of Reviews* for everything else."[32]

Judging by sales, Churchill's comment was not inaccurate. For in its particular field the *Review* consistently overshadowed the newer and imitative *World's Work* and in per issue sales generally remained ahead of the weekly *Literary Digest* for almost the first two decades of their rivalry, which dated from the very founding of the American *Review*. Having held its own during the depression of the 1890s, the *Review* nearly doubled its circulation at the end of the decade, until by 1901 it was distributing over 178,000 copies per month, mostly through subscriptions.[33] The timing of the spurt in sales

[30] Mott, *American Magazines,* IV, 598-619; Peterson, *Magazines in the Twentieth Century,* pp. 57-60, 69-77.

[31] Mott, *American Magazines,* IV, 10, 662; H. P. Hubbard to Shaw, Jan. 3, 1901, Shaw MSS.

[32] William Melville to the *Review of Reviews,* Feb. 16, 1915, Shaw to (Miss) Galentine, Jan. 26, 1901, Churchill to Shaw, Apr. 27, 1898, all in Shaw MSS. For a description of *Scribner's* and other select periodicals, see Dorothy M. Brown, "The Quality Magazines in the Progressive Era," *Mid-America,* LIII (July 1971), 139-59.

[33] One cannot just multiply circulation statistics by twenty-five cents and come out with a round figure for revenue like $500,000 because there were many leakages along the line. School and group subscribers received discounts; country newspapers got free subscriptions in return for a monthly plug; the American News Co., which handled distribution to newsdealers, subtracted about half of every quarter; and so on. The fixed and operating expenses like

suggests that the *Review's* increased popularity stemmed not only from the return of prosperity but also—and perhaps mainly—from the heightened interest in the world situation dating from the Spanish-American War and the quickly breaking developments that followed it. Circulation subsequently edged up to the 200,000 mark, but in 1909 a modest decline set in which lasted until World War I. During this new crisis sales climbed to a peak of almost 250,000 monthly, and readership was probably considerably more extensive. Six people, a prewar survey had estimated, read each copy.[34]

Advertising developments were at least as cheerful. In 1902 a well-wisher noted the happy occasion when advertising (which the *Review* confined in a separate section) filled more pages than text, and that situation became customary. One hundred and twenty-eight pages were then devoted to text, as they had been since 1892. Advertising, which had a posted rate of $200 a page during these years, averaged 150 or more pages per issue, sometimes over 200 even in the slower days of 1910.[35] Its ad manager claimed that the *Review* was carrying "the largest amount of paid advertising in any magazine in the

---

salaries, office rental, and costs of paper, printing, photoengraving, electrotyping, and binding deducted more, so that net income would be a far different figure. Any attempt to pin down advertising revenue runs into similar complications, for there were arrangements for free space in return for some suitable quid pro quo, discounts to preferred advertisers, and so forth. Considerable money was also made by selling sets of books like O. Henry stories as a tie-in to subscribers. For example, from December 1903 through May 1904, the gross profits from the book accounts, advertising, and circulation were respectively $139,621.91; $120,494.85; and $118,699.90. Surplus income was $13,222.53, but substantial deductions had apparently first been distributed to the stockholders. The semiannual balance sheets tabulated by the accountant, Charles Noble, between 1896 and 1904 are useful, but unfortunately no figures are available after those of 1904. The next available financial statements date from the late 1920s. It is therefore impossible to discuss the *Review's* financial situation with precision. About all that can be said is that trends indicate that it was doing well.

34 Mott, *American Magazines*, IV, 21, 661-62; interview with Albert Shaw, Jr., Sept. 3, 1964; William Menkel to A. L. Frisbie, Mar. 30, 1910, Shaw MSS.

35 Henry B. F. Macfarland to Shaw (received), Nov. 9, 1902, Shaw MSS. The growth in advertising is indicated by two volumes published by the Review of Reviews Company as a lure to potential advertisers: *Does Magazine Publishing Pay? 1869 Answers By Concerns That Have Tried It and Found Out* (New York, 1909), and the earlier *The Experiences of 187 Advertisers* (New York, 1898).

world."[36] The tie-in sale of books was another profitable part
of the *Review*'s operations. The fact that the *Review* now
employed more than one hundred people at seasonal peaks
highlights its development.[37]

With success normal the *Review* adhered generally to the
formula it had followed from the start. Shaw gave his particular attention to the cartoon section and to "The Progress of
the World." Despite his caution he unhesitatingly supported
the issues he believed right. In the 1890s he probably had no
superior among editors as a proponent of municipal reform,
and in the first decade of the present century his widely
recognized friendship with Theodore Roosevelt won him
attention as a man who had something important to say. He
was a consistent advocate of an assertive foreign policy; on
domestic matters he enthusiastically seconded whatever Roosevelt proposed and in some instances took the lead, occasionally
using the *Review* as a sounding board for the president. While
he repeatedly insisted that his editorials were nonpartisan,
suffice it to say that his preferences were those of a progressive
Republican.

According to Frank Luther Mott, Albert Shaw's editorial
commentary was characterized by a "high standard of fairness
and unemotional rationality."[38] Shaw did have a lucid and
informed way of writing and discussed many topics in a genial
manner, often presenting both sides of an argument. In fact
it was precisely this quality which he felt was responsible for
much of his success.[39]

But there is another side to the story. Shaw knew that in
the *Review* he had found his métier. He no longer deprecated
his ability but instead boasted of his capacity to interpret
events. He developed a supreme confidence, even arrogance,
that was evident in the way he wrote about public affairs. On
matters where he thought political morality or the national

[36] Mott, *American Magazines*, IV, 661.
[37] Interview with Albert Shaw, Jr., Sept. 3, 1964; Albert Shaw, Jr., to author,
Mar. 15, 1969.
[38] Quoted in Mott, *American Magazines*, IV, 660.
[39] Shaw to Theodore Roosevelt, June 25, 1912, Shaw MSS.

interest was at stake he departed from his vaunted geniality to hit hard. Sure in the knowledge that he was fighting for righteousness, he could not tolerate criticism of his judgment or of his motivation. For instance he was dispassionate in his criticism of William Jennings Bryan in 1896 because he thought Bryan was merely wrong-headed. But toward Tammany Hall in the 1890s, and more flagrantly toward William Howard Taft in 1912 and George Norris and Franklin D. Roosevelt in later years, he made use of invective and innuendo, apparently without realizing that in doing so he was falling short of his own editorial standards.[40]

Staff members continued to handle the other departments of the magazine. "Leading Articles" remained a prominent feature, occupying some twenty pages in the latter part of each issue. Both the "Index to Periodicals" and "The Periodicals [Reviews] Reviewed" were discarded. "The Character Sketch" was retained on an occasional basis, usually appearing in the guise of a featured article. "The New Books," the caricatures, and "The Record of Current Events" were all traditional features.[41]

The contributed articles which had been few at the beginning came to occupy a third or more of the magazine, ten or twelve of these appearing in each issue. Initially they brought their authors no more than a penny a word (except in the case of big names), but then compensation climbed to almost three cents a word during World War I, and rose again in the 1920s. By then the *Review* was budgeting over $1,000 a month for authors' fees, about four times what it once had. The *Review of Reviews* did not use fiction, and if a novelist contributed it had to be as the author of something on the order of Churchill's "The Battle with Cervera's Fleet off Santiago" or Jack London's "The Economics of the Klondike."[42]

40 Shaw to Stead, July 22, 1895, Shaw to the Rev. Dan Freeman Bradley, Apr. 8, 1912, Shaw to Hamlin Garland, Aug. 13, 1912, all in Shaw MSS.
41 Mott, *American Magazines*, IV, 662; Shaw to (Miss) Galentine, Jan. 26, 1901, Shaw MSS.
42 Winston Churchill, "The Battle with Cervera's Fleet Off Santiago," *American Monthly Review of Reviews*, XVIII (1898), 153-67; Jack London, "The Economics of the Klondike," ibid., XXI (Jan. 1900), 70-74. No financial records are extant

Although the majority of the articles—of which many were written by leading scholars like John Rogers Commons, Richard T. Ely, and Jeremiah Jenks—treated domestic and foreign themes in their political and economic aspects, Shaw maintained a planned diversity. A representative month's contents might list such articles as "King Edward in England's Time of Crisis," "The Return of Halley's Comet," "Björnsen, The Poet Reformer," "Lessons from Western Fruit Culture for the East," and "No Tuberculosis in New York State in 1920!"[43] Shaw's specifications that each article be nonargumentative, informative, and timely almost ruled out muckraking and also made most unsolicited contributions unacceptable. Shaw made his policy explicit: not "to invite the general scribbling public to send all kinds of things to be read."[44]

The staff planned each issue carefully, trying to anticipate what would be timely. Each month's copy had to be completed by the twentieth—the day Shaw was so harried that he could not eat dinner—in order to meet a release date which fell on the first of the following month. In case of an emergency the schedule could still be tightened. The death of Queen Victoria on January 22, 1901, furnishes an example. The magazine was then ready to be delivered to the printers, two days late as it was, when Shaw heard the news. Very quickly he prepared four pages with which to introduce "The Progress," secured several illustrations for them, and by having everyone from photoengravers to binders work at an "unprecedented rate of speed," he boasted, had copies ready by the thirtieth.[45] A contributor once noted this ability and asked: "Is there any other magazine in America that gets its produce so quickly from the producer to the consumer?"[46]

that specify the writers' fees over the years, but they can be gleaned from correspondence between the *Review* and its contributors. See, for example, Jack London to the editor, *Review of Reviews*, Dec. 18, 1899, Richard Ballinger to Shaw, Dec. 30, 1909, and J. Russell Smith to Shaw, Sept. 28, 1917, all in Shaw MSS.

[43] All of these articles appeared in the April 1910 issue of the *American Review of Reviews*. The authors are, respectively: William T. Stead, S. A. Mitchell, Edwin Björkman, Agnes C. Laut, and John A. Kingsbury.

[44] Shaw to the Rev. Henry Stimson, Apr. 18, 1902, Shaw MSS.

[45] Shaw to C. W. Ordway, Apr. 13, 1897, Shaw to Louis Stevenson, Aug. 22, 1902, Shaw to Albert Beveridge, Jan. 20, 1901, all in Shaw MSS.

Yet this leaves unsaid the question of whether efficient editing of a monthly news magazine was enough. Even under the best working conditions and with the most favorable postal regulations in effect no current issue of the *Review* could include any news developments from the final week of a month. More often the lag was from ten days to two weeks. In this respect it is instructive to note that the *Review* experienced its sales slump in 1909 just as its old rival, the weekly *Literary Digest,* was finally forging ahead in circulation. This initial decline was not financially harmful, for advertisements remained abundant. Then during World War I sales surpassed the best previous figures by almost 25 percent. Portentous of trouble, however, was the fact that circulation of the *Literary Digest* exceeded one million.[47]

The staff had additional tasks. Tens of thousands and, in some peak years, upward of a half million letters came annually and had to be answered. Much of this correspondence concerned material for the *Review,* for many people submitted manuscripts without waiting for an invitation; some letters brought complaints that deserved an answer; while a few were eccentric and were simply put in the crank file. Shaw's personal mail only amounted to a fraction of the total but was still extensive. He had friends all over the nation, was active socially and in charitable causes in New York, and of course found it indispensable for his editorial work to have sources of information in the federal government and throughout the states. All of these interests involved letter writing. Lanier ably handled the financial aspects of the business, but Shaw as majority stockholder and president had certain other problems to ponder. He had to be concerned with the magazine industry at large, to study the effects upon it of political decisions, and to cooperate with it in lobbying for governmental favors. The price of paper and the rate on second-class

---

46 Carl Vrooman to Shaw, Dec. 26, 1917, Shaw MSS.

47 Mott, *American Magazines,* IV, 573-74. Circulation statistics are available in *N. W. Ayer & Son's American Newspaper Annual* but should be employed with some caution; they are probably more reliable, at least prior to 1916, for trends than for specific circulation.

mail could, for instance, be changed by a decision made in Washington, and Shaw with other members of the Periodical Publishers' Association had to analyze such matters carefully. The importance of this aspect of Shaw's duties is indicated by statistics he compiled for the Post Office Department; they show that during one six-month period in 1916 and 1917 the *Review* was spending almost $15,000 monthly for the various categories of postal service.[48]

Shaw once complained that "the million odds and ends I, as an editor, have to do for other people without thanks have entirely destroyed all my plans for writing books and give me small chance for recreation."[49] The statement is not altogether an exaggeration. Shaw's day was often arduous, and with the additional concern of being president of the Review of Reviews Company his nervous system suffered recurrently.[50]

Nevertheless, Shaw's output as an author, excluding what he wrote for the *Review,* did not decline to the extent he had indicated. A pronounced change did take place in the sort of writing he attempted. The climax of his career as a scholar had come in 1895 with the publication of the well-received *Municipal Government in Great Britain* and *Municipal Government in Continental Europe.* Both books were updated and much expanded versions of the articles he had done earlier, impressively thick and factual and, Shaw hoped, "possibly seductive" in their presentation of civic developments abroad.[51] In the next dozen years his publications numbered a pamphlet, a few reviews, some twenty articles, and three books: *The Business Career in Its Public Relations, The Outlook for the*

---

[48] Cyrus Curtis to Shaw, Dec. 9, 1909, William C. Edgar to Shaw, Dec. 23, 1909, Frank Hitchcock to Shaw, Sept. 8, 1911, Shaw to Beveridge, Nov. 18, 1911, Shaw to Albert S. Burleson, May 15, 1917, all in Shaw MSS.

[49] Shaw to Stimson, Apr. 18, 1902, Shaw MSS.

[50] Interview with Albert Shaw, Jr., Feb. 10, 1965; Shaw to Hawley, Feb. 6, 1894, Aug. 15, 1900, Shaw to Lucy Shaw Stephenson, June 15, 1900, all in Shaw MSS.

[51] Shaw, *Municipal Government in Continental Europe* (New York: Century Co., 1895), and *Municipal Government in Great Britain* (New York: Century Co., 1895); Shaw to G. A. Gates, Dec. 31, 1894, Shaw to Frank Scott (not sent), Dec. 26, 1899, both in Shaw MSS.

Average Man, and *Political Problems of American Development.*[52] These books were all compilations of lectures he had given and represented little effort beyond what had been required to prepare the lectures. Some of these works contain provocative thoughts, but collectively the group falls short of the scholarly promise he had always shown.

Political Problems of American Development, the most ambitious (but not the most perceptive) of the three, grew out of a series of lectures Shaw delivered at Columbia University in 1907 and was a moderately successful effort to discuss the forces underlying the formation of a distinctive American nationality. Its importance in understanding Shaw lies in two areas: in its theme, which reflected his persistent concern with American nationalism, and in its approach, which was altogether different from that of his municipal studies and the other works that had grown out of his Johns Hopkins experience. A letter to Shaw from Harvard's distinguished historian, Albert Bushnell Hart, makes this change apparent. Perhaps a bit miffed that Shaw had come out with a book similar to one on which he himself was working, Hart congratulated Shaw on producing a volume replete with "suggestive ideas" but snidely added that it was not as "objective" as his own study would be nor "riveted throughout to historical occurrences."[53] In effect Shaw's major works had come to resemble his editorials: all were the products of a thoughtful and observant journalist who possessed a keen sense of history. If lack of time had cost him anything, it was the opportunity to do archival research of the depth which had made his municipal studies so successful. Shaw doubtless had many substantial books that he wanted to do, but their undertaking would have to be indefinitely postponed.

To change perspectives, one might say that it was Shaw's

---

52 The works referred to above are listed in the bibliography in order of their publication. Reviews (largely favorable) of the two major books, *The Outlook for the Average Man* and *Political Problems of American Development,* are filed in the Shaw MSS. *The Business Career* appeared again as one of the collection in the former volume.

53 Hart to Shaw, Oct. 30, 1907, Shaw MSS.

prominence, as much as his work on the *Review*, which subtracted from his small budget of free time. Dr. Shaw, as he was usually addressed, was famous as an editor and a municipal expert. People talked of Shaw, who was considered a public figure, and wanted to hear him talk. He was in demand as a lecturer, and newspapers mentioned him as a possibility for the presidencies of the University of California and of Johns Hopkins University, as a likely ambassador to Germany and, while Roosevelt was president, as a member of a reputed kitchen cabinet. He did accept several speaking invitations annually, became a trustee of Iowa College and other schools, a director of the Dobbs Ferry Bank and of the American Press Association in which he had invested, a senator of Phi Beta Kappa, and received by 1912 three honorary doctorates to go with the one he had earned. Shaw served as a delegate to the Chicago Conference on Trusts in 1899 and was at the White House Conference on Conservation in 1908. Roosevelt, as governor of New York and then as president, chose him both times, and he might have held appointive office had he not told T. R. he wished none. He was content to remain an ex officio adviser and a frequent visitor to the White House.[54]

Shaw belonged to more than a score of organizations, some social, like the distinguished Century Club, the Aldine Club, and the Ardsley Golf Club (whose roster included such prominent men as the financier George Perkins and the steel magnate Charles Schwab). Others had civic reform and charity as their purpose, and Shaw participated in such as the Social Reform Club and the City Club in New York and the National Municipal League. He was also a director of the General Education Board and the Southern Education Board. Of course he could not give abundant time to each one. Socially he seemed to prefer a luncheon engagement to a convivial

---

[54] *New York Times*, Mar. 1, 1897, Nov. 21, 1900, Mar. 8, 1915, *Oakland Enquirer*, Dec. 10, 1898, *New York Herald*, Aug. 12, Sept. 15, 16, 18, 1899, *St. Louis Post-Dispatch*, July 8, 1902, *New York World*, Aug. 9, 1902, *Illustrated Buffalo Express*, Aug. 18, 1903, *Norfolk Virginian-Pilot*, May 24, 1907, *Cincinnati Commercial-Tribune*, June 15, 1913, *Phi Beta Kappa Key*, II (Oct. 1913), 27, *J. H. Circulars*, XIX (1914-15), 77-79, all in Scrapbooks, Shaw MSS.

evening. He was proud to be a centurion but normally avoided the club's Saturday soirées of sparkling chatter and good cheer; and as a golfer he liked the game but not too much the clubhouse banter. He sympathized with the goals of the many reform-oriented organizations he had joined, but with some his participation was limited mainly to a constructive speech or some commentary in the *Review*. In others he was active.[55]

Withal Shaw still had a family life. Single when he had moved to New York, and having failed to fulfill his resolution to be married at the age of thirty-one,[56] Shaw had continued to remain a bachelor. But in June 1893, while visiting his sister Lucy during his convalescence, Shaw entered upon what can only be called a whirlwind courtship. At a church social, the story goes, he met and was entranced by Elizabeth "Bessie" Bacon of Reading, Pennsylvania, before he had started on his second piece of shortcake. The twenty-three-year-old Miss Bacon was described by a zealous society columnist as a "prodigy of perfection," beauty, charm, and intellect—all in the superlative—being foremost among her qualities.[57] More striking is her resemblance to Shaw's late mother, for at least after her marriage she possessed the characteristics of devotion, a quiet strength, and a preference for domestic life rather than social gaiety. She had no aspirations to write nor any notable concern with the political and social problems that intrigued Shaw. He proposed only five weeks after their meeting, and their wedding, attended by such of Shaw's friends as Charles Thwing, Woodrow Wilson, and Charles Lanier, took place in Reading in September.[58]

55 Raymond B. Fosdick (with Henry F. Pringle and Katherine Douglas Pringle), *Adventure in Giving: The Story of the General Education Board* (New York: Harper & Row, 1962), pp. 3-7, 337; interview with Albert Shaw, Jr., Sept. 3, 1964. Shaw's organizational correspondence is filed in a separate section of the Shaw MSS.

56 Shaw to Wilson, May 24, 1885, Wilson MSS; Shaw to Susan Shaw, Feb. 15, 1891, Shaw MSS.

57 *St. Paul Pioneer Press*, July 19, 1893, Scrapbooks, Shaw MSS.

58 *Minneapolis Tribune*, Sept. 6, 1893, Scrapbooks, Shaw MSS; interview with Albert Shaw, Jr., Sept. 3, 1964.

Following their wedding trip to Europe the couple established a home in the New York area and eventually settled in
the suburban community of Hastings-on-Hudson, New York.
Hastings is located on the east bank of the river, twenty miles
from Manhattan's business section. It was then a fashionable
town in the midst of a district inhabited by the wealthy. On
the northern edge of the area lies Rhinebeck where one of
the Astors lived, below that is Hyde Park, and about fifty
miles to the south of Hyde Park come Dobbs Ferry, Hastings,
and finally Yonkers, just above New York City.[59] Shaw qualified for the neighborhood. The friends and acquaintances
he made in his professional and philanthropic endeavors were
among the nation's distinguished citizens: college presidents
like Edwin Alderman of Virginia and Nicholas Murray Butler
of Columbia, public-minded businessmen like Andrew Carnegie and the financiers George Perkins and George Roberts,
and politicians of stature such as Theodore Roosevelt, Albert
Beveridge, and, later, Herbert Hoover. He also had the
proper financial attainments. While he probably did not earn
his first million much before 1920, Shaw's fortune, based on
his control of the profitable *Review* and extensive investments
in stocks, grew to six digits in the first decade of this century
and kept increasing. The Shaw home, which was situated
near the river with a splendid view of the New Jersey Palisades,
was large and comfortable without being garish.[60]

The Shaws had a good life. His two sons, Albert, Jr., and
Roger, born in 1897 and 1903 respectively, gave him great
pleasure, and Shaw especially loved to send friends frequent
bulletins about the progress of his eldest. When he had the
time, he tried skating and sledding, or settled for the less
strenuous pursuits of whist and family-singing, and enjoyed
them all. With his wife he had the familiar disagreement
over the mountains and the seashore, went mostly to his choice,

59 Ibid.; *New York Commercial-Advertiser,* Jan. 17, 1903, Scrapbooks, Shaw
MSS.
60 Interview with Albert Shaw, Jr., Mar. 20, 1965. A section of the Shaw
MSS deals with his multiple transactions in the stock market. His account
books with brokerage firms like Carpenter and Company are included in it.

the Adirondacks, and about every fifth year journeyed as far as Mexico or Europe.[61] After buying a farm near Leesburg in northern Virginia, Shaw discovered himself as pleased "as a child with a new toy," and found the role of gentleman farmer, which he played when he could, his favorite recreation.[62]

Shaw turned fifty in 1907; his face was starting to show age, and his hair was graying rapidly. Although he felt unusually well at the time, he soon decided in a sentimental moment that he was heading toward the "sunset" of life; he had, however, almost another forty years to live.[63] Had he paused for retrospection at this time, Shaw would have had no cause for dissatisfaction with his previous years, for he was successful as editor, author, lecturer, citizen, and family man.

He had had to work hard for his success. Intelligent and able as he was, Shaw had still allowed self-doubt to mark the initial phase of his career in journalism. Unhappiness with his positions on the *Grinnell Herald* and *Minneapolis Tribune* and uncertainty about his ability to discharge his duties on these papers had threatened to make him veer off and make scholarship his career. But at the crucial moment he hesitated (as if to change professions would betray the memory of Roger Williams) and wound up remaining in journalism. The years of doubt ended with his decision to buy into the *Review*. In a sense he took advantage of Stead, but he did make the *Review of Reviews* the outstanding monthly of its kind and established close relationships with many of the nation's rising leaders. And when men of his generation reached national policy-making levels soon after the turn of the century he found himself in a position editorially and personally to exert some influence on the course of events.

61 W. Halstead, *Story of the Halsteads*, p. 100; interview with Albert Shaw, Jr., Sept. 3, 1964: Shaw to Stead, May 11, 1895, Mar. 22, 1898, Churchill to Shaw, Aug. 10, 1897, Shaw to Hawley, July 3, 1899, Aug. 15, 1900, Shaw to Lucy Shaw Stephenson, June 15, 1900, Feb. 14, 1908, Shaw to C. Dunham, Dec. 17, 1901, June 17, 1902, Shaw to Charles Bell, Nov. 3, 1902, Shaw to A. J. Montague, Aug. 17, 1903, all in Shaw MSS.

62 Shaw to Beveridge, Nov. 14, 1908, Shaw MSS.

63 Shaw to Lucy Shaw Stephenson, Feb. 14, 1908, Shaw MSS.

5

The Ideal City, 1891-1900

Just as Shaw was establishing himself in New York, a new episode in the history of American reform was beginning. It was progressivism. Although its origins were modest, it was destined to attract the attention of the nation in the early years of the present century and of historians long after. Their interpretations of it have been diverse.[1] The first significant statement placed progressivism within the context of the reform tradition emanating from the midwestern agrarian protest of Populism, the Alliance, and the Grange. The common man was seen struggling against economic depression and against the privileges arrogated by selfish industrial and political bosses.[2]

The most compelling recent evaluations of progressivism, however, are those that distinguish it from the rural protest of the late nineteenth century.[3] Progressivism at its height between 1900 and 1915 existed in an era of prosperity and was less tinged with acrimony than Populism had been. Moreover among the exponents of progressivism was a substantial middle-class element whose interests varied from those of its agrarian predecessors. Its spokesmen, who in 1900 clustered around the age level of forty, were of Protestant, old American stock, more than likely British in origin—a composite into which Albert Shaw neatly fit. As befitting members of the first generation too young to have participated in the sectional struggle, progressives were nationalistic and felt that America had vast potential. They were optimistic about seeing this greatness reached, but they thought that it would have to be resolutely sought for they were acutely aware that shortcomings existed. While they were concerned with all phases of

American life from the farm to foreign policy, their typical anxiety stemmed from the problems inherent in an urban, industrial society. Thus matters like social welfare, the condition of labor, and the disorder of the city received their attention for more than two decades after the commencement in the 1890s of their campaign for municipal reform—the earliest manifestation of this urban-oriented progressivism.[4]

Yet within this sphere of progressivism there were differences of opinion on goals and of assumptions toward reform. For instance Jane Addams, to cite a conspicuous example, learned through her participation in settlement work to view the problems of the underprivileged with solicitude and to think of social justice as the purpose of reform. On the other hand Shaw, who approached the problems of the urban poor from a well-intentioned but considerably more aloof point of view, came to think of reform more as a way to establish social order—as a means to secure a wholesome and less alien environment. Miss Addams believed in racial equality and in aiding the new immigrant to adjust himself to his changed circumstances; Shaw thought more of making the new immigrant conform. Both, however, had much to do with the municipal question and other socioeconomic issues of the day. Thus, however different some of their attitudes, both deserve

1 Of use in pointing out the various interpretations are Samuel P. Hays, *The Response to Industrialism, 1885-1914*, Chicago History of American Civilization series (Chicago: University of Chicago Press, 1957), pp. 198-205; Daniel Levine, *Varieties of Reform Thought* (Madison: State Historical Society of Wisconsin, 1964), pp. vii-viii; Arthur Mann, "The Progressive Tradition," in John Higham, ed., *The Reconstruction of American History* (New York: The Humanities Press, 1962), pp. 157-79; and especially Otis L. Graham, Jr., *The Great Campaigns: Reform and War in America, 1900-1928*, History of the American People Series (Englewood Cliffs, N.J.: Prentice-Hall, 1971), pp. 1-51, 171-79.

2 John Hicks, *The Populist Revolt: A History of the Farmers' Alliance and the People's Party* (Minneapolis: University of Minnesota, 1931), pp. 404-23.

3 For instance Richard Hofstadter, *The Age of Reform* (New York: Vintage Books, 1955); Roy Lubove, "The Twentieth Century City: The Progressive as Municipal Reformer," *Mid-America*, XLI (Oct. 1959), 195-209; and George E. Mowry, *The Era of Theodore Roosevelt, 1900-1912*, New American Nation Series (New York: Harper & Brothers, 1958).

4 Hofstadter, *Age of Reform*, p. 133; Mowry, *Era of Theodore Roosevelt*, pp. 59-105.

to be classified as progressives, not only in that they joined
the Bull Moose party in 1912 but in their belief that betterment could be achieved through the commitment to reform
of right-minded citizens and the appropriate agencies of government.[5]

The urbanization of America was a process that had been
going on, though at an uneven tempo, throughout the nineteenth century. For much of the time the growth of the cities
had been obscured by other developments. Only in the
century's last decade did the phenomenon of urbanization
receive its due attention. Statistics show the enormous importance that cities had assumed by then. Just between 1860
and 1890 the number of cities of more than 8,000 inhabitants
trebled, rising from 141 to 449, with a corresponding gain in
population from just over 5,000,000 to 18,327,987. The pace
continued, and the data for 1910 revealed that urban population had more than doubled since 1890. The total was over
42,000,000—almost half of the nation's 91,000,000 people.[6]
During the same years a dismaying number of problems
became evident: foul slums, dishonest government, spiraling
occurrences of crime and disease, the inadequacy of municipal
services. Not all of these were new, however—for instance in
New York municipal corruption was in the process of becoming systematized prior to 1860, but the existing problems were
almost invariably intensified even as additional ones developed.[7]

[5] On Jane Addams see, for example, Allen F. Davis's important new biography,
American Heroine: The Life and Legend of Jane Addams (New York: Oxford
University Press, 1973), and Christopher Lasch, *The New Radicalism in America,
1889-1963: The Intellectual as a Social Type* (New York: Knopf, 1965), pp. 3-37.

[6] Blake McKelvey, *The Urbanization of America, 1860-1915* (New Brunswick,
N.J.: Rutgers University Press, 1963), pp. 61-63; Frank Mann Stewart, *A Half
Century of Municipal Reform: The History of the National Municipal League*
(Berkeley and Los Angeles: University of California Press, 1950), p. 2; *Thirteenth
Census of the United States: 1910* (Washington: Government Printing Office,
1913), I, 53-54.

[7] McKelvey, *Urbanization of America*, pp. 86-98; Alexander Callow, Jr., *The
Tweed Ring* (New York: Oxford Universitp Press, 1966), pp. 18-24; Roy Lubove,
*The Progressives and the Slums: Tenement House Reform in New York City
1890-1917* (Pittsburgh: University of Pittsburgh Press, 1962), pp. 4-23; Clifford

A reappraisal of urban life was needed and forthcoming. One might say that it began at the Johns Hopkins University, for as Richard Hofstadter has suggested, the remarkable scholars who assembled there to work in the social sciences in the 1880s and early 1890s anticipated the sense of civic responsibility that was soon to become evident among progressive reformers in general.[8] There was the perceptive Englishman James Bryce who pointed out in his *American Commonwealth* that municipal government was the single conspicuous failure of American democracy and who asked why good men did not go into politics. There was the pioneering health expert John Shaw Billings who argued that epidemic diseases could be controlled. There were Ely directing his students to undertake research that had social relevance and Adams whose concept of institutional research furnished a needed model for the study of municipal government. And there were their students who raised many questions and supplied some of the answers: Wilson worked with Congress and also in municipal administration, Bemis and Gould became experts in utilities and housing respectively, and Shaw returned as a visiting lecturer to inspire his own students with notions of what cities could accomplish. Fred Howe, who attended Shaw's lectures and who himself became one of the foremost municipal reformers, recalled the idealized quality of his talks: he "painted pictures of cities that I could visualise—cities that I wanted to take part in in America; cities managed as business enterprises; cities that were big business enterprises, that owned things and did things for people. There was order and beauty in the cities he described. They owned their own tramways

Patton, *The Battle for Municipal Reform: Mobilization and Attack, 1875-1900* (Washington: American Council on Public Affairs, 1940), pp. 10, 13, 19.

8 Although Hofstadter mentions the late 1880s and early 1890s as the period when the sense of civic responsibility became evident in the Hopkins community, the feeling of concern seems to have been developing earlier. Shaw and other disciples of Ely were investigating socially relevant topics by mid-decade (Hofstadter, *Age of Reform*, p. 206). See also William Diamond, "On the Dangers of an Urban Interpretation of History," in Eric F. Goldman, ed., *Historiography and Urbanization* (rpt. Port Washington, N.Y.: Kennikat Press, 1968), pp. 67-78; and Rader, *The Academic Mind and Reform*, pp. 20-27.

and gas and electric lighting plants, and they made great successes of them."[9]

A similar disposition to question the status quo was also becoming evident in the cities themselves. It soon developed into a movement. Beginning in 1892 organizations such as the City Club of New York, the Committee of Fifty of Albany, the National Municipal League (which originated in Philadelphia), and the Civic Federation of Chicago were founded in consecutive years; these were only a few of the scores of similar groups whose goal was reform. Although there had previously been municipal reform campaigns, new developments were taking place in the reformer's approach to the city: the discovery of the city as a subject of scholarly inquiry and the realization that the bleaker aspects of the urban environment could be ameliorated by responsible government action. The new thinking represented a broadening of the earlier outlook, which had rested on the negative and simplistic proposition that whatever was wrong with American cities was essentially political and could be remedied by turning the rascals out of city hall. In essence the genteel reform tradition which had been negative and spasmodic (once the rascals were gone what was there to do?) was yielding to progressivism which was positive, broader in that it did not regard honest government as an end in itself but paid close attention to social and economic matters as well—and which was predicated on the concept that the cities, the coming centers of population, demanded continuous study and attention.[10]

[9] Frederic C. Howe, *Confessions of a Reformer* (Chicago: Quadrangle Books, Quadrangle Paperbacks, 1967), pp. 5-6.

[10] Patton, *Battle for Municipal Reform*, p. 35. William Howe Tolman, *Municipal Reform Movements in the United States* (New York, Chicago, Toronto: Fleming H. Revell Co., 1895), and E. L. Godkin, ed., *The Triumph of Reform: A History of the Great Political Revolution, November Sixth, Eighteen Hundred and Ninety-Four* (New York: Souvenir Publishing Co., 1895), deal extensively with reform groups, although commentary in the latter is limited to those in New York City. John G. Sproat, *The Best Men: Liberal Reformers in the Gilded Age* (New York: Oxford University Press, 1968), exposes the limitations of mugwump reform, while Gerald W. McFarland, "Politics, Morals, and the Mugwump Reformers" (Diss., Columbia University, 1965), pp. 308-72, takes a more favorable view and shows how mugwump reform evolved into municipal

It was in this milieu that Shaw rose to fame as a municipal reformer. Even before he moved to New York his university lectures and his early articles in the *Century,* the first of which appeared in 1890, had begun to win him attention as a man who had somethng important to say. His goal was to develop his studies of foreign cities into book-length format. And although his duties with the American *Review* proved more onerous than he had anticipated, he did manage to complete the task. Additional research done on his wedding trip in 1893 enabled him to expand and update his material, and the two volumes printed in 1895 were impressively informed.[11]

Thematically they were similar to his articles and lectures and had the same didactic purpose of informing Americans of the latest and best accomplishments abroad, to offer them not a blueprint but at least an outline for progress. Not that Shaw was unaware of the possibility of using shame as a goad to action, for less than a year before the first of his own volumes was due to be published, Stead's *If Christ Came to Chicago* had made its notorious appearance. It horrified Shaw, and in a letter referring to another shock the Englishman had recently given him he contrasted his and Stead's approaches to reform:

In the good providence of God it sometimes turns out that the best way to batter down a great stone wall is to blow rams' horns and yell like a maniac. But there are some men whose reasoning faculties are so constituted that they can never heat themselves up to the point of rushing with wild shrieks and butting their heads against the stone wall. While equally determined to get over the wall, they are either proceeding to construct scaling ladders or else are at work upon mechanisms scientifically designed to win the battle.[12]

---

progressivism in New York. For Shaw's own awareness of this change see the *New York Press,* Nov. 11, 1895, Scrapbooks, Shaw MSS.

[11] The two books came out in January and November, *Municipal Government in Great Britain* appearing first and going through three printings. Shaw, *Municipal Government in Continental Europe,* p. v; Shaw to Frank Scott, Dec. 17, 1894, Shaw to G. A. Gates, Dec. 31, 1894, Stead to Shaw, Aug. 5, 1893, all in Shaw MSS.

While Shaw considered restraint to be one of the virtues of his own path to reform, it was nevertheless clear from the outset that he was no sponsor of the status quo. Or as he put it in the introductory chapter of his *Municipal Government in Great Britain,* the elimination of a slum was now as feasible as the drainage of a swamp. "The so-called problems of the modern city," explained Shaw, "are but the various phases of the one main question, How can the environment be most perfectly adapted to the welfare of urban populations? And science [including 'administrative science, statistical science, engineering and technological science, sanitary science, and educational, social and moral science'] can meet and answer every one of these problems."[13] Although the books were arranged in chapters discussing individual cities or groups of cities, the best way to gain an overview of the two volumes is to consider them as a unified whole, stressing, as Shaw did, the functions and administrative methods of enlightened municipal governments.

Consider, for instance, Shaw's emphasis on the efforts to modernize the mazes of archaic city streets that in some instances dated from the medieval past. Vienna provided a classic example of progress in this area. Unlike Chicago, which after the fire of 1871 had squandered its opportunity to rebuild with foresight, Vienna combined private and public action in an inspiring renewal project initiated by the imperial authorities in 1857. The program had begun with the destruction of the venerable fortifications that surrounded the inner city and their replacement in part by the superb Ring-strasse, a boulevard which encircled the cramped, medieval area. A network of smaller streets, public buildings and parks, and

---

12 Shaw to Gates, Dec. 31, 1894, Shaw MSS. Stead's intervention in behalf of George D. Herron, a zealous advocate of the social gospel and a faculty member at Iowa College who was then considered an embarrassment to the school, was the immediate cause of Shaw's indignant outburst. Rader, *The Academic Mind and Reform,* p. 134.

13 Shaw, *Municipal Government in Britain,* p. 3; Shaw to Carl Schurz, Jan. 5, 1895, and his interview in the *New York Press,* Nov. 11, 1895, both in Shaw MSS, are informative on the hopes he held for his books as instruments of reform.

some private developments occupied the remainder of the reclaimed space. Shaw, who consistently indicated the long-term monetary value of municipal improvements (perhaps as a means of convincing dubious readers of their desirability), related how the revenue from the sales to private interests financed a fair share of the public program. The increase in land values stemming from the renewal project and a tax-exemption plan stimulated a city-wide spurt of construction. With a new outlet to a greater Vienna the traditional commercial center of the city prospered as never before.[14]

Another important contributor to a city's economic vitality was public transportation. Shaw found that it was functioning well in the major continental cities he studied, for the opportunities for profit seemed such that business had accepted terms specifying the conditions of service and the payment of reasonable fees to the municipality. Yet there was a trend toward municipal ownership. Berlin and Cologne, among other cities, would acquire ownership of their streetcar lines upon termination of the franchises they had granted; Vienna envisioned the construction of a city-owned rapid transit system. The outlook was equally favorable in Great Britain. There, several cities, including Birmingham and Manchester, followed the pattern of building municipal trackage and leasing operating rights to private corporations that Glasgow had set in 1870. Many of these communities expected to begin municipal operation when the leases, which generally ran for twenty-odd years, expired sometime during the 1890s. In London a dozen companies ran trolleys, yet the metropolis planned on having most service under public management by 1900.[15]

Conditions were similar in the gas and electric industries. Many cities owned these essential utilities, while in those communities like Paris where the private distribution of gas and/or electricity was allowed the entrepreneur had to sub-

14 Shaw, *Municipal Government in Europe*, pp. 410-12, 419-26.
15 Ibid., pp. 77-90, 262-63, 325-27, 335, 350-55, 427-29, 459-60; Shaw, *Municipal Government in Britain*, pp. 156-57.

scribe to shrewdly drawn contracts that protected the public interest.[16] Berlin's privately owned electric company had to agree to illuminate the Unter-den-Linden and two other thoroughfares at a nominal price, to pay the city a percentage of its returns, and to charge consumers only authorized rates. Such contracts, remarked Shaw, always demonstrated a "sense of the first-class legal, financial, and technical ability that the [German] city is able to command"; in contrast the astute bargaining in American municipalities was regularly done by the representatives of the private corporations.[17] Modern communities, to employ one of Shaw's favorite analogies, managed their affairs with businesslike acumen.

Of all the reports Shaw made, he probably considered none more important than those about public hygiene. "The test of material progress with me," he wrote in 1899, "is to be found in sanitary conditions."[18] Although public health was an area in which American communities were making significant advances, much could still be learned by studying sanitation programs abroad. On the Continent the most effective application of the era's increasing hygienic knowledge to municipal conditions had been made in Germany. Inclined to be parsimonious in spending money on public health, the German cities had been moved to take determined action by a ravaging cholera epidemic in 1892. Illustrative of the German progress in the field of health were developments in Hamburg. This thriving port had unusually difficult problems because of its location by the Elbe, a river which carried waste from cities upstream and which served also as the receptacle for the numerous ships present at the Hamburg docks. Since there were no accessible upland sources of fresh water, Hamburg had to draw its drinking supply from this polluted river.

16 Shaw, *Municipal Government in Europe*, pp. 45-54, 263, 346-49, 458-59; Shaw, *Municipal Government in Britain*, pp. 118-21, 155-56, 175-76, 203.

17 Shaw, *Municipal Government in Europe*, pp. 349-50.

18 Shaw to Mrs. E. H. Van Patten, Feb. 28, 1899, Shaw MSS; an informative article on the hygienic advances of American cities is Howard D. Kramer's "The Germ Theory and the Early Public Health Program in the United States," *Bulletin of the History of Medicine*, XXII (May-June 1948), 233-48.

Other cities, including Berlin and New York, had already learned how to check the cholera, but Hamburg's aggressive and intelligent efforts to combat the disease through the construction of a superb filtration system seemed typical of the new German policy.[19]

With the exception of a none too satisfactory sewage system, Hamburg's other sanitary precautions were impeccable, for after 1892 the city made successful efforts to scour the streets, to collect and burn garbage, and to amend the building code. Added to municipal statutes were clauses requiring that court apartments have access to light and air, that tenement houses have sanitary plumbing, and so on. The city also established a hospital for the treatment of contagious diseases, an ambulance service, and public disinfection plants and balanced the new health program with a sensible plan for food inspection. The value of these measures was soon apparent, for within three years following the institution of these and other advances in public health Hamburg's death rate had declined by 20 percent from the average of the preceding decade.[20]

While Shaw's normal approach was to instruct by example, he could not help but reflect dourly upon American urban administration in discussing governmental standards abroad. The governments of many of the great British and continental cities had an important uniformity in that their municipal councils customarily held responsibility for determining policy. The very absence of competing authorities of equal stature helped to facilitate the execution of this policy. There were differences in such other considerations as the function of the mayor and the sources from which talent was recruited, but what was most notable was an almost monotonous similarity in the ability with which these cities were managed. Shaw indicated several other reasons for the existence of such a felicitous situation: nonpartisan elections, the esteem in which public office was held, and, by implication at least, limitations upon the extent of the suffrage. Of course not all of these

19 Shaw, *Municipal Government in Europe,* pp. 378-88.
20 Ibid., pp. 391-97, 401-9.

elements prevailed in every place, but Shaw frequently observed what appeared to be the wholesome effects of one or more of these. For the most part they were conspicuously absent from America.

London was in some sense an exception, for not only did it have its vested interests but a confusing distribution of governmental powers that admitted archaic guilds and over three dozen parishes to some share of authority. The establishment in 1889 of a county council had done much, however, to give the sprawling city a unified and enlightened regime. The council, which inherited from a predecessor jurisdiction over main avenues, bridges, parks, unfit housing, and other matters, was progressive and competent (besides being free of ward bosses and saloonkeepers, Shaw advised his American readers). The conciliar elections of 1892 showed how such a desirable norm could be obtained. Even though the campaign preceded a parliamentary election and could not entirely escape the intrusion of national political topics and parties, local issues remained paramount. The opponents of reform— drawn from such selfish groups as the great landlords and the liquor dealers—lost, for in such a situation they were unable to obscure their true goals with irrelevant matters. Partisan prejudice had not exercised its disturbing influence on voting behavior.[21]

In British cities generally everything seemed to contrast with the prevailing situation in the United States. Suffrage restrictions served to keep the "unattached or floating elements of the population" from participating in municipal elections, while severe penalties discouraged the bribing of those among "the ignorant, vicious, and indifferent" who did have the ballot. Elective offices were few, and the position of councilor—which offered little opportunity for graft and no remuneration—was an esteemed one that attracted able, disinterested candidates, many of whom were reputable businessmen. Appointive offices were also well staffed, for despite their small salary and

21 Shaw, *Municipal Government in Britain*, pp. 222-53.

demanding routine these positions were widely respected and attractive. Executive responsibility belonged to the council, since the mayoralty was merely an honorary office.[22]

Shaw was perhaps most impressed by the administration and activities of German cities—the Germans, he generalized, having "a higher capacity for organized social action than Anglo-Saxon or Celtic peoples."[23] Their municipal councils, chosen in many instances under a three-class voting system, had some resemblance to those of English communities. But German city governments had this significant functional difference: they allotted much responsibility to the mayor or burgomaster. Selected by the councils, burgomasters were career administrators who in turn appointed other qualified professional civil servants to municipal office. This system, observed Shaw, was roughly analogous to that of a railway corporation, "in which the board of directors, chosen by the stockholders, appoint a general superintendent or manager, a general passenger agent, . . . and other general officers, and leave to these highly salaried experts, promoted from inferior places or drawn from the service of various other transportation companies, almost the entire management and operation of the road."[24]

Not given to tinkering with the mechanisms of government to the extent that American reformers were, the Germans were primarily concerned with using their superb administrative system for "new and wonderful purposes." Thus Shaw employed phrases such as "thrifty and progressive," "splendid efficiency," "superb and continuous organization," "symmetrical progress," "organic entity," "sense of human brotherhood and mutual responsibility" in describing the capacity of the German community to ascertain public needs and to provide for them with efficiently administered services. The sum of

22 Ibid., pp. 44-50, 53-61. Later on Lincoln Steffens expressed a much less favorable view of the British system, calling it "class government." Steffens, *The Autobiography of Lincoln Steffens* (New York: Harcourt, Brace, 1931), p. 704.

23 Shaw, *Municipal Government in Europe*, p. 291.

24 Ibid., pp. 312-14.

such activities he called municipal socialism—or housekeeping—an alternative and less controversial word that Shaw preferred to use. He defined socialism as a doctrinaire commitment to public ownership; housekeeping involved instead a sense of practicality and responsibility. For example a socialist would insist on the municipalization of a traction or water company just to eliminate a private enterprise. The resourceful, businesslike leadership of a community would demand such a step only if necessary to give the public better service.[25]

The studies were not without fault. The idealism that was so evident in them and that Howe had noticed in his lectures seems to have led Shaw astray in his assessment of the European city, for as hindsight has made clear he tended to see in the cities he observed those things he wanted to see. For instance, as Roy Lubove has argued, Shaw, in common with many of the early municipal reformers, simply misjudged the German city, confusing administrative control with solicitude for the public welfare.[26] There is a related problem: that Shaw, who had a progressive's faith in the ability of the expert to perfect man's environment, overestimated the ease with which the ideal city could be created. The difficulty seems to be in the fact that he had little insight into the dynamics of change. Although he correctly foresaw the population growth that made municipal reform imperative, he did not appreciate the importance of two factors which have had much to do with the course of urban development: the political with its complicated interaction of interest groups and the technological in which change disrupts even as it benefits.

Shaw's version of the ideal city was also questioned by contemporaries. His opinions were suspect on both sides of the political spectrum. That he had anticipated the rigidly conservative critique is evident from his painstaking efforts to show that municipal activism was not socialistic and that reform could be profitable, but he did not care to counter the judgment that his views on the suffrage were elitist.[27] The

25 Ibid., pp. 289, 304-5, 323-25.
26 Lubove, "The Twentieth Century City," p. 207.

fact, of course, is that they were; along with his moralism and caution they reflected facets of his thought in which the genteel, or mugwump, reform outlook was strong. And even though he would eventually conclude that American traditions made universal white male suffrage an unalterable part of our public life, he did not come to exult in its possibilities as Fred Howe and other reformers did.[28] (How could it have been otherwise with someone who had assisted Bryce in preparing the *American Commonwealth*?) There were also other criticisms. Perhaps the most telling was political scientist Frank Goodnow's charge that Shaw had paid inadequate attention to the relationship between local and central government.[29]

On the whole, however, Goodnow and, in fact, most reviewers found much to praise in Shaw's books and generally espoused the intended lesson that American cities could profit much from the example set by their British and continental counterparts. This sentiment was illustrated well by James Phelan, the California reformer, who after reading what Shaw had written about public ownership in Glasgow chortled in an article of his own: "The Mayor has swallowed the Octopus, and, more than that, it seems to agree with him!"[30]

There was also interest in what Shaw had to say about American cities, and throughout the 1890s he was constantly being importuned to participate in urban reform endeavors.

---

[27] Among the various critics were: *City and State* (Philadelphia), Sept. 19, 1895; *Philadelphia Call*, Nov. 19, 1895; *Nation* (New York), Apr. 9, 1896; *Fabian News* (London), June, 1896; *Saturday Review* (London), Dec. 28, 1895, all in Scrapbooks, Shaw MSS.

[28] For Howe's contrasting opinion on the suffrage see Frederic Howe, *The City: The Hope of Democracy*, Americana Library (Seattle: University of Washington Press, 1967), pp. 1-3.

[29] Frank Goodnow, Reviews of *Municipal Government in Great Britain* and *Municipal Government in Continental Europe*, *Political Science Quarterly*, X (Mar. 1895), 171-74, XI (Mar. 1896), 158-60.

[30] James D. Phelan, "Municipal Conditions and the New Charter," *Overland Monthly*, XXVIII (July 1896), 105. For examples of other favorable commentary see *Denver Republican*, Jan. 13, 1895; *Omaha Bee*, Jan. 20, 1895; *New York Times*, Jan. 21, Nov. 27, 1895; *Washington Star*, Nov. 16, 1895; *Boston Transcript*, Dec. 11, 1895, Feb. 6, 1896; *Chicago Advance*, Jan. 9, 1896; and *New York Tribune*, Jan. 22, 1896, all in Scrapbooks, Shaw MSS.

He joined over a dozen of the various reform organizations that were being launched in New York City and on a nation-wide level, accepted several out of dozens of speaking engagements proferred each year by such groups in major American cities, and also wrote numerous editorials in the *Review* on the state of government in American municipalities.[31]

The lessons he expounded on these occasions were like those contained in his formal studies of municipal government, but unencumbered by the scholarly apparatus, they were at times revealingly frank. Nowhere is this more apparent than in his extensive commentary on Tammany Hall, New York City's infamous Democratic machine. Shaw and other reformers had taken hope in 1894 that Tammany's grip on New York politics might be broken, for in the wake of some particularly damning exposures an upsurge of revulsion at Tammany had secured the election of a good-government ticket headed by mayoralty candidate William Strong. But their euphoria was short-lived; in the next municipal election Tammany made a comeback, its candidates sweeping to victory to the chant of "Well, well, Reform has gone to hell."[32]

In his postelection analysis the editor expressed his bitter realization of where reform had gone. He lashed out at those he presumed had voted for Tammany: the "positively vicious, belonging to the criminal and semi-criminal classes"; petty politicians with a pecuniary stake in an organization victory; the city's fifteen thousand saloonkeepers and their hangers-on; and those "private interests that wish to violate municipal ordinances or break the State laws, and that seek the connivance of public officials." Shaw's sweep was wide; in this last category he included anyone who sought special privilege, from the poor workingman on up to the franchise-manipulators and their dependents.[33]

A few years before in another such eruption Shaw had also

---

[31] The Shaw Manuscripts have complete sections on his organizational correspondence and on his speaking invitations and engagements.

[32] Lloyd Morris, *Incredible New York: High Life and Low Life of the Last One Hundred Years* (New York: Random House, 1951), pp. 215-33.

[33] *American Monthly Review of Reviews*, XVI (1897), 651.

charged the so-called new immigration with responsibility for the urban crisis. Referring to the 1891 lynching in New Orleans of eleven imprisoned Italian immigrants suspected of the murder of the local police superintendent, Shaw filled a page of his first "Progress" with denunciations of foreign influences. Although his anger had been aroused by the subsequent appeals of Italian-Americans that the government of Italy demand satisfaction for the incident, Shaw also took advantage of it to attack in this and following columns America's liberal immigration and naturalization policies. He blamed them for the influx into our cities of masses of easily influenced voters from Bohemia, Ruthenia, and other exotic European regions (many of which he had visited).[34] He accused Italy of "dumping its bandits, assassins, and paupers upon Western shores, to the disturbance of labor markets and the demoralization of cities,"[35] and predicted that "the American people will soon begin to make very urgent demands for a restriction or a careful sifting of immigration. . . . Why," he asked rhetorically, "should they consent to spoil their breed of pedigree-stock by allowing the introduction of the refuse of the murder-breeds of Southern Europe?"[36] Alarmed by the prospect that the United States might lose its traditional identity, he later queried in headlines: "Is English To Be Our Speech?"[37]

Shaw followed up the accusations he made by urging patriots to conduct special evening classes in citizenship in order to safeguard American mores. "There must," he wrote, "be a voluntary but general and aggressive movement in all our towns and cities for the propagation of Americanism among the non-English-speaking immigrants [even including the Germans of Milwaukee]."[38] He further demanded that such weak laws as existed should be strictly enforced to check the continued influx of people of undesirable races and quick

---

34 *Review of Reviews* (Amer. ed.), III (1891), 228.
35 Ibid.
36 Ibid., p. 331.
37 Ibid., p. 448.
38 Ibid., p. 228.

enfranchisement of those already here and that a positive policy of restriction should be adopted.[39] According to Lee Benson, Shaw's pleas for restriction contained the "first *effective* linkage" between the recent awareness that the supply of free land was nearing exhaustion and the alleged discovery that the new immigration was less wholesome than the old.[40]

Aggravated by the rebuffs that even disinterested reformers received, Shaw allowed these two incidents of the lost election and the lynching to lead him into vituperative outbursts. It does not justify such racist convictions as Shaw held to say that they were common among educated people of his day, but at least he did not normally express them so vehemently. His subsequent comments on immigration were tepid indeed. He deplored our past importation of Negroes and hailed the Chinese Exclusion Act of 1882 as a landmark of American history, but he retreated in his stand vis-à-vis the new immigrants to the position that they would be welcomed in the United States as long as they proved assimilable. Temporarily coming to feel that among whites Anglo-Saxon institutions mattered more than Anglo-Saxon lineage, he mentioned the desirability of restriction with propriety if he mentioned it at all.[41]

Shaw likewise discussed the problems of the urban masses more sympathetically. Some weeks after Tammany's victory he prepared an address on the results of the balloting that contrasted sharply with his abusive editorial. Its thesis was the complexity of reform. Reform always caused "a good deal of disturbance" for somebody, for it involved changes. To illustrate his point, he cited the case of some thirty thousand truckmen who prior to Strong's election had traditionally been allowed to park their vehicles overnight on streets

[39] Ibid., pp. 228, 331, 449.

[40] Lee Benson, *Turner and Beard: American Historical Writing Reconsidered* (Glencoe, Ill.: The Free Press, 1960), pp. 71-72; Billington, *Frederick Jackson Turner*, p. 110.

[41] *American Monthly Review of Reviews*, XXVIII (1903), 657, XXXIII (1906), 264; Shaw, *Political Problems of American Development*, pp. 45, 62-70; Shaw, "Government and the Social Welfare" (n.p., n.d.), pp. 11-12 of typescript of speech, Shaw MSS.

throughout the tenement district. Denied this privilege by Colonel George Waring, the reform street commissioner, who felt that the parked trucks were a detriment to public health and morals, they had sought compensation on the grounds that the new ruling had forced them to rent expensive garage or yard space. Their request spurned, they voted for Tammany. In the immediate aftermath of the election, Shaw had been infuriated by their alleged abuse of the ballot and had bluntly written so in his editorials, but he now saw things differently. The regulation that they complained of was undoubtedly proper, he thought; but reformers had been wrong to refuse the truckers even a sympathetic hearing of their grievances.[42]

Sometimes the law itself was unjust. The state law that ordered the closing of New York City's saloons on Sundays was an example of one. The editor maintained that there was nothing criminal in wanting a beer on Sunday and explained that the enactment of the law had been motivated by political opportunism. Republican state boss Tom Platt (whose political standards he held in contempt) had contrived its passage in a hypocritical effort to pose as the champion of morality before the upstate constituency of his party. The well-to-do could still go to their luxurious clubs for refreshment and relaxation, but the new establishments that called themselves clubs so that they too could remain open on Sundays and cater to the workingman were harassed into closing by the Strong administration, which had been burdened with enforcing the law. In this, as in the dispute with the truckers, reformers had disdained the ordinary voter and as a result had earned widespread displeasure. They had been too aloof in the past and should become less "amateurish and unpractical," suggested Shaw. The city had a cosmopolitan population whose varying needs required sympathetic attention.[43]

---

42 Shaw, "Speech on New York City Affairs after Election of Van Wyck in 1897," (n.p., n.d.), pp. 7-10 of typescript of speech, Shaw MSS.
43 Ibid., pp. 11-15.

One of the first goals of reformers should be the provision of a sound educational system. "After all," Shaw remarked, "the ideal city cannot exist without a very large number of ideal citizens."[44] At the time the greatest need was for public kindergartens and manual training schools. Shaw emphasized that it was especially important for the American-born children of immigrants to have the opportunity to learn a trade. Those who could not complete school would thus be able to earn a living and would be less likely to become street corner idlers than if their only recourse were to the traditional education. Schools, of course, could also teach the meaning of citizenship and of good government. Education and the public health were the foremost obligations of municipal government.[45]

A proponent of municipal activism, Shaw specified that government had other tasks as well. The maintenance of public baths, beaches, parks, libraries, and art galleries, the renovation of slums and streets, the promotion of improved public architecture were all included in his definition of estimable civic endeavors.[46] Caution, however, was always apparent in Shaw's references to municipal ownership; about the only categorical statement he made on the topic was that public control was a question of expediency which each community had to resolve for itself. His evaluation was that a municipality should own its waterworks, should operate its gasworks if practical, and should at least secure a revenue and competent service from its transportation facilities which might

[44] Shaw, "Lecture on Public Ownership" (Philadelphia, Feb. 28, 1902), p. 15 of typescript, Shaw MSS.

[45] Shaw, "Government and the Social Welfare," pp. 13-19; Shaw, "The Opportunity of the Publicist in Relation to Efforts for Social Betterment," in Alexander Johnson, ed., Proceedings of the National Conference of Charities and Corrections . . . June 9th to 16th, 1909 (Fort Wayne, Ind.: Press of Fort Wayne Printing Co., n.d.), p. 328; Shaw, "The Higher Life of New York City," Outlook, LIII (Jan. 25, 1896), 134-36.

[46] Shaw, "Government and the Social Welfare," pp. 22-26; Shaw, "Speech to Congregational Club of Yonkers" (Yonkers, N.Y., Oct. 21, 1901), pp. 16-32 of typescript, Shaw MSS; Shaw, "The City in the United States: The Proper Scope of Its Activities," in Clinton Rogers Woodruff, ed., Proceedings of the Indianapolis Conference for Good City Government and Fourth Annual Meeting of the National Municipal League Held November 30, December 1, 2, 1898 (Philadelphia: National Municipal League, 1898), pp. 82-93.

or might not be publicly owned. As the years passed, Shaw seems to have concluded that the last could be operated most efficiently by private enterprise, yet until the 1920s when he repudiated the theory of municipalism altogether his judgment was flexible.[47]

Once called to Albany to testify before a legislative committee, Shaw had been asked a loaded question about utilities that was designed to label him a doctrinaire advocate of public ownership and discredit the influence he felt was his. His hedging answer, Shaw explained to a pair of worried Philadelphians who wanted to solicit his backing, did not mean he had repudiated municipalism. In Philadelphia's circumstances it was desirable.[48] Shaw made a fine assessment of himself: some would call him a socialist because he believed so much in public operation of certain municipal services while others would brand him a reactionary because he retained so much faith in private initiative.[49]

The structure of government, as contrasted to its functioning, held only secondary interest for Shaw, but he was not lacking in suggestions for its improvement. Aside from some reforms like odd-year balloting, general-ticket elections, and proportional representation, which he hoped might weaken the grasp of urban machines, it seemed to Shaw that home rule and the simplification of charters would best work to the advantage of good government. The prevailing European system that centered on a strong municipal council—the mayor often chosen from its ranks—was a well-integrated and effective one that merited attention.[50]

---

[47] *American Monthly Review of Reviews*, XXXIII (1906), 139-40; *American Review of Reviews*, XL (1909), 17-18; Shaw, "Lecture on Public Ownership," pp. 4, 35; *New York Times*, Apr. 9, 1905; Shaw to George W. Ochs, Nov. 11, 1895, Shaw to C. W. Ordway, Apr. 13, 1897, Shaw to Sir Robert Donald, Sept. 24, 1930, all in Shaw MSS.

[48] Shaw to Leo S. Rowe, Oct. 26, 1897, Clinton Rogers Woodruff to Shaw, Oct. 28, 1897, both in Shaw MSS.

[49] Shaw, "Government and the Social Welfare," p. 1.

[50] Shaw, "The Municipal Problem and Greater New York," *Atlantic Monthly*, LXXIX (June 1897), 733, 736-39, 744-48; Shaw, "The New San Francisco Charter," *American Monthly Review of Reviews*, XIX (1899), 569-75; Shaw to Bryce, May 25, 1894, Shaw MSS. For a perceptive interpretation of charter

By 1900 Albert Shaw's reputation as a municipal reformer was declining, for after the publication of his two books on municipal government he undertook no investigations of comparable significance. His editorials and speeches received the attention they did largely because of the acclaim the books and the articles that preceded them had won. By themselves they could not sustain his reputation. He did not seem to care, however. He would maintain his affiliations with reform organizations and even deliver an occasional speech on civic affairs, but the sense of urgency he had felt about the condition of American cities was gone. The 1890s had generally been a triumphal decade for reformers, and by its end he regarded the campaign for municipal betterment as substantially won. The nation was now aroused to the need for honest government, efficiently administered public services, and effective training in citizenship and would not forget it. (Even Tammany, despite its predictable inefficiency, would have to bear this in mind in governing New York City.) The cause of municipal reform seemingly secure, Shaw grew alert to what seemed to him more pressing matters: to the rise of big business and of organized labor and to the decline of the small farmer.

---

reform see Samuel P. Hays, "The Politics of Reform in Municipal Government in the Progressive Era," *Pacific Northwest Quarterly*, LV (Oct. 1964), 157-69.

6

The Average Man

The Progressive era was a time of far-reaching economic change in which industrial trusts were being established with an unprecedented rapidity while organized labor was struggling for overdue benefits. Even farmers followed the pattern set by business and formed cooperative marketing and distribution associations to pursue commercial gains.[1] Bigness seemed to be the hallmark of things, and people asked about the possible consequences: were massive combinations of capital and aggressive organizations of labor necessary? And if so, how was the traditional faith that the man of competence could make his own way in the business world and become an entrepreneur to be squared with this new situation?

In 1907 several of Shaw's addresses that attempted to resolve such questions were published in one volume titled *The Outlook for the Average Man*. Each of the selections had been delivered to college audiences within the five years preceding the date of issue,[2] so they have a restricted scope and an invariable tone of optimism. Though they deal far more in possibilities than in realities, they are not inconsistent with Shaw's analysis of the Progressive era's unfolding social and economic developments.

The most spectacular of these matters that Shaw and his contemporaries pondered was that of trusts—the popular, if imprecise, designation for sizeable commercial and industrial combinations formed from several component companies for the purpose of dominating the market in their respective fields. Railroads, which already had monopolistic aspects, had formed trunk lines and were threatening to consolidate regionally. Anyone who had read Henry D. Lloyd's *Wealth Against*

Commonwealth knew that the Standard Oil Company of the Rockefellers was symbolic of these unwholesome and sinister forces. For each merger, much of the public seemed to think, had been preceded by a commercial Little Big Horn at which scores of small honest entrepreneurs had been wiped out by the greedy chieftains of capital. There had been some mergers in the 1880s; and, after a lapse of a few years in which depression, labor violence, and free silver successively became domestic issues, there came a bold series of consolidations. Between 1897 and 1903 capital combined in amounts that dwarfed previous conceptions of size: the number of manufacturing trusts increased from 12 to 305 as their capital resources rose from less than one billion dollars to nearly seven billion dollars. The United States Steel Company, formed in 1901 from the already formidable Carnegie interests and other concerns, alone accounted for about one-fifth of the total capital. Several Wall Street financial houses, like those of J. P. Morgan and Kuhn, Loeb, had a key role in these dealings, and they remained influential in corporate affairs thereafter.[3]

For more than a decade prior to this time Shaw had been editorially exploring the trend to economic bigness. Personally he probably leaned to the view that it was a legitimate development, as did most of his generation of political economists,[4] but his available statements on it are contradictory. The consolidation movement itself was still so novel as conceivably to cause him genuine uncertainty about how to treat it. Most of the time Shaw had been critical of trusts, suggesting that such combinations as the anthracite, beef, and school book interests should be denied tariff protection and otherwise harassed.[5] There was, however, a minor theme to his editorials. In it he

[1] Hays, *Response to Industrialism*, pp. 48-70.

[2] The fifth selection, "Jefferson's Doctrines under New Tests," was largely concerned with imperialism. The other four treated economic problems.

[3] Hays, *Response to Industrialism*, pp. 48-52; Mowry, *Era of Theodore Roosevelt*, pp. 6-8, 82.

[4] Fine, *Laissez Faire and General-Welfare State*, pp. 232, 338; Rader, *Academic Mind and Reform*, pp. 104-5.

[5] *Minneapolis Tribune*, Nov. 26, Dec. 20, 1884, Aug. 11, 1885, Oct. 7, 1886, Sept. 10, 17, Dec. 14, 1889, July 1, 8, 10, 1890.

held that business combination was not of itself repugnant; while there should be governmental regulation of it, some forms, like railroad pools to divide the available traffic, were perhaps beneficial. The public frequently suffered from excessive competition.[6]

In his discussions of business affairs, both in the *Tribune* and in the early issues of the *Review,* Shaw did not speak of any sacrosanct rights of property.[7] Instead, he assumed, as in his municipal studies, that the public welfare, asserted through institutions of government, was superior to that of property and that trusts had to be considered in their social aspects. Within this framework he was, therefore, able to accept or reject trusts, or deal in the same way with certain of their features.

At the onset of the second wave of mergers in 1897 Shaw took a decisive stand: "There are economic tendencies making for the concentration of productive capital which it is worse than idle to oppose."[8] Two years later when he was appointed by Governor Roosevelt of New York as a delegate to the Chicago Conference on Trusts and Combinations, it was clear in advance what position he would take.[9] Asked what he thought of trusts, Shaw replied: "What do I think of the heavenly system? I think that they are both inevitable. What we have to do is to correct any defects there may be in such trusts."[10]

Elaborating his views in the *Average Man* essays, Shaw distinguished between the old competitive era and the contemporary one that was still ill-defined. The earlier period, from which the Rockefellers had emerged as the representative capitalists, had been ruthless and wasteful. The successful

6 Ibid., Dec. 13, 1884, Jan. 19, 1886, Sept. 9, 1887, Mar. 3, 1888.

7 *Review of Reviews* (Amer. ed.), IV (1891-1892), 251-52, VII (1893), 266-67, 518-19.

8 Ibid., XV (1897), 18.

9 Fine, *Laissez Faire and General-Welfare State,* p. 337; Shaw, "The President and the Trusts," *Century,* n.s. XLV (Jan. 1903), 382. Shaw had indirectly informed T. R. he would be willing to attend. Roosevelt to Shaw, July 29, 1899, Shaw MSS.

10 Quoted in *New York Times,* Sept. 14, 1899.

industrialists—men of vision, Shaw said in their behalf—had not been the only ones to use rebates and the other under-handed devices of the competitive era: they had just employed them more adroitly.[11] "The fact is, of course, that the old-fashioned competitive system, carried to a logical extreme, is closely analogous to warfare; and the whole tendency of our civilization," he had once generalized, "is away from Ishmael-itish methods, and is moving nobly and wholesomely in the direction of cooperative and peaceful methods."[12]

This new age, maintained Shaw (who in this context all but ignored the evils of the present), was to be a more orderly one in which the great administrator would replace the great capitalist and in which planning would replace chance, as had already occurred in the case of the railroads.[13] The public would profit from such stability, he reasoned: "If one or two traveling salesmen can really do all the business that thirty or forty were struggling and competing for under the old system, the community as a whole must certainly reap the benefit when the necessary readjustments have been made; and what is good for the community as a whole will not fail to be good also for most of the individuals concerned."[14]

The images Shaw held of the new business era resembled the ones he had formed of the ideal municipality: efficiency, order, and applied science were its distinctive features.[15] He readily conceded that traditional standards would have to be redefined, for the margins within which would-be Rockefellers might operate were diminishing. His prognostication was nevertheless encouraging. As usual he emphasized character and pointed out that the future managerial recruits then in college were sure to be socially responsible. There was little likelihood that the young century would turn out to be an age of plutocracy. Although Shaw's "Average Man" would probably not become wealthy himself, he would earn a steady

11 Shaw, *Average Man*, pp. 67-79.
12 *American Monthly Review of Reviews*, XIX (1899), 644.
13 Shaw, *Average Man*, pp. 16, 28-29, 37-38, 70-74, 162.
14 Ibid., p. 29.
15 Ibid., pp. 4, 13-14, 28, 38, 158, 163.

income and have new opportunities to enjoy leisure and obtain cultural edification: in short, professional status.[16]

Labor shared in the organizational rally of the period. Under the determined leadership of Samuel Gompers, the American Federation of Labor was in the process of establishing itself in the 1890s. Composed of already existing national craft unions like the Cigar Makers and Typographers, the A. F. of L. sought to improve hours and wages through the use of collective bargaining. Such other unions as the four railway brotherhoods remained unaffiliated. Although the total strength of organized labor was estimated at only 250,000 men in 1897, just surviving the depression had been a feat. Between then and 1904, when a mild slump caused by the successful counterthrust of capital set in, roughly five times as many men enlisted in unions. They as well as unorganized laborers benefited from the passage in over two dozen states of workmen's compensation and maximum hours statutes during the years before World War I. Laws that protected women and child laborers by limiting their hours of employment and prescribing standards for health and safety were widely enacted too.[17]

Despite this well-intentioned legislation the attitude of the average progressive toward organized labor was generally ambivalent. "Unions were grudgingly recognized as a necessary evil," notes one of progressivism's more informed students, "but the monopolistic closed shop was an abomination not to be tolerated with or without government regulation."[18] Caught between the advance of organized labor on one side and of consolidating capital on the other, the average middle-class citizen regarded both as threats to his status and individuality.

Shaw's own economic and social position was rising enviably throughout the period, but the notion of status seems relevant in that he was much concerned with the assault of the new

[16] Ibid., pp. 10-17.
[17] Foster Rhea Dulles, *Labor in America: A History,* 2d rev. ed. (New York: Crowell, 1960), pp. 128-63, 183, 193, 201, 203; Hays, *Response to Industrialism,* pp. 66-67.
[18] Mowry, *Era of Theodore Roosevelt,* p. 102.

economic forces upon old values.[19] His *Average Man* essays represented a perceptive effort to resolve these tensions and to offer encouragement for the future. Shaw regarded organized labor in much the same way as he regarded the trust movement, for he wondered of both whether they contributed to industrial efficiency and how they affected the public. What did they mean to familiar standards, he was asking. What would become of the old America of sturdy farmers, proud craftsmen, and the self-employed middle class?

Shaw had recognized the labor movement from both a scholarly and editorial viewpoint when he was in Minneapolis. There appears little doubt that his interest in the working-man's aspirations for betterment was genuine, but he allowed labor few weapons for self help. The cooperative technique that he analyzed in his monograph on Minneapolis labor groups appeared for a time to offer prospects for improvement. He expected too much of it, though: "It develops and strengthens all the worthiest elements of manhood, while its disciplines and restraints are invaluable."[20] When he discussed the more irritating union weapons of the strike and the boycott, he was not so idealistic and mellow. "Its operation is sweeping and tyrannical," he wrote of the boycott. "It interferes with the rights of neutrals, and punishes a hundred innocent people to make sure of slaying one enemy. The disposition to abuse the power of perfected organization is some thing that every thoughtful workingman should recognize and guard against."[21] Shaw applied the same analogy to strikes: "The strike is warfare; and it ought to be superseded by peaceful modes of settling disputes."[22]

On several occasions Shaw suggested that arbitration be used to protect the public and effect justice. The violent Homestead

[19] Hofstadter, *Age of Reform*, pp. 131-73, presents the most enlightened discussion of status. Otis L. Graham, Jr., ed., *From Roosevelt to Roosevelt: American Politics and Diplomacy, 1901-1941*, The Literature of History Series (New York: Appleton-Century-Crofts, 1971), pp. 41-47, 53-67, surveys scholarly opinion of this significant but controversial argument.

[20] Shaw, "Cooperation in the Northwest," p. 305.

[21] *Minneapolis Tribune*, Dec. 27, 1885.

[22] Ibid., Jan. 23, 1886.

steel strike of 1892 particularly alarmed him, since neither capital nor labor could be relied upon to follow the "principles of Christianity" and as a result he recommended compulsory arbitration to settle subsequent industrial disputes of such magnitude.[23] Shortly afterward he said of a railroad strike which the stubbornness of the owners appeared to be prolonging: "If the corporations are more afraid than the labor unions of so just and fair a remedy as arbitration, we have only to remark that the discerning public may draw its own inferences and act accordingly. . . . The rights and the supreme dignity of the State itself are what chiefly need attention and reinforcement."[24]

Shaw toned down his most advanced opinions about the use of compulsory arbitration, but he did continue to suggest that in some circumstances it was reasonable.[25] Strikes still seemed to be no better than warfare, and in many instances he felt that the public was unduly afflicted by them. Shaw's reaction to the strike at the Pullman car works in 1894 and the subsequent sympathy strke by the American Railway Union was typical of his median attitude. "I have no more sympathy with lawlessness or with violence on the part of labor leaders than you have," he explained to a friend who expressed surprise at Shaw's judgment that capital bore some responsibility for the conflict. "On the other hand I do not find it necessary in every case to sympathize deeply with a corporation or an employer simply because his striking employees have conducted themselves improperly."[26] He condoned the Cleveland administration's decision to use federal troops against labor rowdyism and, in effect, to break the strike by the A.R.U., but he condemned the arrest of leader Eugene Debs. Although Debs had been morally wrong, leading a strike was no more

---

23 Ibid., Dec. 27, 1885, Jan. 23, 1886, Mar. 10, 1888; *Review of Reviews* (Amer. ed.), VI (1892-1893), 13.

24 Ibid., p. 133.

25 Ibid., IX (1894), 5. 648, X (1894), 135; *American Monthly Review of Reviews*, XXII (1900), 399-400; Shaw to the editor of the *Voice*, Mar. 20, 1895, Shaw MSS.

26 Walter Scaife to Shaw, Sept. 23, 1894, Shaw to Scaife, Dec. 26, 1894, both in Shaw MSS.

criminal than striking. The public—"the innocent third party"—had suffered most from it.[27]

Shaw later tried to assess the relationship of organized labor to the trust movement. The chances were that unions and trusts would cooperate more readily than labor and small enterprise, surmised Shaw, hoping that regular procedures of discussion and arbitration would be established. The diffusion of stock ownership among the workers themselves might also lead to greater rapport. But when strikes kept recurring Shaw's analysis became less favorable. In those trades—like construction—where manual skill counted a great deal, unionism actually had harmful aspects, for it tended to set as a lowest common denominator of efficiency the ability of the least able workers. Strikes which had the achievement of union recognition and the closed shop as their purpose were not justifiable; only severe provocation in the form of low wages, long hours, and poor working conditions furnished a sufficient reason for inconveniencing the public. Yet the nonunion man, or scab, should not be exalted to the position of a hero; sometimes it seemed objectionable for the scabs to accept the gains won by organized workers. Shaw hoped that unionism would not crystallize occupational differences into class lines. The ideal to maintain was that of mobility: to join or not to join a union, to rise within one's craft or above it. Success should depend on competence and character.[28]

Shaw was not, however, regarded as an enemy of labor.[29] He did expect organized labor to behave responsibly just as he expected business to submit to regulation. Though he made unfavorable comments at times, he then was probably quicker to reprimand capital.

[27] *Review of Reviews* (Amer. ed.), X (1894), 132-36.

[28] *American Monthly Review of Reviews,* XXIII (1901), 390, 526, XXV (1902), 652, XXVII (1903), 645, XXXIII (1906), 142-43, 393; Shaw to S. S. McClure, Dec. 13, 1902, Shaw MSS.

[29] Shaw, *Average Man,* pp. 14, 163; Shaw to Jesse Macy, June 8, 1894, Shaw to Stead, June 12, 1894, Shaw to Samuel Gompers, Dec. 17, 1895, Albert Beveridge to Shaw, Apr. 12, 1901, Paul Kennady to Shaw, Oct. 16, 1911, all in Shaw MSS; *Chicago Evening Post,* Mar. 19, 1902; *Grand Rapids Herald,* Mar. 23, 1902, both in Scrapbooks, Shaw MSS.

Agriculture, broadly interpreted, was the third great economic question that Shaw studied at length. It was not unusual for city people to concern themselves with rural culture, for the years around 1900 were ones of transition between an old and a new society. Some of the most confirmed urbanites retained an affection for rural life and its storied virtues of yeoman individualism, simplicity, and morality. Perhaps like Shaw they had been reared in a pastoral setting themselves or had at least enjoyed easy access to the unspoiled countryside. Municipal reformers, acting through such organizations as the American Civic Association, labored to obtain parks for their cities and for the nation, so that theirs and generations to come would be able to draw inspiration from this precious heritage. Barely a decade after the municipal reform movement had reached its height the Country Life Movement began.[30] It was not a back-to-the-land crusade, its chronicler asserted, but an attempt to make rural life more satisfying by overcoming its acknowledged handicaps of isolation and backwardness.[31] As Shaw later explained it: "We had become acutely aware of the so-called city problem before we had realized that a not less formidable problem of the countryside was presenting itself."[32] To remedy it he joined others in supporting a multi-faceted program that included rural free delivery, good roads, better schooling, conservation, and improved farming.

[30] For an extended discussion of these matters, see Peter J. Schmitt, *Back to Nature: The Arcadian Myth in Urban America,* Urban Life in America Series (New York: Oxford University Press, 1969).

[31] Hays, *Response to Industrialism,* pp. 82-83; Liberty Hyde Bailey, *The Country-Life Movement in the United States* (New York: Macmillan, 1911), p. 1; Kenyon Butterfield, *Chapters in Rural Progress* (Chicago: University of Chicago Press, 1908), pp. 9-41. For a short time in 1905 Shaw, in association with publisher J. Horace McFarland, head of the American Civic Association, issued a magazine about this subject, *The Country Calendar.* In the first issue Grover Cleveland wrote: "All but the absolutely indifferent can be made to realize that outdoor air and activity, intimacy with nature, and acquaintanceship with birds and animals and fish are essential to physical and mental strength." Quoted in *American Monthly Review of Reviews,* XXXI (1905), 628.

[32] Shaw, Introduction to Harlean James, *Land Planning in the United States for the City, State and Nation,* Land Economics Series (New York: Macmillan, 1926), p. xiii.

Not much need be said about Shaw as a conservationist, for his relationship to the conservation movement consisted of little more than joining the proper societies and giving it a favorable hearing in the *Review of Reviews*. He argued that scenic beauty had to be preserved and in keeping with his attitude toward reform generally advanced the contention that the use of America's resources had to be governed by the principle of efficiency.[33]

Shaw was probably more concerned with improving modes of agriculture than with any other aspect of country life, for on it, he believed, depended the viability of the family farm and ultimately the dignity of rural America. Despite his midwestern background Shaw's closest involvement with agrarian society was with the South and came about largely after 1900. The story of this commitment belongs to that of the educational revival that swept the South in the first decade of this century.

What there was of the southern public school system was deplorable, for regional poverty, an unusually high proportion of children to adults, and the provision of separate facilities for both whites and Negroes proved a crippling handicap for education.[34] It was said of rural schools in Virginia that "pupils could literally sit in the classrooms and study astronomy through the roof and geology through the floor."[35] Half the Negroes and over a tenth (an incidence more than double the national average) of the native whites in the South were illiterate. An educator starkly summed up the South's statistical plight of 1901: "In the Southern states, in schoolhouses

---

[33] Shaw, *Political Problems of American Development*, pp. 101-15; *Review of Reviews* (Amer. ed.), VIII (1893), 63-66, X (1894), 359; *American Monthly Review of Reviews*, XXXIII (1906), 141-42, 396; *American Review of Reviews*, XLI (1910), 136, XLII (1910), 402. For the relationship between conservation and efficiency see Samuel Hays's admirable monograph, *Conservation and the Gospel of Efficiency: The Progressive Conservation Movement, 1890-1920* (Cambridge: Harvard University Press, 1959).

[34] C. Vann Woodward, *Origins of the New South*, A History of the South, Vol. IX (Baton Rouge: Louisiana State University Press, 1951), pp. 398-400, 406.

[35] James W. Patton, "The Southern Reaction to the Ogden Movement," in R. C. Simonini, ed., *Education in the South*, Institute of Southern Culture Lectures (Farmville, Va.: Publications of Longwood College, 1959), p. 68.

costing an average of $276 each, under teachers receiving the average salary of $25 a month, we are giving the children in actual attendance 5 cents' worth of education a day for eighty-seven days only in the year."[36]

The educational upsurge of the South can be traced to a school campaign that began indigenously in North Carolina in the 1890s and to the intervention of outside reformers, one of whom was Shaw. In 1898 a conference on southern education had been held at Capon Springs, West Virginia. Most of the participants were primarily concerned with church schools for Negroes, but some interest in other educational matters was displayed. It resulted in the calling of a session of wider scope for the following year. Several New Yorkers including the municipal reformers George McAneny and William Jay Schieffelin; Robert C. Ogden, who was John Wanamaker's business associate and a veteran trustee of the Hampton Institute; and the banker and philanthropist George Foster Peabody went to the 1899 gathering. Attending as Peabody's guest, Shaw wrote the resolutions for it and thus commenced a career as a draftsman of manifestoes on southern education.[37] The resolutions stressed the need for secondary and industrial education and, in contrast to northern philanthropic efforts theretofore, also emphasized the schooling of whites.[38]

The intention was to educate the backward whites of mountain areas, "our contemporary ancestors," as they were called.[39] This had an especially poignant appeal, for their Anglo-Saxon lineage was impeccable, if hidden under a cracker exterior. But this limited conception soon was transformed

36 Quoted in Woodward, *Origins of the New South*, p. 400.

37 On these developments see the Southern Education Board Papers, University of North Carolina, and Charles W. Dabney, *Universal Education in the South*, 2 vols. (Chapel Hill: University of North Carolina Press, 1936), which is based on them.

38 Ibid., II, 8-10; Louis Harlan, *Separate and Unequal: Public School Campaigns and Racism in the Southern Seaboard States, 1901-1915* (Chapel Hill. University of North Carolina Press, 1958), pp. 45-80; *American Monthly Review of Reviews*, XX (1899), 131-37; W. H. Sale to Shaw, May 14, 1899, Robert Ogden to Shaw, June 3, 1901, Apr. 22, 1903, all in Shaw MSS.

39 Quoted in *American Monthly Review of Reviews*, XX (1899), 137.

into a general plea for the education of whites.[40] Walter Hines Page best expressed the rationale for this change: "We want to train both the white boy and the black boy, but we must train the white boy first, because we cannot do anything for the Negro boy until his white friend is convinced of his responsibility to him."[41] However, this deference to southern racial prejudices was also congenial to many of the Yankees involved, for it was a time of frank bigotry in both sections. Jim Crow laws were enacted in the South and at least tacitly approved by the North. Shaw, for one, had the firmest convictions about white superiority and consistently approved of schemes to disfranchise Negroes, saying that the South should be allowed to work out its own destinies.[42] Although he personally knew such Negro spokesmen as Booker T. Washington, Shaw had little or no insight into the life of the ordinary black American and simply took it for granted that any racial injustices would be worked out in due time. Seemingly his greater concern was to see the wrongs perpetrated on the white South during Reconstruction rectified. He showed no inclination to disturb segregated education and would hardly have questioned another journalist's reassurance to the South that save for visits to the famed Negro schools at Hampton, Virginia, and Tuskegee, Alabama, the only contact northern educational philanthropists had or wanted with blacks in the South was with those who served them as porters and waiters.[43]

[40] Dabney, *Universal Education*, II, 46. Shaw became a trustee of the Martha Berry School, a Georgia institution that catered to poor whites from Appalachia. Martha Berry to Shaw, Oct. 19, 1909, John J. Eagan to Shaw, Dec. 21, 31, 1909, all in Shaw MSS. Tracy Byers, *The Sunday Lady of Possum Trot* (New York: Putnams, 1932), tells the story of Miss Berry and her schools.

[41] Quoted in Dabney, *Universal Education*, II, 46.

[42] C. Vann Woodward, *The Strange Career of Jim Crow* (New York: Oxford University Press, Galaxy Books, 1957), pp. 49-95; Shaw, *Political Problems of American Development*, p. 125; *American Monthly Review of Reviews*, XXII (1900), 520, XXIII (1901), 643-44. Of course Shaw also insisted that such disfranchisement would enable the South to divide politically. One day qualified Negroes would be allowed to vote. The *Richmond Times*, May 3, 1903, and the *New Orleans Item*, May 5, 1903, favorably mention his views on Negroes, both in Scrapbooks, Shaw MSS.

[43] *Raleigh News and Observer*, June 4, 1902, Scrapbooks, Southern Education

By 1901 the idea of educational regeneration was catching hold. The conference met at Winston-Salem, where it was resolved to establish the Southern Education Board to serve as the executive committee for the annual meetings and more importantly to try and rally opinion behind the public school campaign in the South. Ogden, who every year led a junket of northerners to the conferences, touring school facilities en route, was the dominant figure in the movement. Associated with him on the new board were Shaw, who customarily accompanied his tours; Page, Peabody, Jabez L. M. Curry (a distinguished educational reformer), William H. Baldwin, Jr. (who was president of the Long Island Railroad), and the southern educators Edwin A. Alderman, Charles W. Dabney, and Charles D. McIver. The latter three in addition to Edgar Gardner Murphy of Alabama, who joined in 1902, were the principal policy-makers. Acquiescing in the disfranchisement and segregation policies of the South, the board hoped, un-realistically as it proved, that Negro opportunities for educa-tion would be advanced along with those of whites through the protection of responsible state leaders.[44] The board re-garded the South, Louis Harlan has stated, as an "under-developed region" for which it would "furnish technical assistance and a little money if the South would supply the educational enthusiasm and local leadership."[45]

Philanthropic funds were made available in 1902 when the General Education Board was established. John D. Rocke-feller, Jr., a recent convert to the idea that white education should receive primacy, called the first meeting and pledged the new panel a million dollars on behalf of his father. Eleven

Board Papers. Numerous newspaper clippings in these scrapbooks reveal the concern with the race question that both school reformers and southern observers of the education revival felt.

[44] Dabney, *Universal Education*, II, 32-43; Harlan, *Separate and Unequal*, pp. 75-84; Ogden, Curry, and the three southerners were among the original eight members of 1901. Shaw, Baldwin, and Page joined later that year. Hugh C. Bailey, *Edgar Gardner Murphy: Gentle Progressive* (Coral Gables, Fla.: University of Miami Press, 1968), pp. 138-85, provides the best brief account of the board's work and accomplishments.

[45] Louis Harlan, "The Southern Education Board and the Race Issue in Public Education," *Journal of Southern History*, XXIII (May 1957), 192.

members of the Southern Board served as trustees of this new
foundation during its early years including Shaw, Ogden,
Peabody, and Baldwin, who was the first chairman. Unlike the
Southern Education Board, which it helped finance, this new
organization was to control sufficient funds to subsidize on a
matching basis various programs including summer school for
teachers, teacher training for both races, industrial and agricultural education, and improvement of secondary and rural
elementary schools' facilities. It also aided colleges both South
and North. The General Education Board dispensed money
slowly at first as it explored the possibilities open to it, but
later it acted more decisively and by 1914 felt free to let
the Southern Education Board lapse, taking over the functions
of the other panel itself.[46] When Andrew Carnegie joined it
in 1908, Shaw chuckled that the General Education Board had
become "an educational trust with a vengeance,"[47] but it never
did pry substantial funds from anyone but the Rockefellers
who contributed almost $130,000,000 in its first twenty years.[48]

Grants to the diverse school programs could not fill the
needs of southern education, for these needs were too
enormous. The General Education Board early in its career
undertook a highly creative supplemental program—farm
demonstration work. "In the Southern States," Shaw later
wrote in explaining the rationale for the board's involvement
in this new activity, "it was almost impossible to secure proper
local support of common schools until neighborhoods had
become sufficiently prosperous to pay school taxes. Agricultural prosperity seemed even more urgent than improved
schools."[49]

Its interest in farming led the General Education Board
to Seaman Knapp, the so-called "Benjamin Franklin of the
countryside," who as a special agent of the Department of

46 Dabney, *Universal Education*, II, 143-52; Fosdick, *Adventure in Giving*,
pp. 3-38, 63-98; Harlan, *Separate and Unequal*, pp. 76, 85-88; *The General
Education Board: An Account of its Activities, 1902-1914* (New York: General
Education Board, 1915), pp. 3-18.
47 Shaw to Newton Hawley, Mar. 25, 1908, Shaw MSS.
48 Fosdick, *Adventure in Giving*, pp. 9, 327.
49 Shaw to Sen. William S. Kenyon, May 5, 1914, Shaw MSS.

Agriculture had perfected the demonstration method of agricultural education in 1903 and was already conducting a small campaign in its behalf in weevil-infested areas of Arkansas, Louisiana, and Texas. The demonstration program depended for its success on the cooperation of selected local farmers who (guaranteed against loss) would introduce scientific modes of cultivation on part of their acreage. Once it was seen what impressive results the new techniques such as crop rotation brought about, others copied them, increasing in turn their own harvests and the reputation of the methods advocated by Knapp. In 1906 the Board, in an effort to upgrade farm productivity generally, began financing his projects in other southern states, paying the salaries of demonstration agents who were appointed and controlled by the Agriculture Department. As substantial gains became evident, the government kept assuming greater responsibilities until by 1912 demonstration projects were being conducted in over half the counties of the South. New hope seemed to be sweeping the region.[50]

Shaw was a staunch supporter of the demonstration program and kept Theodore Roosevelt informed of its achievements, leading to some worthwhile publicity for it.[51] His interest in scientific methods of cultivation caused him to embark on a farming venture of his own. Attending the White House Conference on Conservation in 1908, Shaw chatted with Knapp, who persuaded him to buy a farm. Since Shaw normally traveled to Washington at least monthly, Knapp went with him to the nearby Virginia countryside to select some land. Shaw bought a farm in Loudoun County, some twenty-five miles from Washington. With additions it soon comprised 1,600 acres and was large for the area. Aided by Knapp and men from the Department of Agriculture, Shaw hired a

[50] Joseph C. Bailey, *Seaman A. Knapp, Schoolmaster of American Agriculture* (New York: Columbia University Press, 1945), pp. 149-68, 214-48; Dabney, *Universal Education*, II, 177-89; Fosdick, *Adventure in Giving*, pp. 39-62; Woodward, *Origins of the New South*, pp. 408-14; Wallace Buttrick, "Seaman A. Knapp's Work as an Agricultural Statesman," *American Review of Reviews*, XLIII (1911), 683-85.
[51] Hugh C. Bailey, *Edgar Gardner Murphy*, p. 170.

manager and began improving the barren soil through the introduction of proper methods of drainage and fertilization, reserving part of the farm for a demonstration project. The farm became both a hobby and, after several years worth of expensive improvements had been added, a source of modest, albeit sporadic, profit. Shaw solicited advice from experts and tried to wangle modern equipment from International Harvester in exchange for free advertising.[52] "I have not had much experience in these matters," he said of his farming ability, "but I try to bring as much intelligence to bear upon the development of a dairy farm as I have put into my editorial work in the Review for a good many years."[53]

Shaw came to resent the imputation that his farm was only a branch of the Department of Agriculture, and he severed his close connections with it, reserving the right to ask the advice of its experts on specific problems. His particular aims were to raise livestock and to improve the soil to grow silage. He gave close personal attention to the plans for building a manure pit and a piggery, the latter to be so placed, he understood from books, "as to give the pigs a chance to get down to the water and wallow." Shaw was also proud of his oak pasturage for pigs, but his emphasis was upon cattle. He sold milk in the Washington market and after fifteen years had the satisfaction of selling one of his steers for a record price in Loudoun County.[54]

In addition to his practical interest in agriculture, Shaw also developed an intellectual concern for it. In 1913 he presented a paper on modern methods of farming before an assemblage of the American Academy of Political and Social

[52] Interview with Albert Shaw, Jr., Sept. 3, 1964; Shaw to F. C. Moultrop, June 5, 1911, Mar. 12, 1912, Shaw to L. H. Bailey, Dec. 8, 1911, Shaw to Carroll Dunham, Dec. 21, 1911, Shaw to William D. Saunders, Jan. 31, 1913, William Dodd to Shaw, Dec. 13, 1915, all in Shaw MSS; Shaw, "Memorandum Regarding Book on Farming in Virginia," July 22, 1939, in possession of Albert Shaw, Jr. Also available in the Shaw collection are the account journals of his Sterling Farm.

[53] Shaw to W. D. Hoard & Sons Company, Feb. 27, 1913, Shaw MSS.

[54] Henry St. George Tucker to Shaw, June 27, 1924, Shaw to F. C. Moultrop, June 5, 1911, Mar. 12, 1912, Shaw to L. H. Bailey, Dec. 8, 1911, Shaw to Dunham, Dec. 21, 1911, Shaw to James Ricketts, Sr., Mar. 29, 1912, all in Shaw MSS.

Science, and the following year successfully urged the National Civic Federation to hold a symposium on agriculture.[55] On the assumption that modernization would prove the salvation of the family farm in the United States (whereas it merely confirmed its obsolescence), he approached his subject with something of the zeal he had once shown in his works on municipal reform. "We must needs industrialize agriculture," he declared in his paper. "Farming must be put upon a modern basis and capitalized." In order to eliminate the waste inherent in competition and in needless duplication of facilities, he recommended that farmers explore the advantages of cooperation. Consolidated rural schools should be constructed. Through common action farmers could obtain good roads. Farm machinery and knowledge could be shared. He emphasized the potential of marketing cooperatives in obtaining higher prices. Citing an instance where urban consumers paid forty cents a dozen for eggs while farmers marketed them locally for only twelve or fifteen cents a dozen, he speculated that cooperative action would allow farmers to ship their products to more distant outlets where they could obtain better prices. By eliminating some of the middlemen, they would probably help the consumer and also themselves. But even if higher prices resulted in the short run, the ultimate outcome of modern agriculture would be to cheapen the unit cost of production as farmers used their extra profits to employ better methods of cultivation. The economies and the greater productivity of efficient agriculture would thus assist the consumer too.[56]

The resurgence of southern agriculture that Shaw participated in did not have more than temporary results. The aim of the farmer was to grow more cotton, and the wisdom of that was already being disputed by those who believed that crop limitations were the surest path to prosperity. The

[55] Shaw, "Cooperation as a Means of Reducing the Cost of Living," *Annals of the American Academy of Political and Social Science*, XLVIII (July 1913), 225-37; *New York Times*, Mar. 24, 1914; Shaw to Ralph Easley, Mar. 12, 1914, Easley to Shaw, Apr. 7, 1914, both in Shaw MSS.

[56] Shaw, "Cooperation as a Means of Reducing the Cost of Living," pp. 226-37.

achievements in education were heartening but by 1914 had still not brought southern standards up to those of the nation. Still, the estimated value of public-school property more than tripled, and teachers' salaries, school attendance, and length of sessions also advanced. Illiteracy declined among both white and Negro children of school age, but the racial disparities increased. A disproportionate share of the additional education funds went to the white schools, for fair-mindedness or paternalism was not as prevalent as the members of the two school boards had believed.[57]

Shaw served on the Southern Education Board until it disbanded in 1914 and on the General Education Board until he reached its retirement age in 1929.[58] He was an enthusiastic and faithful supporter of both but not a leader of either one. His contributions came in good measure as a publicist. Shaw's participation does, however, underline the range of his interests which spanned business, labor, conservation, education, and agriculture. Although on the surface of things these matters appear to have little in common, Shaw's treatment of them centers on certain themes: the need to apply to them the latest advances in efficiency, knowledge, and organization and their relationship to the national well-being.

While he touched upon them recurrently, it was in one of his *Average Man* essays, "Our Legacy From a Century of Pioneers," that Shaw integrated the two ideas most explicitly. The focus of this address was on the need for reconciling the rural, pioneer past—the period when the subsistence farmer had been the "typical American citizen"—and the urban-industrial present in which the trained professional would predominate. Americans had to recognize that theirs was a mature society, declared Shaw, for the century of vigorous westward expansion that had begun about 1785 had come to an end in the 1890s. Maturity, however, did not mean stagnation but a period of growth and challenge under novel social conditions.[59]

57 Woodward, *Origins of the New South,* pp. 405-6, 408-12.
58 W. W. Brierley to Shaw, June 16, 1930, Shaw MSS.
59 Shaw to Kenyon Butterfield, Sept. 12, 1923, Shaw MSS; Shaw, *Average Man,*

Even though the pioneer period during which America's distinctive characteristics of individualism, independence, and self-reliance had been shaped was gone, social conditions could be ameliorated and made more equitable without sacrificing these national traits. While socialism was to be rejected, various agencies of government still had many legitimate functions to perform: promoting education, regulating the common carriers, protecting the public health through the control of epidemic diseases and the enactment of food and drug statutes. But since the expansion of government in these and other areas would demand unprecedented expenditures, the public revenues would have to be administered more efficiently and the sagging areas of the economy (as the members of the General Education Board had already perceived) would have to be revitalized in order to provide the requisite tax base. Ample challenges in both public and private pursuits thus faced the young citizen, challenges that could be solved without betraying America's pioneer forefathers.[60]

Unwittingly Shaw had mired himself in a contradiction that plagued not only this particular address but ultimately his whole reformist posture. It centered on the question of individualism. He had first encountered it in his municipal studies where the problem had been to show how the operations of local government could be expanded without encroaching upon individual liberties. Shaw neatly resolved it by arguing that the new activism was intended to provide a safe and attractive environment for people to live in; as such it was merely an extension of the traditional police power and hence quite compatible with individualism.[61] But he now was involving himself in the problem more deeply and with less satisfactory results, for in his discussion of the pioneer legacy individualism had assumed almost mystical attributes as one of the determinants of the national character. Individualism

---

pp. 95-118, 126-27. The address also appeared as an article, "Our Legacy from a Century of Pioneers," *South Atlantic Quarterly*, V (Oct. 1906), 311-32.

[60] Shaw, *Average Man*, pp. 119-33.

[61] Shaw, "Municipal Socialism in Scotland," *Juridical Review*, I (Jan. 1889), 33-34; Shaw, *Municipal Government in Britain*, pp. 7-8.

had produced the atomistic society he deplored, but he nevertheless expected it to be maintained even as a bureaucratic
state in which America's hitherto self-seeking individuals would
conduct themselves with social consciousness was being erected.
He did not even try to explain what sort of alchemy other than
the dawning of a new social epoch was to bring about this
conversion of the individualistic impulse or to show how individualism and the new bureaucratic apparatus were to co-
exist.[62] Was there an answer?

In effect Shaw had defined his progressive credo: a combination of reform and Americanism. Since it meant substantially the same thing to Theodore Roosevelt, Albert
Beveridge, and a few others who comprised the leadership of
what has become identified as the New Nationalist wing of
progressivism, it was only natural that Shaw found congenial
friends in these men and worked closely with them in the early
years of the present century to secure the enactment of policies
that would promote what they defined as the national health.

[62] Shaw, *Average Man*, p. 134. For an illuminating discussion of individualism
in the Progressive era see Theodore P. Greene, *America's Heroes: The Changing
Models of Success in American Magazines* (New York: Oxford University Press,
1970), pp. 232-84. Also pertinent are Robert Wiebe, *The Search for Order,
1877-1920*, The Making of America Series (New York: Hill and Wang, 1967),
and James Weinstein, *The Corporate Ideal in the Liberal State: 1900-1918*
(Boston: Beacon Press, 1968). The latter deals with the corporate, as opposed
to the individual, vision of society and furnishes a different but nevertheless
useful perspective on the social outlook of Shaw's generation.

7

Hand in Hand with T. R., 1901-1908

In 1942 Shaw began writing a book about his long-time friend Theodore Roosevelt. About three-fourths of the unfinished manuscript deals directly or by digression with Roosevelt, the mugwumps, and the events of 1884, the year in which this group of eastern Republicans earned immediate opprobrium and lasting fame by supporting Democrat Grover Cleveland for president rather than their own party's candidate, James G. Blaine. Shaw (who prominently included himself in asides) was bent on proving that Roosevelt, "the fearless and hard-hitting young New Yorker," was as righteous as the mugwumps and vastly more practical in his decision to remain a Republican during this controversial campaign. Shaw acknowledged the personal decency of individual mugwumps, several of whom befriended him after he moved to New York, but still he could not justify their switch to Cleveland. Mugwump leaders like George William Curtis, E. L. Godkin, and Carl Schurz, argued Shaw, had only tenuous affiliations with the Republican party by 1884 and had no right to accuse Roosevelt and others like him of betraying principle in refusing to bolt.[1]

Shaw also spoke of his own commitment to the GOP. It seems that in 1884 he had favored Senator George Edmunds of Vermont as a prospective presidential candidate—partly out of a sentimental attachment to his mother's native state and partly because Edmunds represented ability and integrity. Blaine, no matter what the mugwumps thought of him, had been an acceptable alternative, especially admired by westerners for his nationalism. They had understood his interest in railroad projects, and they had hailed his foreign policy goal of securing Latin American markets for our commerce. In contrast, easterners from whom the mugwumps had been recruited had no longer maintained a lusty Americanism.[2]

Shaw had not met Roosevelt in 1884; he only knew of him. They became acquainted about a decade later when T. R. was serving in Washington as United States Civil Service Commissioner but did not meet frequently until 1895 when Roosevelt moved to New York to head the city's police board during Mayor Strong's reform administration. Soon after they were having luncheon engagements, became lifelong friends, and, in Shaw's words, went "hand in hand" through public affairs. Roosevelt, who was a year the younger, was an easterner, while Shaw's connections were with the Midwest. The former was a politician, the latter an editor, but they had much in common. They were well-bred, well-educated, semiprofessional scholars. Their notions about literary and personal standards of propriety were compatible and conventional. Winston Churchill, Shaw's warm friend and favorite novelist, was also much admired by Roosevelt. Churchill's heroines were pure, his outcomes usually happy, his plots either historical romances or, after 1904, more sophisticated explorations of the Progressive era's typical problems.[3] The family was the anchor of institutions. When Shaw once broke an appointment to remain home with his indisposed sons, T. R. characteristically replied: "I should think mighty little of you if you had not gone home to your wife and the quarantined small people."[4] They were moralists and expected the most elevated deportment from one another. "I should be ashamed indeed to do anything base and look you in the face afterwards," Roosevelt said of his regard for Shaw's standards. "I hope I

---

1 Shaw, "Reminiscences of Theodore Roosevelt" (unpublished typescript, 1942), pp. 52, 92, 111-12, 166, 168, Shaw MSS.

2 Ibid., pp. 83, 100, 144.

3 Mowry, *Era of Theodore Roosevelt*, pp. 106-15; John Morton Blum, *The Republican Roosevelt* (New York: Atheneum, 1962), pp. 24-36; Robert W. Schneider, *Five Novelists of the Progressive Era* (New York: Columbia University Press, 1965), pp. 205-51; Shaw to James H. Pound, Dec. 20, 1912, Shaw to Herman Hagedorn, July 28, 1924, both in Shaw MSS.

4 Roosevelt to Shaw, Sept. 13, 1907, Shaw MSS.

would not do anything base anyhow, but I simply could not do it when I have friends like yourself."[5] Politically they thought alike; they were ardent nationalists; they had friends in common. Nicholas Murray Butler, president of Columbia University, and Frederick William Holls, a prominent attorney, comprised with Shaw the New York "trio" of T. R.'s cronies. George Perkins and especially Albert Beveridge were also political supporters of Roosevelt who were close to Shaw.[6]

When T. R. and Shaw disagreed about politics, it was apt to be over tone rather than substance. Roosevelt was often blunt, and Shaw measured his words. Beveridge, for instance, usually submitted the drafts of his speeches to Shaw for criticism. Normally Shaw's advice was to qualify a statement. " 'Never' is such a very long time," he said in one typical instance.[7] Although Shaw was hard-hitting in attacking Tammany Hall and in asserting America's claim to empire, he preferred to eschew political controversy and within the limits of his own Republicanism gave the other side a fair hearing. He was committed to a modified protective tariff and the gold standard and opposed the income tax,[8] but he was particularly conscious of his western background and throughout the 1890s, a decade of severe social disturbance, pointed out that such groups as the Coxeyites, the Populists, and the Bryan Democrats were not the incarnations of evil that their more fervent detractors seemed to think. Any number of times he called for the reestablishment of sectional good will. "The East has come to distrust Kansas, Nebraska, Colorado, and to some extent Iowa," he explained to Jesse Macy in requesting a statement for the *Review of Reviews*. "What

---

[5] Ibid., July 31, 1902.

[6] Ibid., Sept. 20, 1899, Dec. 20, 1900; Nicholas Murray Butler, *Across the Busy Years: Recollections and Reflections*, 2 vols. (New York: Scribners, 1939-40), I, 312-13, 347, 351; John Braeman, *Albert J. Beveridge, American Nationalist* (Chicago: University of Chicago Press, 1971), pp. 39-41.

[7] Claude G. Bowers, *Beveridge and the Progressive Era* (Cambridge: Houghton Mifflin, 1932), p. 177; Shaw to Beveridge, Feb. 11, 1902, Albert Beveridge MSS, Library of Congress.

[8] *Review of Reviews* (Amer. ed.), IX (1894), 521-22, X (1894), 244-46, XIV (1896), 135; *American Monthly Review of Reviews*, XVI (1897), 267.

should be said for the essential rightmindedness of the people of the great American region to which you and I belong?" He told Stead why he was sure the Coxeyites were not revolutionaries: "You may not quite realize it, but I know the kind of fellows who are in these industrial armies almost as well as you know the kind of lads you grew up with in the north of England." And to Roosevelt who had recently told him that western radicalism "was fundamentally an attack on civilization; an appeal to the torch," he replied: "Our political situation just now is a very queer one. You Republicans of the reforming tendency are fiercely brave against the Populist bugaboo, while you have nothing to say at all against the Platt system of politics."[9]

Shaw was soon to get a more intimate look at New York politics, for Roosevelt's highly publicized derring-do in the Spanish-American War made him a prime candidate for the governorship. It happened that the Platt machine was in some difficulty at the time and for practical reasons was willing to accept Roosevelt at the head of the Republican slate in 1898. Fragile from the start, the alliance between them began crumbling when T. R. threw his support behind a measure which imposed a franchise tax on utilities.[10]

The editor once reminisced about his part in this incident, which, by considerable stretch of the imagination, could be said to have made T. R. president. It seems that the sponsor of the bill, Democratic state senator John Ford, had been a student in Shaw's lectures on municipal administration at Cornell a decade earlier. It was there that Ford was exposed to the idea of taxing franchises. The Ford bill was repugnant to Platt and his business allies who resented Roosevelt's backing of it. Although other incidents would pit Platt and T. R. against each other, the controversy over the Ford bill was one of the first, and certainly one of the most serious, arguments between

[9] Shaw to Macy, June 8, 1894, Shaw to Stead, June 20, 1894, Roosevelt to Shaw, Nov. 4, 1896, Shaw to Roosevelt, Dec. 31, 1896, all in Shaw MSS.

[10] William Henry Harbaugh, *The Life and Times of Theodore Roosevelt,* rev. ed. (New York: Collier Books, 1966), pp. 110-11.

the governor and the party boss. Platt ultimately decided to oppose Roosevelt's bid for renomination, but his popularity was so great it would be difficult just to dump him. Nominating him for the vice-presidency offered a way out of the dilemma, for westerners were especially enthusiastic about having him on the national ticket in 1900 as McKinley's running mate.[11]

The traditionally meaningless position of vice-president had no appeal for T. R., who tried to discourage thought of his being nominated for the post. But support for him persisted, and his attendance at the Republican national convention at Philadelphia made it more likely than ever that he would receive the nomination; the delegates were overwhelmingly behind him. Shaw was alone with him in T. R.'s hotel room when Boies Penrose and another party leader entered and told Roosevelt that Pennsylvania Republicans wanted him on the ticket. (Shaw surmised that they were under instructions from the traction interests to do so.) With misgivings Roosevelt accepted the nomination, campaigned vigorously, and helped McKinley win the presidency. A year later he became president when McKinley was assassinated.[12]

The relationship between Shaw and T. R. continued to be close after the latter became president, and the editor made frequent trips to the White House or to Roosevelt's home at Oyster Bay, Long Island. On Roosevelt's accession to the presidency Henry Cabot Lodge (for unexplained reasons) was supposed to have advised him not to bring his New York intimates—Shaw, Butler, and Holls—to Washington in any official capacity. Shaw claimed he wished no office but did hope that he could be of aid to Roosevelt. For instance he made two visits to the White House during Roosevelt's first month in office to relay information from Newton Hawley about personal currents in Minnesota politics. Shaw also acted

[11] Ibid., pp. 114-26; Shaw to John Ford, Nov. 16, 1932, Shaw MSS.
[12] Ibid.; Harbaugh, *Life and Times of Theodore Roosevelt,* pp. 130-34; G. Wallace Chessman, *Governor Theodore Roosevelt: The Albany Apprenticeship, 1898-1900* (Cambridge, Mass.: Harvard University Press, 1965), pp. 135-57.

as an adviser to Roosevelt and counseled him on various matters: foreign affairs, labor problems, and primarily, Shaw remembered, on the trust question, the one that turned out to be the most significant domestic issue of the Roosevelt administration.[13]

Although Roosevelt was once applauded for the trust-busting activities of his administration, his feelings about business consolidation were sophisticated, and like Shaw he accepted the existence of bigness. But he did think that the contemporary magnates were too arrogant and not sufficiently subservient to a superior national interest. Thus, through the Justice Department, the Roosevelt administration initiated over three dozen antitrust suits under the Sherman Act, several of them spectacular, for they challenged corporate giants like the Northern Securities and Standard Oil companies. The intent of these moves was to meet a public demand for anti-trust activities and also to emphasize the need for more flexible and effective regulatory legislation than existed under the Interstate Commerce Act of 1887 and the Sherman Law of 1890.[14]

The administration's first antitrust suit came in early 1902 against the Northern Securities Company, a New Jersey holding company which brought into a community of interests the three major northwestern railroads—the Great Northern, the Northern Pacific, and the Burlington—that dominated traffic between Chicago and Seattle. An early stockholder in the organization, Shaw had admired its president, James J. Hill, since his Minneapolis days. He regarded the Northern Securities Company as a legitimate combination and disliked seeing it challenged and eventually dissolved in federal court. "The modern business principle," he observed at the time the adverse decree was delivered, "is not that large industrial combinations should be broken up, but that they should be

13 Butler, *Across the Busy Years*, I, 312; Ely, *Ground under Our Feet*, pp. 277-78; Theodore Roosevelt to Shaw, July 28, 1899, Shaw to Newton Hawley, Oct. 14, 1901, Shaw to Frederic Delano, Jan. 13, 1937, all in Shaw MSS.
14 Mowry, *Era of Theodore Roosevelt*, pp. 130-33.

so regulated as to prevent them from doing any act of harm or oppression."[15] But personally close to T. R. as he was and usually informed of presidential matters, Shaw justified the prosecution from its inception, even though he held that the law under which suit was instituted was unsatisfactory. It obstructed business operations instead of guiding them into proper channels, and improvements in it were therefore needed. However, until they were made, the existing provisions would have to be enforced as Roosevelt was correctly doing in the Northern Securities proceedings.[16]

In the January 1903 issue of the *Century* there appeared an article by Shaw, "The President and the Trusts," that was thought to be officially inspired. It was.[17] Shaw attempted to interpret Roosevelt's reasoning in the Northern Securities affair in a favorable light, his purpose being to allay the fear of business that Roosevelt was something of a fanatic. He told how responsible Roosevelt really was and reminded his readers that when Roosevelt had been governor he had formulated an intelligent policy toward big business. In contrast Bryan had not even thought of regulating trusts. To do so would have been to concede them a legitimate existence; the "Commoner" and his followers thought "they should be outlawed."[18]

Continuing to show his usual good sense as president, Roosevelt had been subjected to unwarranted attacks by those journals responsive to the interests. Shaw indicated that the trusts had taken their attitude of "concerted hostility" toward Roosevelt because of his administration's involvement with the Northern Securities case. Reiterating the point that he had made in the *Review,* Shaw insisted that the president had

[15] E. R. Johnstone to Shaw, Apr. 7, 15, 1902, Shaw to Howard Elliott (not sent), May 12, 1927, all in Shaw MSS; *American Monthly Review of Reviews,* XXV (1902), 398-99, XXVII (1903), 525.

[16] Ibid. Beveridge and Perkins both commended Shaw for his discussion of the case. Shaw to Beveridge, May 9, 1903, Beveridge MSS.

[17] Shaw, "The President and the Trusts," *Century Magazine,* n.s. XLIII (Jan. 1903), 381-87; Roosevelt to Shaw, Dec. 26, 1902, Shaw MSS; *Baltimore American,* Dec. 21, 1902; *Ithaca Journal,* Jan. 6, 1903, both in Scrapbooks, Shaw MSS.

[18] Shaw, "President and Trusts," pp. 382-83.

shown no animosity toward the trusts but was only seeing that the Sherman Law as it stood was enforced, leaving specific legal decisions to Attorney General Philander Knox. While deciding to prosecute this case, the administration had rejected pleas from outsiders to break up the United States Steel Company and the anthracite monopoly precisely because these combines did not appear illegal within the framework of the same statute. All honest businessmen should really have been grateful for Roosevelt's decision to enforce the law impartially, since it was "the one safeguard against undiscriminating attacks upon the part of sincere though unwise masses of men, led either by demagogues or by honest fanatics and agitators." A continued display of perversity by the interests might well increase this threat of fanaticism, for Roosevelt was highly popular.[19]

If any of the right people read Shaw's article, the evidence would seem to indicate that few heeded it, for the battle between the trusts and Roosevelt continued for the remainder of his presidency. Holding firm to his view that economic combinations in transport and industry were to be accepted, Shaw, through his unflinching support of Roosevelt, entered into persistent editorial sniping with the trust magnates and then with their political allies who were not responsive to T. R.'s program.[20] Ideally Shaw would have liked to see laws providing for the federal incorporation or licensing of companies doing interstate business enacted as the core of any national regulatory program. But circumstances directed attention to specific abuses in the railroad, meat-packing, and food-processing industries, and Shaw enthusiastically endorsed the various laws that Roosevelt supported as a way of policing them. The railroads "have had their innings for a long time" and should accept the proposals for federal rate-making power then being discussed, Shaw advised the president of the

[19] Ibid., pp. 384-87.
[20] American Monthly Review of Reviews, XXVII (1903), 266-67, 396-97; XXXI (1905), 12-13, 395-96; American Review of Reviews, XXXVII (1908), 269-70; Shaw to Beveridge, Dec. 9, 1903, Beveridge MSS.

Louisville and Nashville. And all the while in the *Review of Reviews* he insisted with a variety of synonyms that Roosevelt was conservative and that to accept his ideas was only common sense.[21]

Labor furnished the occasion for another of Roosevelt's most memorable acts—his intervention in the 1902 anthracite strike. The strike began in May 1902 when 50,000 miners walked off their jobs, asking for a 20 percent wage boost, an eight-hour day, and recognition of their union, as well as protesting a threatened change in the manner of weighing coal. Closing down the mines completely and rejecting all offers of conciliation, the six railroads that controlled the struck anthracite fields in northeastern Pennsylvania waited for the union to submit but forfeited their claim to public sympathy as fear of a winter coal shortage mounted. Their insistence on the absolute rights of property seemed unreasonable. The press demanded government intervention, but until October Roosevelt refrained from interfering.[22]

Dubious of the strike's merits at first, Shaw stood more decisively behind labor as time went on, noting its calm behavior, its right to be organized, and its support by the public.[23] "Monopoly on One Side—Means Union on the Other Side," he instructed the coal barons. If only they would heed what he had written, Roosevelt responded.[24] Shaw also played something of an inside role, for the responsibility for resolving the protracted strike was finally assumed by Roosevelt. Instead of threatening to send in federal troops to break the strike as one of his predecessors might have done in similar circumstances, Roosevelt established a precedent by summoning both sides to a conference at the White House.

[21] Shaw to Milton H. Smith, Jan. 17, 1905, Shaw to Frederic Delano, Jan. 13, 1937, both in Shaw MSS; *American Monthly Review of Reviews*, XXVII (1903), 397, XXXI (1905), 14, 270, 516, XXXIII (1906), 387-89, 648-52, XXXV (1907), 388, 515, 522.

[22] Harbaugh, *Life and Times of Theodore Roosevelt*, pp. 165-70.

[23] *American Monthly Review of Reviews*, XXV (1902), 652, XXVI (1902), 405-6, 515-16, 518-23.

[24] Ibid., p. 518; Roosevelt to Shaw, Oct. 29, 1902, Shaw MSS.

When the operators proved as stubborn as ever, Roosevelt with the cooperation of J. P. Morgan pressed management to agree to binding arbitration, a procedure which union leader John Mitchell had previously suggested.[25]

During one of his periodic visits to the White House, Shaw telegraphed Mitchell his advice to listen to the president when it came to resolving the strike. The following day, October 8, in a letter to Mitchell that he decided not to send (perhaps because it anticipated decisions that were still several days away), Shaw explained his reasoning. If the miners first met at their various local headquarters to sustain the union leadership in its conduct of the strike, the decision to return to work pending arbitration would be interpreted as freely made and public spirited. Finding that the owners had been "as stupid as the nobility of France on the eve of the great Revolution" and deficient "in the essentials of patriotism," Shaw requested the men to sacrifice their right and interest on the "altar of patriotism." Work was resumed, and the arbitral award of March 1903, while not conceding union recognition, did give the workers half the raise they had wanted, a reduction of hours to eight or nine, and a favorable verdict on the work rules dispute. Though there were some who believed the miners could have gained more, Roosevelt's moves seemed equitable and gave his unfolding Square Deal what would now be called credibility.[26]

Following the launching of the Square Deal, the attention of Roosevelt and of the nation turned to a foreign question—to the complex and controversial series of events preceding American acquisition of the Panama Canal Zone. This was another of the matters over which T. R. and Shaw were both vitally concerned, for an isthmian canal represented the potential hub of America's expanding overseas interests and a vital link in her defense posture.

A member, together with Roosevelt and Beveridge, of a

[25] Harbaugh, *Life and Times of Theodore Roosevelt,* pp. 174-78. T. R. did have Grover Cleveland's backing.

[26] Ibid., p. 179; Shaw to John Mitchell (not sent), Oct. 8, 1902, Shaw MSS.

group Richard Hofstadter has identified as the "dynamic element" in American imperialism, Shaw was a nationalist of intense dedication and had an outlook on foreign affairs much like that of his two friends and compatriots in the advocacy of imperialism. The three inevitably differed in particulars but were united by a desire to see the United States conduct its foreign policy in a manner that would safeguard American interests and advance American ideals. Reluctant to urge permanent American retention of the Philippines—in this, for instance, he differed from Beveridge—the editor nevertheless believed that expansion in East Asia, in the Pacific, and especially in the Caribbean and Central America was mandated both by altruism and by the national interest. Although his moralism made him uncomfortable with the appellation of *imperialist* (for he regarded imperialism as an extension of Europe's sordid power politics and as such qualitatively different from America's benevolent expansionism), suffice it to say that by most acceptable definitions of the word Shaw must be considered an imperialist.[27] He arrived at this position, as did Roosevelt and Beveridge, through a vigorous sense of nationalism.[28] It led all three to progressivism—and to imperialism.

Shaw's life is studded with examples of incidents that might well have inculcated this sense of nationalism: his youthful acquaintance with surviving pioneers, his father undermining his health through his work on the draft board, his own

[27] Shaw to Percy Bunting, Jan. 3, 1896, Shaw to Amos Hershey, Nov. 10, 1898, both in Shaw MSS; Braemen, *Albert Beveridge*, pp. 42-67; Richard Hofstadter, "Manifest Destiny and the Philippines," in Daniel Aaron, ed., *America in Crisis* (New York: Knopf, 1952), p. 183; William E. Leuchtenburg, "Progressivism and Imperialism: The Progressive Movement and American Foreign Policy, 1898-1916," *Mississippi Valley Historical Review*, XXXIX (Dec. 1952), 483-504; John Milton Cooper, Jr., "Progressivism and American Foreign Policy: A Reconsideration," *Mid-America*, LI (Oct. 1969), 260-77; John P. Mallon, "Roosevelt, Brooks Adams, and Lea: The Warrior Critique of the Business Civilization," *American Quarterly*, VIII (Fall 1956), 216-30.

[28] Shaw was the only one of the three to admire Thomas Jefferson. Looming large among his reasons for doing so was his conviction that Jefferson had delineated the basic concepts of American foreign policy—expansion throughout North America and its environs and adherence to what became known as the Monroe Doctrine. Shaw, *Average Man*, pp. 199-219.

marching in Lincoln rallies, his residence in Minneapolis when that city was seeing its first rail line pushed to the Pacific Coast. Similarly his economic writings stressed greater productivity and regulation in behalf of a national interest, and his political commentary told of the patriotism that was manifested by the people of the Mississippi Valley. Out of this staunch nationalism, his firm moral attitudes (there were several missionaries in his family),[29] his convictions about Anglo-Saxon superiority, and his political heritage of Blaine Republicanism, he wove a sturdy fabric of imperialist commitments.

Shaw's vision was a large one and included development of a strong navy and merchant marine, the construction of an isthmian canal, and the acquisition of strategically situated colonies. "With the control of the Hawaii group for naval and political purposes," he wrote in 1894, "the United States would assume in the Pacific ocean the position that its dignity requires and that consistency with its past course no less plainly necessitates."[30] In successive headlines directed at President Cleveland's disinclination to commit the United States to expansion he soon made it plain that this country also had a duty to civilize the natives of the Pacific: "Shall We 'Scuttle' Out of Samoa?," "What England Has Done for Fiji," "Shall We Do Our Part, or Shirk?"[31] Perhaps nowhere did Shaw detail his aspirations more candidly than in a letter to a fan of his who happened also to be a scholar of international affairs:

The thing I demand in my August [1897] number is a deliberate rather than an accidental policy of expansion. I am in favor of the

---

[29] They were an aunt and uncle on his mother's side of the family who had worked as missionaries in Turkey and among the Chippewa Indians respectively, a younger cousin of his who did educational work in Turkey and Greece, and his brother-in-law, John C. Fisher, who had once been affiliated with the Protestant College in Beirut. See Shaw to Raymond B. Fosdick, Mar. 6, 1924, Shaw MSS.

[30] *Review of Reviews* (Amer. ed.), IV (1891-92), 125, 499-501, IX (1894), 135-37, 515-16.

[31] Ibid., pp. 517-18.

annexation of Hawaii, but I would make that annexation a part of a policy which would include the acquisition of a strip of land in Central America whereon to build the inter-oceanic canal, and would further aim as a part of that same policy to acquire interests in the West Indies. I wonder what you would think of my suggestion that the United States lend its influence towards the building up of Mexico by the annexation first of Cuba, and then of the Central American states. Our ownership of the canal and of a naval station or two in Cuba and the West Indies would of course bring the Mexican confederation under our virtual protectorate. Mexico has in actual fact of course been under our protection for more than thirty years. The annexation of the South American states to Mexico would effectively keep out hostile European influences. You will, by reading between the lines of the paragraphs in which I discuss the Canadian situation, understand that my theory is that the Dominion will some day go to pieces, and that individual provinces will apply for admission to the United States. We ought to have financed and secured Newfoundland two or three years ago.[32]

During the months preceding the Spanish-American War, Shaw wrote in a firm but responsible interventionist manner. Soon after the fighting commenced he repeated his former demands for expansion and, taking advantage of the new opportunities that the conflict presented, spoke glowingly of an imperial future. He presented his arguments in his editorials and also in a speech he delivered at Grinnell. In it he spoke principally of duty. He mentioned the "moral jurisdiction" we had assumed under the Monroe Doctrine and how beneficently it had evolved from a negative policy to the positive one under which we took to police the hemisphere. In regard to the Pacific he could only make predictions but felt that we would come to exert influence there on behalf of a higher law. The implication was present that we would assume responsibility for the Philippines. "There must, therefore," he also wrote, "come into existence, if needless and harmful disputes—perhaps bloody wars—are to be avoided,

32 Shaw to Lindley M. Keasby, July 28, 1897, Shaw MSS.

some *tertium quid,* some distinct scheme of international oversight for the regulation of such questions as that of Corea, the spheres of influence in China, etc. . . . We must hold ourselves subject to such an evolution of a higher international oversight of affairs in the Pacific." Just before he addressed a closing message to the youth of Iowa to be staunch in their devotion to duty, he connected overseas expansion and domestic reform by remarking that future professional administrators who would receive their training abroad would return home to raise our crass political standards. Shaw also deplored the selfishness of the Wall Street interests who had opposed war for fear of jeopardizing investments and then had sought to profit from it by making fresh investments. "But, at least, let us keep ourselves unstained by greed" was his appeal.[33]

The cardinal theme in Shaw's design was for an interoceanic canal which would facilitate development of the navy, stimulate commerce, and solidify our influence in Central America and the Caribbean. Nearly twenty years after he had written about this very topic for the *Minneapolis Tribune* the Clayton-Bulwer Treaty still remained an obstacle to Shaw's hopes for the realization of such a project, but McKinley's secretary of state, John Hay, negotiated a new treaty with England, granting us the exclusive right to construct a canal while specifying that it be neutralized and unfortified. Shaw, however, was not satisfied with it. He diplomatically exposed what he considered some of the faults of the new arrangement in an editorial: "Why should the United States Government spend American money to dig a canal on alien soil over which it is pledged never to acquire or exercise sovereignty, in which its own warships are to have no advantage over those of an enemy, and through which American merchant ships are forever denied any better terms than those of all other countries?" But in correspondence with influential Senator Cushman Davis

[33] *American Monthly Review of Reviews,* XVI (1897), 135-36, XVII (1898), 261-63, 397-98, XVIII (1898), 15-20, 123-29, 259, 633-35, XIX (1899), 14-18: Shaw, "Speech at Grinnell" (Grinnell, June 21, 1898), pp. 14-15, 19, 23, 26-31 of typescript, Shaw MSS.

of Minnesota, an opponent of the treaty, Shaw revealed just how angry he was: "Let international commerce dig its own ditches. The United States Government should concern itself with the national defense, and public policy in the high sense. The only right solution of the Nicaragua Canal question lies in the acquisition of full political sovereignty over a Central American strip." A few days later he wrote: "If the Hay-Pauncefote treaty should be ratified, the country will distinctly understand that this means that you gentlemen at Washington do not really intend to provide any Nicaragua canal at all."[34]

Roosevelt and the rest of the New York triumvirate were equally troubled by the proposed treaty. Shaw's efforts to discredit it probably did not accomplish enough, for the authorities at Washington procrastinated about it for months. On consultation the group, abetted by a subordinate of Secretary of State John Hay, decided that T. R. should issue to the press a statement criticizing it on the ground that it jeopardized defense preparations and undermined the Monroe Doctrine. Butler believed that Roosevelt's public intervention saved the day. Whatever the reason, the dilemma was favorably resolved in the end, for the Senate amended the treaty in a way that caused Britain to reject it. A second Hay-Pauncefote pact concluded and ratified in 1901 gave the United States the explicit right to own and operate a canal and by implication the privilege of fortifying it.[35]

Roosevelt was president two years later when the United States acquired the land across which to construct the canal. He and Shaw were fundamentally in accord in respect to the complicated situation that developed out of this country's efforts to secure this land, but, as chief executive, T. R. in this instance had to speak more discreetly than his friend. Although Congress on the recommendation of engineers chose

---

[34] *American Monthly Review of Reviews*, XXI (1900), 280-81; Howard K. Beale, *Theodore Roosevelt and the Rise of America to World Power* (New York: Collier Books, 1962), pp. 101-8; Shaw to Davis, Feb. 10, 19, 1900, both in Shaw MSS.

[35] Butler, *Across the Busy Years*, I, 310-11; Beale, *Roosevelt and Rise of America to World Power*, pp. 102-3.

Panama instead of Nicaragua as the site for the project, the outcome pleased Shaw immensely.

The story of the acquisition of the canal zone is perhaps as familiar as any episode in American diplomatic history.[36] Colombia exercised sovereignty over the Panamanian territory in question and was willing to lease the valuable rights. Its representative in the United States had already negotiated the Hay-Herran convention, transferring construction rights to the U.S. while retaining for Colombia nominal sovereignty over a canal zone. Colombia was to receive $10,000,000 and an annual rental, but the successor to the old De Lesseps Company, which held a franchise that would soon expire, would get four times the cash settlement. The Colombian legislature, as was its right, stalled in ratifying the treaty, hoping to make a better deal when the French rights lapsed. Some Panamanians, with conspiratorial aid from the representatives of the French interests who stood to profit from a quick commencement of the enterprise, carried out a midget revolution. Acting on presidential orders to protect overland transit across the Isthmus of Panama, marines from a United States warship which happened to be at hand prevented Colombian troops from quelling the revolt.

Dwight Miner has shown that although Roosevelt did not instigate the revolution, he welcomed its occurrence as the surest means to hasten construction of the canal. He was aware of the possibilities of a revolt by September, two months before it occurred. Shaw was thinking along similar lines, for the likelihood of a Panamanian insurrection was by no means idle speculation. In July Shaw surmised that a revolt was "not unlikely" should Colombia reject the pending Hay-Herran treaty. Two months afterwards he noted that the American press was openly discussing the various contingencies—including rebellion—and repeated his opinion that Panama would be better off without her degenerate Colombian

[36] Dwight C. Miner, *The Fight for the Panama Route: The Story of the Spooner Act and the Hay-Herran Treaty* (New York: Columbia University Press, 1940), pp. 340-89, is particularly useful for the details.

tutor. Chafing at the delay which Colombia was causing, he conveniently forgot how he had fumed against ratification of the first Hay-Pauncefote treaty. In October, armed with tips leaked by an official in the State Department and by other Washington sources, he discussed the affair in detail. Shaw made it clear that he scorned the pending treaty, for it reserved ultimate sovereignty to Colombia, an unthinkable suggestion. The proposed canal should be as American as if it were to be dug across Florida. In any case it was unseemly for the U.S. to deal for a franchise like a private corporation. The analogy was probably more meaningful than he intended, for in this instance American ethics turned out to be not unlike those of the municipal interests he was accustomed to deriding. "Up to date," Shaw asserted, "the Washington authorities have simply succeeded in making a bad muddle."[37]

Roosevelt tried to correct Shaw's unfavorable opinion of the State Department. Sending him a copy of a report from our minister at Bogata, Colombia, T. R. reminded Shaw that treaties were objects of give and take between two parties. Under the circumstances nothing more could have been accomplished. The alternatives had been to revert to the Nicaraguan route, of which competent engineering authorities had disapproved, or to seize the Panamanian territory. "I cast aside the proposition made at this time to foment the secession of Panama," T. R. declared. "Whatever other governments can do, the United States cannot go into the securing by such underhand means, the secession. Privately, I freely say to you that I should be delighted if Panama were an independent State, or if it made itself so at this moment; but for me to say so publicly would amount to an instigation of a revolt, and therefore I cannot say it."[38]

Less than a week after he received Roosevelt's pronouncement of October 10, Shaw made an appointment to spend

[37] *American Monthly Review of Reviews*, XXVIII (1903), 17, 279, 393-97; Shaw to Francis Loomis, Jan. 19, 1933, Shaw MSS.

[38] Roosevelt to Shaw, Oct. 10, 1903 (with enclosure of A. M. Beaupre to John Hay, Sept. 5, 1903), Shaw MSS.

a night at the White House. About this time Shaw was probably finishing his November editorials. In them he formulated a plan for revolution. His essential point was that the Colombian government was incompetent and had no pretext to disrupt Panamanian progress in particular and hemispheric welfare in general. The time was ripe for a revolution, he maintained, significantly adding that no American marines would be employed—ostensibly to maintain transit but actually to hold "the situation for the benefit of" Colombia. Within a few days after this column appeared in the *Review,* the predicted uprising occurred. Only marines were used; however, their presence did serve to obstruct Colombia's chances of thrashing the insurgents. The United States promptly recognized the new Panamanian regime and negotiated a favorable canal pact (about which Shaw was consulted) with it.[39] Three days after the revolt of November 3 occurred, the still enthusiastic Roosevelt congratulated Shaw for the prescience of his editorials: "You are all right in every way! When people come to compare what has happened in the Isthmus, with what you said in the *Review of Reviews,* they will come to the conclusion that you are the seventh son of a seventh son!"[40]

The following year politicking Senator Charles Culberson from Texas obtained a copy of the letter in which Roosevelt had written Shaw, "I cast aside the proposition." Roosevelt had in fact authorized its release to prove that he had rejected the thought of instigating a revolt. Culberson quoted it at length, embellishing matters with remarks about presidential rashness and a conjecture about a conspiracy with Shaw. He wondered how Shaw had so uncannily predicted the outbreak of rebellion, and the *New York Evening Post,* which made much of the charges, speculated that Shaw had personally proposed to lead a filibustering expedition to Panama.[41] The

39 William Loeb, Jr. (for T. R.), to Shaw, Oct. 14, 1903, Shaw MSS; *American Monthly Review of Reviews,* XXVIII (1903), 524-26; Harbaugh, *Life and Times of Theodore Roosevelt,* p. 204.
40 Roosevelt to Shaw, Nov. 6, 1903, Shaw MSS.
41 *New York Evening Post,* Oct. 21, 1904, Scrapbooks, Shaw MSS.

Post's tale was fantasy. Although he was patriotic and sometimes given to outbursts of Darwinian vocabulary, Shaw, unlike Roosevelt, was not the martial type.

Culberson's query about Shaw's prophecy was vastly more plausible. In an interview Shaw, who had once boasted to Stead of his "rather uncommon power" to ascertain the course of events, dismissed the senator's remarks about his prophetic talents by saying that he took them as a compliment to the profession of journalism.[42] Exciting as it would be to imagine that Shaw was officially expounding Roosevelt's policy, as he had in respect to the Northern Securities affair, or that his November editorials were a prearranged signal to the conspirators,[43] common sense indicates that Shaw's observations did no more than combine a legitimate topic of speculation with much wishful thinking. They pleased Roosevelt so much because he had been thinking the same things.

Nothing quite as exciting happened to Shaw again. He continued in close association with T. R. throughout his second term and supported his chosen successor William Howard Taft at the beginning of the latter's unhappy administration. But he eventually broke with Taft and had not been an intimate of his to begin with. Although Shaw would have warm contacts with members of the Wilson and Hoover administrations, he never regained a position that enabled him to exert direct personal influence on the course of political events.

Yet granted that he was an adviser to T. R., even a close one on the trust question, how much and what kind of influence did he actually have on major decisions? It is impossible to say. Their views were frequently in close accord, but their

[42] Shaw to Stead, July 22, 1895, Shaw MSS.

[43] Shaw did say: "I was earnestly in favor of sticking to Nicaragua, and I refused to meet Bunau-Varilla or to have any parley with the active agents of the French Panama Company who promoted the revolution in Panama and who busied themselves most industriously in New York and Washington, with W. Nelson Cromwell as their very able and indefatigable legal counsel. . . . Nor have I ever discovered any corruption or wrong doing in . . . their eager endeavor to sell the property of their clients to Uncle Sam." Shaw to M. R. Scott, July 16, 1914, Shaw MSS.

most significant exchanges of ideas, one must assume, took place in conversation and not in correspondence. As he grew older Shaw understandably liked to recall the closeness of his relationship with T. R., but he did not try to pinpoint exactly how he had helped shape presidential decisions. In any event the problem of sorting out sources and degrees of influence is about as difficult to resolve as the old chicken-egg conundrum. Did Shaw mold Roosevelt's general views on the trust question or on Panama, or were his own statements on these and other matters formulated with the desire to support his friend? How many reliable consultants did Roosevelt have? The logical answer is that Roosevelt was an intelligent and forceful person, well able to form his own conclusions or at least to select the politically realistic alternatives from the abundance of advice he was offered. Albert Shaw was only one of many conferees.

8

At Odds with Taft, 1909-1912

Albert Shaw had never considered himself a machine Republican. Although he regularly supported the party's national tickets and fundamental policies, he rarely hesitated to denounce a state or local boss. As much as he disliked Tammany, it is not inconceivable that he thought even less of Republican organizations like those that dominated politics in New York and Pennsylvania. In his opinion they represented an unholy alliance between corporate interests and professional politicans intent on profiting from their positions of responsibility. "They are institutional and organic," he wrote of parties. They "exist simply because the great business of politics in America is so extended, so complex, and so continuous, that it requires permanent organization." "The machine," generalized Shaw, "was supplied with money by the corporations and various private interests, seeking either favors or immunity. The object of the system was to put in control leaders [like Platt] who knew how to maintain discipline and secure desired results." Fashioned in the late 1880s as a substitute for the declining spoils system, the partnership between organized politics and the interests had flourished throughout much of the 1890s. Thereafter it had been placed on the defensive. The basic honesty of the people, Shaw believed in 1907, made it inevitable that the reformer would succeed in the long run.[1]

Shaw was soon to enter into his most bitter fight with organized politics. His list of political bogeys was already compiled when William Howard Taft succeeded Roosevelt as president in March 1909. All that remained for him to do was to link Taft with them in order to define a villain of formidable proportions. Reluctant at first to think ill of Taft, by late 1910 Shaw had become convinced that he personified politics at its worst. As a consequence he labored to prevent Taft's renomination and, failing in that, jumped the Republican party in 1912 to back the Progressive ticket of Roosevelt and California's Hiram Johnson.

The editor's praise of Taft had once been high. During the early weeks of the Taft administration, Shaw promised in the *Review* that it would rival Roosevelt's in efficiency and in progressive spirit. There is nothing to indicate that Shaw's private opinion of him was less favorable. In fact much of Taft's subsequent difficulty with Shaw, and perhaps also with the public at large, appears to stem from the initially high expectations of him. As the hand-picked successor of Roosevelt he was thought to be vigorously progressive.[2]

It was not long until doubts about him were raised, for the special session of Congress that he called in March 1909 to revise the tariff failed to enact any fundamental improvements over the existing high rates. Some reductions were secured, but close examination of the Payne-Aldrich bill that was passed by Congress at the end of July and signed by Taft showed that it was basically a reenactment of the now obnoxious Dingley Tariff of 1897. The new law aroused mild opposition in the East and concerted antagonism among midwestern Republicans. Among the dissidents—or insurgents—were two of Shaw's friends, Indianan Albert Beveridge and Iowa Senator Albert Cummins.[3] At this time Beveridge was probably Shaw's most intimate informant about political issues; he and Shaw were in close touch throughout the ensuing political upheaval.

Shaw paid careful attention to each phase of the tariff struggle. A moderate protectionist himself, he thought that reform was imperative at this point in history and expected

[1] Shaw, *Political Problems of American Development*, pp. 136, 148, 150-54; Shaw to Roosevelt, Dec. 31, 1896, Shaw MSS.

[2] *American Review of Reviews*, XXXIX (1909), 524.

[3] George E. Mowry, *Theodore Roosevelt and the Progressive Movement*, American Century Series (New York: Hill and Wang, 1960), pp. 35-65. Donald F. Anderson, *William Howard Taft: A Conservative's Conception of the Presidency* (Ithaca, N.Y.: Cornell University Press, 1973), offers a sympathetic reassessment of Taft's administration.

Taft to work for it. He promised as much in the *Review*. By June, though, the editor was criticizing the emerging tariff. Its high duties appeared to be so nearly prohibitive as to deprive the Unted States Treasury of needed customs revenue. What could one expect of politically motivated tariff-making, he asked, as he himself called for the future establishment of an impartial commission that would set rates scientifically. But he also disagreed with the Senate insurgents for their proposal of an income tax. The next month he pointed out that Taft had tried to do right and would still attempt to secure the anticipated revisions from the conference committee. Once the bill was enacted, Shaw said that the public had been "bamboozled" and that the tariff was a "hodge-podge" of selfish demands. He now questioned Taft's role in the proceedings and in addition took special pains to applaud the seven Republican senators who had persisted in voting negatively. He also disapproved of the new corporation tax that the president had sought and won, saying that its taxation of net profits rather than gross income would lead to various accounting tricks and that it was too inquisitorial. He also published in the September issue of the *Review* an anonymous article that exposed the new tariff's inequities in detail and told Beveridge that "I have also struck fairly hard myself. . . . It seemed right to be a little emphatic." Wrote Butler, "Accept my hearty congratulations upon the clearness and blunt truth of your setting forth of the enormities of the new tariff bill in your September issue."[4]

More incidents followed. Taft, on a continental tour, said in a speech at Winona, Minnesota, that the new tariff was the "best" ever passed. The noted dispute between T. R.'s friend, Chief Forester Gifford Pinchot, and Taft's secretary of the interior, Richard Ballinger, began. "He has been junketing for months, and now that he is back, he starts out on a series of one- and two-day junkets in all directions," Shaw com-

4 *American Review of Reviews*, XXXVIII (1908), 134, XXXIX (1909), 652-53, XL (1909), 6-10, 259-64, 341-47; Shaw to Beveridge, Aug. 20, 1909, Beveridge MSS; Shaw to Beveridge, June 16, 1909, Butler to Shaw, Sept. 6, 1909, both in Shaw MSS.

plained of Taft. "Beneath the surface everything is seething at Washington. All over the country men are talking about the Crane-Knox episode. They are still talking about the Nagel-North matter in Washington. The Winona speech still rankles. Everybody continues to wonder why the fool corporation tax was sprung upon a surprised public. I have never known such a messy situation."[5]

Even as thoughts of the tariff battle were still festering, the Ballinger-Pinchot dispute began. Destined to last for more than a year, it involved some of the biggest names in the annals of progressivism—Gifford Pinchot and James R. Garfield, both chums of T. R., as well as the same senators who had rebelled at the Payne-Aldrich Tariff. Its significance was to unite two of Roosevelt's closest friends and the dissident midwesterners in opposition to Taft, to win the first considerable eastern Republican support for their cause, and to tarnish further Taft's reputation as a progressive.[6]

It had begun innocuously enough, with Taft's appointment of attorney Richard Ballinger to his cabinet in place of Garfield, who had been Roosevelt's conservation-minded secretary of the interior. Trouble soon started. Annoyed at Ballinger for overruling some of his decisions on conservation practices, Pinchot readily listened to accusations brought against the secretary by an investigator in the Department of the Interior named Louis Glavis. The charges indicated that Ballinger had betrayed the cause of conservation, and Pinchot used them to denounce the secretary of the interior in public. On studying the accusations, however, Taft exonerated Ballinger and discharged Glavis and eventually Pinchot, who had refused to let the issue die. Even so it endured. Congress had already

[5] Shaw to Beveridge, Nov. 13, 1909, Shaw MSS; Mowry, *Theodore Roosevelt and the Progressive Movement*, p. 70. The Crane-Knox and the Nagel-North episodes both involved appointments to office. Charles Crane of Chicago, a friend of Shaw and Roosevelt, was named minister to China but soon recalled. Charles Nagel, Taft's new secretary of commerce and labor, got into a hassle with his strong-minded subordinate, Simon North, chief of the Census Bureau, and replaced him. The Taft-Nagel side seems to have been the "right" one in this case. *American Review of Reviews,* XL (1909), 140, 267; Shaw to Roosevelt, May 29, 1912, Shaw MSS.

[6] Mowry, *Theodore Roosevelt and the Progressive Movement,* pp. 86-87.

begun a lengthy investigation of it, while the progressive press, starting with *Collier's Weekly*, which published an exposé of the case by Glavis in November 1909, made a cause cèlébre of it. When Ballinger was finally and rightly cleared of actual corruption, it no longer mattered, for the public had come to consider him a foe of conservation. What is more, too much vituperation had already passed between the alliances that had formed around Ballinger and Pinchot.[7]

During the crucial early months of the controversy, Shaw appeared to lean toward Pinchot's side of the case but was careful not to impugn Taft's or Ballinger's motives. Shortly after Glavis's article appeared in *Collier's* he advised Beveridge: "Last Friday Ballinger was in New York, telephoned to me, and I went to his hotel. I greatly desire to believe him straight and all right. Pinchot's friends have got to stand by Pinchot." He blamed Taft, who had been on his tour, for not making a firm settlement of things before they got out of hand. His information was that *Collier's* was supplied with "a pile of anti-Ballinger ammunition."[8] Finally discussing the situation at length in the February *Review*, Shaw held that he preferred to believe the decision of Taft and of Attorney General George Wickersham as to Ballinger's innocence. Pinchot had behaved improperly; although he was a superb forester and conservationist, his dismissal was justified. He was too much the militant crusader. Pinchot's replacement, Henry Graves, would execute his policies well. The public was disposed to believe Ballinger innocent.[9] In the same issue Shaw derided the muckraking press and praised Taft's annual message which

[7] Ibid., pp. 70-85. Harold L. Ickes, "Not Guilty! Richard A. Ballinger—An American Dreyfus," *Saturday Evening Post*, CCXII (May 25, 1940), 9-11, 123-28, considers Ballinger wronged.

[8] *American Review of Reviews*, XL (1909), 398-400; Shaw to Beveridge, Nov. 13, 1909, Shaw MSS.

[9] *American Review of Reviews*, XLI (1910), 131-39. Ballinger's article, "Water-Power Sites on the Public Domain," had appeared in the previous issue. Wickersham approved of Shaw's views on the affair, and Shaw later confessed that, although always sympathizing with Pinchot's motives, Wickersham had misled him. At the time, however, he did claim to have done much research on the dispute. Wickersham to Shaw, Jan. 13, 28, 1910, Shaw to Bolton Smith, Feb. 11, 1910, Shaw to Amos Pinchot, Jan. 5, 1911, Shaw to Roosevelt, May 29, 1912, all in Shaw MSS.

called for further regulation of railroads. The next month he wrote of Republican unity, admitted that the Payne-Aldrich Tariff had created some discord, but concluded that basically the United States was a protectionist nation. He did include a subtle warning to Taft and a firm plea on behalf of the dissidents, but his first editorial headline, "Tuning Up the Republican Orchestra," was a sure clue to his desire to see harmony prevail in the upcoming elections.[10]

Shaw was ready to support Taft. His previous disgruntlement with Taft and the regulars, while probably not forgotten, need not remain a point of contention. But other incidents kept the political waters roiled, and when Taft threatened to deny the insurgents patronage in an effort to restore party discipline, Shaw aligned himself firmly with them. The president, he observed in the April *Review,* had come under the "delusion of this idea of party authority. . . . The only salvation for the Republican party lies in tolerating insurgency, so called, and proclaiming full freedom of opinion and speech." The next month Shaw reported a speech in which Wickersham had demanded regularity from the mavericks. They could not be antiadministration Republicans. Beveridge complained of the ultimatum to Shaw. Shaw's public rejoinder to the administration was pointed: "And who would ever have supposed that a man of Mr. Taft's [Unitarian] religious affiliations would have become in politics an almost fanatical heresy-hunter?" He soon indicated that Roosevelt and Charles Evans Hughes, who had recently made a splendid reputation through his reform work in New York, were being thought of as presidential possibilities in 1912. Taft had just named Hughes to the Supreme Court. Shaw discreetly mentioned that the public was wondering whether this nomination meant that Taft was shelving a possible presidential rival. The thought was that this might be a repetition of the situation in 1900 when Roosevelt had been shunted into the vice-presidency by the disgruntled Boss Platt. He said the cause of reform would continue without Hughes.[11]

[10] *American Review of Reviews,* XLI (1910), 143-44, 259-65.

Roosevelt returned from an African tour in June, having already received the insurgents' version of political affairs from Pinchot, who had traveled abroad to meet him. Shaw was in the welcoming committee that greeted Roosevelt on his return to New York. "I wish to see you as soon as possible after returning to America," T. R. had written.[12] Roosevelt attracted enormous attention as he undertook a speaking tour. He wanted to unite the party in time for the fall elections but became involved in a factional fight in New York where progressive Republicans grumbled at him for still speaking well of Taft while their standpat adversaries—the so-called "Black Horse Cavalry"—fumed at him for talking to the progressives. Shaw supported the progressives in the state, but he still had an occasional good word for Taft, who had been acting perversely but seemed about to change his ways. Taft was not a good judge of people and would have made a better justice. There were stories that he was cooperating with the bosses and reactionaries in New York. Perhaps they were not correct, for Taft would hardly want to see his party crushed in the elections. Aligning himself with the standpatters would only accomplish that. Shaw declared in October: "The progressives are the Republican party itself, minus its bosses and their henchmen and minus those rather blundering persons in high place who have thought that the only way to get along well was to cultivate the bosses rather than to ignore them and cultivate the people."[13]

As Shaw expected, the Democrats won the congressional and state elections handily in 1910. (Undercut by standpatters within his own party, Beveridge was one of the casualties.) Shaw interpreted their victories as a rebuke to Taft's handling of the tariff question and his clash with the insurgents. The

---

11 Ibid., pp. 396, 525, 653-57; Mowry, *Theodore Roosevelt and the Progressive Movement*, p. 100; Braemen, *Albert Beveridge*, pp. 185-86.

12 Mowry, *Theodore Roosevelt and the Progressive Movement*, pp. 116-25; Roosevelt to Shaw, Apr. 16, 1910, Shaw to James H. Pound, Dec. 20, 1912, both in Shaw MSS.

13 Mowry, *Theodore Roosevelt and the Progressive Movement*, pp. 135-42, 148-58; *American Review of Reviews*, XLII (1910), 5, 137-43, 259-62, 387-90, 394-96, 400.

Republicans were out of favor with the people. Their debacle in New York in no way reflected on T. R. but was part of the general reaction toward Taft.[14]

In speeches at Osawotomie, Kansas, and other western communities, Roosevelt had recently announced a doctrine called the New Nationalism which approved of federal intervention in the economy and in the states in order to achieve social, regulatory, and conservation programs designed to invigorate the nation's well-being. The "national need" claimed precedence over "sectional and personal advantage," and property mattered less than human welfare, he asserted. He criticized the courts for obstructing needed reform.[15]

Standpatters vehemently denounced the formula, some of them instinctively invoking the sanctity of states rights. Shaw held that Roosevelt was being misrepresented. His criticism of the courts was relatively mild; his proposition envisioned no disruption of Constitutional relations; his views contained "no assault upon the States in the exercise of their appropriate functions." He was a practical reformer and not a Utopian dreamer. The regulation of interstate commerce and of natural resources was a legitimate and traditional federal function. All the states from Ohio west were "mere subdivisions created by the government at Washington, out of its own territory, on plans that we in this country have adopted as convenient and useful in the distribution of powers between central and local authorities."[16]

Spurred on by the impetus of the quarrel with the standpatters, Shaw was defending thinkers even more advanced than Roosevelt. A Socialist government had been chosen in Milwaukee. Business interests denounced it. Shaw's retort was that as long as this administration gave an honest and efficient performance the political persuasions of its leaders should be of no more concern "than the color of their hair."[17]

14 Ibid., pp. 515-23, 643-49; Braemen, *Albert Beveridge*, pp. 186-96.
15 Harbaugh, *Life and Times of Theodore Roosevelt*, pp. 364-71; Mowry, *Theodore Roosevelt and the Progressive Movement*, pp. 143-46.
16 *American Review of Reviews*, XLII (1910), 402, 524-25.
17 Ibid., p. 407.

Shaw soon acquired a personal reason for disliking Taft when the administration unveiled a plan to raise the second-class mail rate from the standard one cent a pound to four cents a pound on just the advertising sections of magazines. The proposal, Shaw promptly complained to Beveridge, was based upon the theory that "after you have killed the goose it will still go on laying eggs." Its enactment would mean the bankruptcy of the leading periodicals, he insisted. His fear was prompted by the fact that advertising usually comprised the bulk of the *Review*'s contents. Although his editorial position toward Taft was already negative and thus not materially altered by the new feud, it placed Shaw in an incongruous position where he acted like a trust tycoon defending a cherished privilege. For while he would not admit it, there was another side to the story.[18]

The existing rate structure had been instituted in the 1880s as an indirect subsidy to stimulate the development of newspapers and periodicals. The industry in general had begun flourishing in the 1890s, but, like a manufacturing establishment which had received tariff protection since infancy and wanted to retain it even when it had become a trust, the periodical publishers wished to keep their own privileges. It should have been obvious to them that changes were going to be made sooner or later, for Congress had begun talking of increasing the rates during the latter part of Roosevelt's presidency, and Taft had mentioned it again in his annual message of 1909. Both times Shaw had been quick to protest. Roosevelt had had no personal involvement with the scheme, but Taft persisted in the idea that something should be done. His first statement on the subject had it that the multi-million dollar postal deficit could be substantially reduced if the losses on second-class mail were cut. The estimate was that it cost the government nine cents a pound to handle this mail while revenue accumulated at but a cent a pound. Rates should

---

[18] Mowry, *Era of Theodore Roosevelt*, p. 259; Henry Pringle, *The Life and Times of William Howard Taft: A Biography*, 2 vols. (New York & Toronto: Farrar & Rinehart, 1939), II, 624-25; Shaw to Beveridge, Feb. 9, 1911, Beveridge MSS.

be uniformly increased for both newspapers and periodicals, it was argued.[19]

Taft let this sensitive subject lapse for a time, but in 1911 he renewed his efforts to have the rates raised. The circumstances appeared strange. Shaw insisted that Taft had promised to consult the publishers about rate revisions sometime in April but had broken faith by having the increases inserted in a rider to an appropriation bill in February. This time they affected magazines but not newspapers. A reciprocal trade bill with Canada that would allow the grade of paper used by newspapers to enter the United States duty free was undergoing discussion in Congress at the same time. (A form of bribery, Shaw wondered.) A few months later the government began antitrust action against the Periodical Clearing House, an association whose purpose was to regularize the discounts allowed advertising and subscription agencies. Then an administrative edict banned the general monthlies in the East from their traditional right of using fast mail trains for shipment. They would have to resort to freight trains instead. Shaw figured that the new rule would add two or three weeks to transportation time to the Pacific Coast and would force him to revise his printing deadlines at the expense of the timeliness that he rightly prized. It appeared that he might even have to convert the *Review of Reviews* to a weekly in order to qualify it for admittance to the fast mails again.[20]

The quarrel between the publishers and Taft dragged on in one form or another for over a year. Shaw discussed the reciprocity bill and the pound-rate revisions in one lengthy

19 Paolo E. Coletta, *The Presidency of William Howard Taft* (Lawrence: The University Press of Kansas, 1973), pp. 124-25; Shaw to Beveridge, Jan. 26, 30, Feb. 9, 1907, all in Beveridge MSS; William C. Edgar to Shaw, Dec. 23, 1909, Shaw MSS; Report of Commission on Second-Class Mail Matter to the President, Jan. 1912, pp. 7-14 of printed statement, William Howard Taft MSS, Library of Congress.

20 *American Review of Reviews*, XLIII (1911), 14-15, 260-64; Shaw to Beveridge, Feb. 9, 1911, Beveridge MSS; Shaw to Stead (not sent), July 7, 1911, Shaw to Charles Lanier, Jan. 23, 1912, Dec. 2, 1913, Shaw to Ellery Sedwick, Apr. 10, 1912, Memorandum prepared by Albert Shaw for the postmaster general to be handed through Mr. Charles D. Lanier to Mr. Stewart, second assistant postmaster general, Sept. 30, 1913, all in Shaw MSS.

segment of his editorials and reached conclusions of varying pertinence. If Taft were interested in tariff reform, he should have put his efforts into securing lower Payne-Aldrich rates in 1909. Before the Post Office Department could legitimately raise rates, it should be managed efficiently and not be operated as a haven for political appointees whose aim was to secure renomination for the incumbent president. Through the response to the advertisements they carried, magazines generated a great volume of first-class mail on which the postal service profited. Already agricultural journals had been classified so they might avoid paying the proposed new rates on advertisements. Such administrative discretion could be used arbitrarily to punish the muckraking journals and others of the standpatters' adversaries and to reward their friends. Both prospective measures discriminated between newspapers and periodicals. If rates had to be increased, why not raise them a uniform 25 or even 50 percent for magazines and papers?[21]

In his correspondence Shaw explicitly stated that there was a conspiracy aimed at punishing insurgent magazines. He claimed to have heard this directly from Postmaster General Frank Hitchcock, who was on amicable terms with him and in addition owed favors to some of his friends. In this same letter to Stead, that he admittedly wrote to let off steam and that he decided not to mail, Shaw employed the words "wicked," "perfidious," and "hypocritical" or their variations twice each. Exercising considerable semantic resourcefulness, he added such words or phrases as "reckless," "diabolic," "foolish," "despicable," "crooked," "persecute," "abuse," "misrepresentation," "conspiracy," and "big moneyed interests" once each in his description of the plot against the periodicals. In 1912 Taft and Shaw revealed their considerable disenchantment with one another in letters to confidants. The administration, Shaw told Butler, was "punk."[22] Taft's opinion of Shaw was somewhat less pithy. His complaint was against "these hogs of

21 *American Review of Reviews*, XLIII (1911), 260-71.
22 Shaw to Stead (not sent), July 7, 1911, Shaw to Butler, Mar. 21, 1912, both in Shaw MSS.

magazine publishers, of whom Albert Shaw is the leading one."[23]

It is no wonder that Taft thought so little of Shaw, for not only did he attack the president politically but he also exerted himself in marshalling opposition to the projected postal changes. He contacted such senatorial friends as Beveridge and Cummins, fellow progressives Jonathan Bourne and Joseph Bristow, Democrat Hoke Smith, Murray Crane—Taft's own ally from Massachusetts, and various other congressmen and editors in efforts to rally support. Although there is no escaping the conclusion that he hated any and all methods of increasing postage rates, Shaw's exertions to get his magazine back on the fast mails seem fully justified. The need to ship by freight cost him a full five days in his tight publishing schedule. This situation was not rectified until 1914. Taft finally appointed a commission headed by Justice Hughes to study the pound-rate problem. Its recommendation was to double rates across the board. Taft got his way, George Mowry points out, but the cost was high: the featured speakers at the 1912 banquet of the Periodical Publishers' Association were rival presidential aspirants Robert LaFollette and Woodrow Wilson.[24] After the election Taft recognized his folly: "It was not necessary for me to run amuck among the magazines."[25]

Angered by Taft's seeming duplicity in the postal controversy and convinced that the president had betrayed his mandate for reform, Shaw was determined to oppose his bid for a second term in 1912. The successes of reform in the preceding decade had apparently persuaded Shaw that the voters had sound political instincts after all, and in the hope of advancing the cause of progressivism he now called for the employment on at least a trial basis of such devices as the

[23] Taft to Murray Crane, Aug. 3, 1912, quoted in Pringle, *Life and Times of Taft*, II, 625.

[24] Mowry, *Era of Theodore Roosevelt*, p. 259; Pringle, *Life and Times of Taft*, II, 625; Report of Commission on Second-Class Matter, pp. 95-100, Taft MSS Shaw to Lanier, Jan. 23, 1912, Jan. 10, 1914, Shaw to Bristow, June 1, 1912, Shaw to Smith, July 8, 1912, Shaw to Crane, July 8, 1912, all in Shaw MSS.

[25] Quoted in Pringle, *Life and Times of Taft*, II, 625.

initiative, referendum, recall, and direct primary.[26] He openly welcomed the people as allies against Taft. Much depended on them, for the state machines in the South and East had already arranged to send delegates to the forthcoming Republican national convention committed to Taft. But victory could still be denied him. "If we get the Republican voters thoroughly aroused we are likely to have a convention out of which something valuable may come," Shaw advised a friend. "What I want to see is the Republican party exercising itself, . . . to find a strong candidate and make a live, up-to-date platform." The electorate needed to get "limbered up and influential," he instructed Butler.[27]

In the event that neither Taft nor the likeliest contenders, Theodore Roosevelt and Senator Robert LaFollette, secured the nomination, Cummins appeared a possible alternative. Along with Beveridge and Hughes he received some favorable mention from Shaw in the first months of 1912. Roosevelt remained Shaw's favorite.[28] He presented Roosevelt as the most logical and most popular of the potential candidates. Troubled by the third-term question and worried by the political climate which presaged a Democratic sweep of the November elections, at the start of 1912 Roosevelt was still ostensibly uncommitted but nevertheless moving closer toward his eventual decision to challenge Taft. Shaw declared in the year's first issue of the *Review*: "He is in every sense available for the nomination if the Republican party wants him."[29] Through a prearranged ruse designed to make him appear as the choice of the people, Roosevelt officially entered the race in February by responding affirmatively to a petition from seven Republican governors requesting him to run. Picking up many of La-

---

[26] *American Review of Reviews*, XXXIX (1909), 276, XLI (1910), 657, XLIII (1911), 273, XLIV (1911), 17; Shaw to William S. Barnes, Aug. 13, 1912, Shaw MSS.

[27] Shaw to James E. Rhodes, Jan. 3, 1912, Shaw to Butler, Mar. 21, 1912, both in Shaw MSS.

[28] Shaw to Rhodes, Jan. 3, 1912, Shaw to Sen. William Borah, Jan. 30, 1912, both in Shaw MSS; *American Review of Reviews*, XLV (1912), 19-21, 266.

[29] Ibid., p. 21; Mowry, *Theodore Roosevelt and the Progressive Movement*, pp. 200-201.

Follette's erstwhile supporters, he quickly established himself as Taft's strongest opponent.[30]

As expected, critics of the former president charged that Roosevelt should not run for an unprecedented third term. Shaw's rebuttal was contained in an unsigned article in which he maintained that the argument against a third term was based only on custom. The people had every right to end it if they so wished. It applied to consecutive terms anyhow. To show the opposition's hypocrisy, he quoted journals which after Roosevelt's victory in 1904 had begun speaking favorably about still another term. The same regular party leaders who had pleaded with T. R. to run in 1908 now strenuously opposed his candidacy. Shaw interpreted the question of Roosevelt's nomination as an issue between the politicians and the people. The article seemed to thrill Roosevelt: "It is conclusive. . . . It leaves the third term people without a leg to stand upon. Good luck, and many thanks."[31]

In boosting Roosevelt, Shaw frequently used Taft as a foil. He also struck at Taft independently, employing various stratagems. Once he used the better part of a page to praise Taft's executive nonpartisanship in order to deride him more effectively for failing to act as a party leader in his dealings with Congress. His failure in 1909 to secure the tariff reductions that his party had pledged proved this. An irate reader complained: "Kick him if you enjoy it so very much, but be honest, and don't kiss him first."[32] A favorite contemporary epithet was the word *trusts,* for it implied greed and conspiracy and posed a question of the people against privilege. Shaw used it to intimate that Taft was in league with a politicians' trust backed by the trusts themselves.[33]

The Democrats were also having a preconvention campaign.

30 Ibid., pp. 205-19.

31 "Roosevelt and the Third Term," *American Review of Reviews,* XLV (1912), 699-704; Shaw to Roosevelt, May 29, 1912, Roosevelt to Shaw, June 5, 1912, both in Shaw MSS. Shaw sent copies of this issue to each member of the Republican National Committee.

32 *American Review of Reviews,* XLV (1912), 260-64; James S. Ricketts, Sr., to Shaw, Mar. 26, 1912, Shaw MSS.

33 *American Review of Reviews,* XLV (1912), 387-90.

To his credit Shaw commended Woodrow Wilson as their best candidate. He artfully blended praise of Wilson, cheers for Roosevelt, and jibes at Taft in one series of editorials. He recounted how the professional politicians on each side tried to see that the other party chose the weakest possible candidate. The Democrats were hoping that Taft would be named, so their partisan press made feverish denunciations of Roosevelt. Allies of the Republican machine similarly concentrated on lampooning Wilson, for it was evident that he would be the most formidable Democratic nominee. "The situation would be an amusing one on both sides, if only the voters had some reasonable opportunity to take part in the selection of candidates," Shaw ruminated.[34]

The editor's intention was to preserve an air of impartiality and to present Roosevelt as the people's choice, yet some did fathom that the ex-president was his personal favorite. Shaw, however, was adamant that the contention for the Republican nomination was a question of principles and not of personalities. Positive that morality was at stake, Shaw utterly resented a minister's charge that he was an "ardent Roosevelt man." It meant that he was not disinterested. He replied with conviction:

It is always a hard thing in a political fight like this, involving moral principle, where one is fighting for conscience sake and for righteousness as against great wrong and evil, that the intelligence of a moral leader like yourself should have become confused and swung over with the innocent but easily swerved men of business, who move like a flock of sheep under the leadership of the subtle minds that control our affairs.

Your letter to me is as removed from a real understanding of what is going on this year in politics as if you lived in another planet. I am writing about things that I know and understand thoroughly. . . . I have never taken the fraction of one of my views from Mr. Roosevelt. I have direct sources of information, and I have always done my own thinking.[35]

---

34 Ibid., pp. 142-43.
35 Shaw to the Rev. Dan Freeman Bradley, Apr. 8, 1912, Shaw MSS.

Feelings were of unusual intensity, and the preconvention campaign from its beginning appeared a "saturnalia of scurrility." Shaw's belief that morality was at issue was widely shared by Rooseveltians; their adversaries felt that treachery was rampant. The personal feud of Taft and Roosevelt was an added element. The old friends had come to despise each other so much that when their campaign cars chanced to be parked on adjacent tracks in Steubenville a crowd gathered expecting to see the Republican rivals break into fisticuffs. The specious story circulated that Roosevelt was a drunkard.[36] Roosevelt claimed that Taft's presidential accomplishments constituted "the crookedest kind of a crooked deal" and that personally he was a "fathead" with an intellect that did not quite equal a guinea pig's.[37]

The Republican convention was held at Chicago in June. Eleven hundred legal delegates were in attendance. Of these the Roosevelt forces (with the support of Cummins and LaFollette) could expect to control about five hundred. In addition they contested 254 of the majority of delegates lined up for Taft. If Roosevelt could succeed in replacing about fifty of the disputed delegates with his own people, he could in conjunction with the Cummins and LaFollette groups stop Taft's likely victory on the first round and probably gain the nomination himself on a later poll. But the immediate situation was precarious, for Taft supporters dominated the National Committee and the Credentials Committee which would make the crucial organizational decisions about the contested delegates and the convention's chairmanship in advance of the actual nominating and balloting.[38]

The National Committee, chaired by Shaw's long-time acquaintance, Omaha journalist Victor Rosewater, made up the temporary roll and awarded Taft 235 of the disputed delegates, more than enough to guarantee his control. There followed a display of the steamroller tactics that Shaw had

---

[36] Mowry, *Theodore Roosevelt and the Progressive Movement*, pp. 220-35.
[37] Quoted in ibid., pp. 222, 234 respectively.
[38] Ibid., pp. 233-44.

feared and hoped to forestall. Each subsequent decision of importance went to Taft, and by the time the actual voting for candidates began the issue was sealed. Most Roosevelt supporters refused to vote, signifying by their silence during the roll call that they no longer considered themselves Republicans. The decision was made at a separate meeting to form the Progressive party.[39]

Shaw was active at Chicago, discussing matters with Roosevelt, attending meetings of his forces, working until 2 or 3 A.M. each day. He thought Roosevelt's adherents had received shabby personal treatment. Some of Roosevelt's important followers had even had a difficult time getting tickets to the convention. Society girls or local people of no consequence had received the tickets. Shaw himself had been snubbed by a man he had known for years. "It was a crime around Chicago to be in sympathy with Colonel Roosevelt," he complained to Newton Hawley.[40] Since the convention was not concluded until the latter part of June, he had had to write his July "Progress" in a preliminary way. His analysis, which he thought held up well, struck the usual blows at Taft. "Flouting the Popular Verdict," " 'Obtuseness' in an Acute Period," and "Offending the Public Conscience" were titles intimating how Taft had secured his delegates. Before the convention Shaw had written Rosewater to ask for fairness and to say that in a close contest neither side should be allowed to use southern delegates; they represented no substantial segment of Republican voters. Ignoring the fact that T. R. had made effective use of them in 1904, he repeated this thought in his editorials and added that Taft's other large group of delegates had been provided by the bosses.[41] These remarks at least vindicated his preconvention observations.

Shaw was convinced that the Taft forces had done little

---

[39] Ibid., pp. 239, 244-55; Rosewater to Shaw, Jan. 1, 1911, Shaw MSS.

[40] Victor Rosewater, *Back Stage in 1912: The Inside Story of the Split Republican Convention* (Philadelphia: Dorrance & Company, 1932), p. 181; Shaw to Hawley, June 25, 1912, Shaw MSS.

[41] Rosewater to Shaw, Jan. 1, 1912, Shaw to Rosewater, May 27, 1912, June 25, 1912, all in Shaw MSS; *American Review of Reviews*, XLVI (1912), 1-14.

but cheat. He explained the circumstances to Hawley: "The Roosevelt people made a clean, plucky fight, but they were defeated by a technical situation that took the form of a vicious circle. Delegates whose title was in dispute were used at all points to hold together a working majority and thus to make the temporary roll permanent."[42] His analysis in the *Review* was intended to aid the cause, he wrote Roosevelt: "Of course you understand that the value of it lies in the fact that with my readers throughout the nation I am regarded as a sort of oracle who looks upon these political movements with sagacity and sincerity, and then tells the truth for all sections of the country and for all political factions." The publisher of the *Coon Rapids Enterprise*, on the contrary, believed that what Shaw wrote was either "far fetched" or "misleading." What could one expect, he retorted on behalf of Taft, "when one remembers that the Review of Reviews belongs to the magazine trust."[43]

The editor's full discussion of the convention appeared in his August issue. He claimed again that Taft had stolen the nomination and then introduced the notion that Roosevelt's floor leader, Governor Herbert Hadley of Missouri, had inadvertently helped him do it. If Roosevelt had had a more effective floor leader—for instance, Beveridge—he might have triumphed anyhow. Shaw also held that the idea of boycotting the final vote was Hadley's and that it was a mistake: "It was a course that fixed responsibility, and made it impossible for the majority to escape from the logical results of its conduct. It created a situation from which nothing but defeat could follow." Hadley demurred.[44]

Shaw corresponded with Cummins about the prudence of the bolt. Cummins, who had continued to remain a Republican while supporting Roosevelt, pointed out that splitting the party would ruin the careers of many able and principled

42 Shaw to Hawley, June 25, 1912, Shaw MSS.

43 Shaw to Roosevelt, June 25, 1912, Sam D. Henry to Shaw, July 9, 1912, both in Shaw MSS.

44 *American Review of Reviews*, XLVI (1912), 132-38; Hadley to Shaw, Aug. 13, 1912, Shaw MSS.

men within the GOP by facilitating Democratic victories. Shaw conceded this possibility and said to Cummins and in the *Review* that it was well to remain a Republican in states like Iowa where the party itself was progressive. But in New York where the trade mark belonged to the machine there was really no alternative but to bolt. He considered the Progressive party a regeneration of Republican principles.[45]

In general the new party did not attract politicians with careers at stake. Some did join it as did factional politicians, ardent social reformers, and assorted admirers of Roosevelt. Revulsion at Taft and at the trend of politics and friendship for Roosevelt attracted Shaw to it, but its immediate aims and principles provided a positive appeal as well. Among the planks the new party chose to stand on were ones recommending the broadened use of the initiative, referendum, and recall; the promotion of agricultural and industrial education; and the extension of federal authority to secure the prohibition of child labor and the enactment of workmen's compensation, old-age insurance, and other social justice measures. Along with Roosevelt's call for the establishment of a national industrial commission to regulate the trusts, these represented the "live, up-to-date" issues Shaw had wanted the GOP to endorse.[46]

Although he did have some minor role in the preliminary drafting of the Progressive platform, Shaw decided not to attend the party's convention, feeling generally overworked from his editorial tasks and from the additional burdens placed on him by his membership on a board impanelled to arbitrate a crucial railroad dispute.[47] The controversy had begun in early 1912, when the Brotherhood of Locomotive Engineers asked fifty-two eastern railroads for wage increases and modifications in work rules. The engineers overwhelmingly voted

45 *American Review of Reviews*, XLVI (1912), 397; Cummins to Shaw, July 20, 30, 1912, Shaw to Cummins, July 23, 1912, Shaw to Roosevelt, Aug. 2, 1912, all in Shaw MSS.

46 Mowry, *Theodore Roosevelt and the Progressive Movement*, pp. 256-73.

47 Shaw to Sen. Moses E. Clapp, Aug. 2, 1912, Shaw to Roosevelt, Aug. 2, 1912, Shaw to William H. Hotchkiss, Aug. 12, 1912, Shaw to Jesse Macy, Oct. 5, 1912, Shaw to Medill McCormick, Nov. 29, 1912, all in Shaw MSS.

to strike upon the refusal of the railroads to meet their demands.[48]

After mediation efforts by two federal officials failed, it was agreed to maintain service and to name an arbitration board; the threatened strike would have stalled all rail traffic in an area where 42 percent of the population of the United States lived. Daniel Willard, president of the Baltimore and Ohio, and P. H. Morrissey, representing the engineers, were selected as members of a proposed seven-man board. Failing to agree on the additional members, they compiled a roster of candidates from which the remaining arbitrators were chosen by Chief Justice White and two other federal officials. The five named were Shaw, Oscar Straus, who during the proceedings was nominated Progressive candidate for governor of New York, Otto Eidlitz, ex-president of the New York Building Trades Association, President Charles Van Hise of the University of Wisconsin, and St. Louis attorney Frederick Judson.[49]

The board heard testimony from both sides during the latter half of July and then dispersed for the members to give what time they could to the study of relevant data and to the resolution of the conflicting arguments. The panel met again in September to discuss findings and recessed from September 14 to October 28 when it assembled a final time to study the revised report which was issued November 2.[50]

The decision that was binding for one year (retroactively from May 1) was a compromise. Willard signed it but briefly stipulated that he disapproved of certain unspecified details; Morrissey formally dissented. He conceded that gains in salary—over two-thirds of the sum demanded—and in standard-

---

[48] "The Railway Arbitration: A Review," *Outlook*, CII (Dec. 1912), 753-54; *Report of the Board of Arbitration. In the matter of the controversy between the Eastern Railroads and the Brotherhood of Locomotive Engineers* (Washington: Published under the Direction of the Secretary to the Board, 1913), pp. 1-8.

[49] Ibid., pp. 2-6, 89; Oscar Strauss, *Under Four Administrations: From Cleveland to Taft* (Boston and New York: Houghton Mifflin, 1922), pp. 199-203; *New York World*, July 16, 1912, Scrapbooks, Shaw MSS.

[50] *Report of the Board of Arbitration*, pp. 8-11, 14-16; *Kansas City Journal*, July 16, 1912, *New York World*, July 16, 1912, both in Scrapbooks, Shaw MSS; C. W. A. Veditz to Shaw, Aug. 3, 9, 13, 20, 24, 31, 1912, all in Shaw MSS.

ization of work rules among the fifty-two railroads had been made, but held that in general the new provisions did not go far enough. And he emphatically rejected the board's gratuitous contention that future salary adjustments be determined for railroad employees by a government commission. The panel had insisted that the rails were a public utility on which widespread work stoppage would jeopardize the popular welfare.[51] Its analogy had been incisive: "A strike in the army or navy is mutiny, and universally punished as such. The same principle is applied to seamen because of the public necessity involved."[52]

Since much of the panel's work was completed by early fall, Shaw was able to pay more attention to political developments during the climactic weeks of the campaign. The editor refrained from taking any conspicuous role in the Progressive party but did participate in it behind the scenes, believing, as he told Hamlin Garland, that he could be of most service to it "by standing for the right things with an air of calm and dispassionate judgment in my monthly review." Shaw, of course, had done anything but this in the preceding two years, but sure of his righteousness he remained blinded to the fact that he had already committed himself to a highly partisan stance. Commitment, however, did not affect his political judgment, for he realized that the split in Republican ranks would be of substantial benefit to the Democrats. He voted for Roosevelt in the November elections but doubted that the Progressive ticket could triumph. Shaw was thus readily able to accept Wilson's victory in the presidential contest and to follow it with warm wishes and editorial support for the success of his former classmate's new administration.[53]

---

[51] *Report of the Board of Arbitration*, pp. 90-123.

[52] Quoted in *United Presbyterian* (Pittsburgh), Dec. 5, 1912, Scrapbooks, Shaw MSS.

[53] Shaw to John C. Shaffer, June 25, 1912, Shaw to Hotchkiss, Aug. 12, 1912, Shaw to Garland, Aug. 13, 1912, Shaw to Butler, Sept. 27, 1912, Shaw to Mrs. Katherine R. West, Nov. 12, 1912, Shaw to William Sulzer, Dec. 4, 1912, Shaw to Will H. Hays, Dec. 29, 1919, all in Shaw MSS; Shaw to Wilson, Mar. 5, 1913, Wilson MSS.

9

Return to Republicanism, 1913-1920

In 1913 Albert Shaw and Woodrow Wilson were no longer as close as they had been during their stay at the Johns Hopkins and during the decade or so thereafter, but they were still on cordial terms. Taking a personal and professional interest in Wilson's administration, Shaw was enthusiastic about his initial moves, particularly in his selection for the cabinet of singularly able men like Franklin Lane and David Houston (both of whom Shaw considered friends). In fact everything he knew of Wilson led him to predict success for his administration. "You may be sure," Shaw wrote Jesse Macy, "that Wilson is going to tie together the executive and legislative as no President has done it before, and that this administration is going to do some things that will interest you very much as a student of parties and a student of our federal system."[1] Indeed, until 1914, Shaw's backing of Wilson was sincerely and generously given. But just at this moment—when foreign policy issues began to dominate the news—Shaw began to reverse his course, joining Theodore Roosevelt in stressing the issue of Americanism and returning with him to the Republican party and the political orthodoxy that, purged of its most progressive elements, it once more represented.

From the very beginning of his presidency it was recognized that Wilson's efforts to secure tariff reform would be a good index of his leadership, for tariff politics only four years before had prompted the insurgent movement in the Republican party. Wilson himself helped give central attention to the issue by going before Congress in April, 1913, to advocate a reduction of the tariff. Shaw was in his corner from the start of what proved to be a protracted controversy, confiding to Wilson that "I find myself able to go the full length of this bill."[2] Reviewing at length the tariff problem under Taft, Shaw concluded that the Republicans' failure to secure meaningful reform had given the Democrats "a mandate to revise the tariff sharply and unsparingly." While he conceded that in the opinion of some the Underwood-Simmons bill that emerged after months of argument was too radical, Shaw thought it represented what the public wanted, for it lowered duties extensively but retained the protective principle.[3]

Shaw had misgivings about some domestic legislation—especially the new graduated income tax which he considered "arbitrary and undemocratic"—but on the whole regarded Wilson's first year in office approvingly. A full year before the 1914 congressional elections, Shaw even predicted in an editorial that the return of a Democratic majority would serve to endorse Wilson's leadership.[4] But developments soon began taking place in foreign affairs that led Shaw to reexamine Wilson's conduct of the presidency. Controversies over the Panama Canal and over the proper American policy toward the Mexican revolution made for acrimonious debate in Congress and in journals of opinion throughout the United States.

In most discussions of these issues America's interference in the Mexican revolution would rank first, for it even threatened to involve the United States in a major military commitment below the Rio Grande. But until the punitive expedition of 1916-17 Shaw was not overly disturbed about the situation in Mexico and, anxious to support the president if he could do so in good conscience, professed to discern some

---

[1] Shaw to Macy, Mar. 24, 1913, Shaw to Wilson, Apr. 18, 1913, Shaw to Charles Shinn, May 9, 1913, all in Shaw MSS. Although almost twenty years old, Arthur Link, *Woodrow Wilson and the Progressive Era, 1910-1917*, New American Nation Series (New York: Harper & Brothers, 1954), remains the best source for a general understanding of the Wilson administration during the period prior to America's declaration of war. Any information in this chapter not otherwise noted is to be found therein.

[2] Shaw to Wilson, Apr. 18, 1913, Shaw MSS.

[3] *American Review of Reviews*, XLVII (1913), 522, XLVIII (1913), 390.

[4] Ibid., XLVII (1913), 524, XLVIII (1913), 140-43, 390-91, 517.

coherent pattern behind the apparent vagaries of Wilson's policy toward Mexico.[5]

The Panamanian questions represented something else, for in Shaw's opinion any matter that touched upon American sovereignty over the Canal Zone represented a threat to our most vital interests. Two issues that seemed to pose such a threat developed almost simultaneously. One concerned a treaty of apology and indemnity between the United States and Colombia. To atone for whatever wrongs the United States had done to Colombia at the time of the Panamanian revolt in 1903, this country agreed to pay a $25,000,000 indemnity and to extend Colombia rights equal to ours in the use of the canal. The pact, which failed of ratification, not only impugned Roosevelt's integrity by reviving doubts about his actions in the canal imbroglio of 1903, but also—and this was what really angered Shaw—appeared to prejudice America's exclusive control of the Canal Zone. What if the rights accorded Colombia were to be used by some other power under the guise of the Colombian flag, he fretted in his correspondence. Shaw's editorial criticism of the treaty was mild, purposely so he informed T. R., but on the whole he found it "the most astounding and offensive treaty ever negotiated in the history of the United States."[6]

The other matter concerned Great Britain's protest of a blanket exemption from canal tolls granted American-flag ships engaged in commerce between the Atlantic and Pacific coasts of the United States. Britain's action was based on the fact that the Hay-Pauncefote Treaty of 1901 guaranteed equal treatment to all ships using the canal. Despite the fact that Wilson had favored the tolls exemption in his campaign statements, he now reversed himself and persuaded a reluctant Congress to repeal the statute granting tolls exemption. Shaw gave the controversy much editorial attention, concluding that

[5] Shaw to Sen. Morris Sheppard, Mar. 11, 1914, Shaw MSS; *American Review of Reviews*, XLIX (1914), 387-92, 516-18, 644-50, L (1914), 131-33.

[6] Ibid., XLIX (1914), 651, L (1914), 10-12; Shaw to Lewis Hosea, Mar. 6, 1914, Shaw to Roosevelt, May 21, 1914, Roosevelt to Shaw, Feb. 10, 1916, Shaw to Albert Cummins, Mar. 25, 1917, all in Shaw MSS.

the exemption was actually unsound economically, for it discriminated against our railroads in their competition with shipping interests for transcontinental traffic. Nevertheless Wilson's insistence that Congress yield to the contention "whether we were right or wrong" was inexcusable, for it jeopardized our sovereignty over the canal and its use. Conceding that Wilson's leadership in domestic matters had been masterful, Shaw revealed the extent of his dissatisfaction with the handling of foreign affairs by suggesting that the 1914 elections might go against the Democratic party after all. Just months before, he had expected them to serve as testimony to Wilson's success as president.[7]

The tolls dispute had hardly been settled when the outbreak of World War I in August 1914 posed a new and vastly graver dilemma for the United States. To Shaw the war was a product of the old world's outmoded statesmanship and governing cliques. He assigned the Central Powers by far the largest share of responsibility for the war, but believed that none of the belligerents could be absolved of guilt since militarism and imperialist rivalries—in which all had participated—had much to do with the coming of the war. Although incensed by Germany's immoral invasion of neutral Belgium, Shaw immediately and unequivocally gave editorial support to America's proclamation of neutrality.[8] Even when Britain and Germany made the sea into a war zone, Shaw remained steadfast in backing neutrality. He regarded it as the only realistic policy: "We have no shipping interests in the North Sea or the waters around Great Britain that are of any relative importance; and we have no occasion to become embroiled either with Great Britain or with Germany. . . . For us," added Shaw some pages later, "the war at worst is a mere inconvenience. Neither duty nor advantage calls us abroad."[9]

[7] *American Review of Reviews*, XLIX (1914), 260-64, 527-28, L (1914), 6-10.

[8] Ibid., pp. 259-70, 394-98, 525; Shaw to Adam Schauss, Oct. 31, 1914, Shaw MSS.

[9] *American Review of Reviews*, LI (1915), 267, 270. J. A. Thompson, "An Imperialist and the First World War: The Case of Albert J. Beveridge," *Journal of American Studies*, V (Aug. 1971), 133-50, takes note of Shaw's anti-interven-

Not even the torpedoing of the *Lusitania* changed Shaw's mind. He thought the attack on it unwarranted but did not feel that American citizens who had lost their lives during the sinking of the *Lusitania* should have been sailing on a belligerent-flag vessel that was known to have frequently transported munitions. The president was to be congratulated for avoiding a break with Germany, especially in view of the hysteria aroused by the press. (And by Theodore Roosevelt, Shaw might have added.)[10]

Shaw, nevertheless, found reason to secondguess Wilson. His primary oversight was in failing to take steps which might have caused the belligerents to observe the accepted standards of warfare more faithfully. For instance, had he convened a meeting of the United States and other neutrals at the outset of war or in early 1915 when encroachments upon the freedom of the seas had initially been made, a joint declaration of policy might have been formulated that would have earned respect for neutral rights and that would have precluded incidents of the *Lusitania* type. Wilson would have been wise to embargo the sale of munitions abroad at the war's commencement. The imposition of an embargo at that point would have been neutral in spirit and would also have furthered the national interest by preventing close links from developing between the American economy and English military fortunes.[11]

Shaw became more insistent in his criticism of Wilson. By the end of 1916 he was even writing to an English friend to whom he customarily spoke frankly: "I have not approved of any important step that the government of the United States has taken at any time since the outbreak of the European War, in so far as its foreign policies are concerned."[12] Shaw seems to have overstated the case in so far as Wilson's European

---

tionism. Also useful is Charles Hirschfeld, "Nationalist Progressivism and World War I," *Mid-America*, XLV (July 1963), 139-56.

10 *American Review of Reviews*, LI (1915), 644-48. Roosevelt's attitude toward World War I is ably discussed in Harbaugh, *Life and Times of Theodore Roosevelt*, pp. 439-89.

11 *American Review of Reviews*, LI (1915), 389-95, 655, LII (1915), 527-28.

12 Shaw to Sir Henry Lunn, Dec. 29, 1916, Shaw MSS.

diplomacy was concerned, for throughout the war's first year his editorial criticisms of Wilson rarely assumed more than a reproachful nature. The hardening of his attitude came in 1916, a year which to Shaw seemed to mark the nadir of American diplomacy. The Colombian treaty was still pending; there was talk of withdrawing from the Philippines; Pershing's invasion of Mexico with relatively weak forces was ill-advised and was hampered in its execution by decisions made at Washington; the continuing crises caused by warfare on the Atlantic produced only irresolution among our leaders.[13] Shaw increasingly focused his criticisms on two matters: the lack of military preparedness and Wilson's failure to be consistent in his actions toward Great Britain and Germany.

The preparedness controversy, which lasted in its most intense form from the summer of 1915 to the summer of 1916, engaged much of Shaw's attention. To him and to many concerned citizens it seemed evident that the United States lacked the military capability to support Pershing's expedition in case of increased trouble with Mexico and to gain respect for its European diplomacy. To remedy this immediate shortcoming and to promote physical vigor and civic-mindedness among a populace that was given to sloth and self-indulgence Shaw advocated a complete reconsideration of our military program. The army's fundamental weakness was that it was narrowly based and regarded almost as a form of servitude. But Shaw argued that it did not have to remain so. If it were enlarged and if short-term enlistments, varying in most cases from three months to one year, were introduced, military service would be made so attractive that it would be seen as an honorable way of discharging one's civic duty. Moreover the rapid turnover of personnel would provide the manpower for a large, partially trained reserve such as peace-loving Switzerland maintained. When buttressed by coordinate programs that would be offered by institutions such as the land grant colleges, private military academies, and even the

---

[13] Shaw to Harry Pratt Judson, May 3, 8, 1916, Shaw to David Houston, July 21, 1916, all in Shaw MSS.

Boy Scouts (where for example instruction in first aid would
be given), the system Shaw championed would give the United
States an army that was defensively oriented, as it should be,
yet modern and effective.[14]

Although not as broadly based as the program Shaw advocated, the plan favored by Secretary of War Lindley Garrison
seemed reasonable. It called for the augmentation of the
regular army, the recruitment over a three-year period of a
reserve force of about 400,000 men, and the disbandment of
the National Guard. The plan, however, got caught up in
politics with the result that Wilson retracted the promise of
support he had given Garrison. Following Garrison's angry
resignation a compromise bill was passed which strengthened
the army and reformed the National Guard. But it was not
enough to placate Shaw who wrote of the new law: "The
measure calls for the largest possible looting of the Treasury,
for the smallest possible military results."[15]

The debate over naval preparedness also exasperated Shaw.
A modern navy, second only to Great Britain's in size, was a
bargain at any price, he reasoned. After all there would have
been no war with Spain in 1898 had the United States only
possessed two or three more battleships. As he succinctly put
it: "We want a navy that will make our pacifism respected
and respectable." Particularly irksome were those who opposed
naval expansion only to grudgingly accept a compromise proposal. The construction of two new battleships when four
were needed was a waste of money.[16]

While the outcome of the preparedness controversy resulted
in considerable improvement in America's armed forces, the
whole episode—especially the wrangling over the reform of
the army—confirmed Shaw's belief that Wilson was too vacil-
lating to be an effective leader during a period of international
crisis. Additional proof was forthcoming in the armed ship
controversy of early 1916. It began when the State Department,

14 *American Review of Reviews*, LII (1915), 260-64, 403-4, LIII (1916), 132.
15 Ibid., pp. 263-70, 527-29, 650.
16 Shaw to N. M. Butler, Apr. 17, 1913, Shaw to Frances Leffler, Oct. 20, 1913,
both in Shaw MSS; *American Review of Reviews*, LIII (1916), 138, 653-54.

with Wilson's backing, initiated a campaign to persuade the Allies to disarm their merchant vessels as part of a larger plan designed to contain German submarine warfare. The idea seemed reasonable, but its implementation would have necessitated a change in the rules of international law that would have been detrimental to the Allies' ability to control the Atlantic. The Allies firmly rejected the proposal. The administration thereupon reversed its course, blundering into a new dispute with Germany and touching off an acrimonious debate with Congress.[17]

Domestic issues had to be subordinated to the handling of the international crisis, Shaw now declared. If the United States was to succeed in remaining neutral, more effective leadership was needed. "It might be fortunate for Wilson if he were defeated," Shaw wrote with the 1916 election in mind. "His talent is not for armies, navies, and diplomacy." Or as Shaw perceptively stated on the eve of the election: "We ought to have accumulated no grievances against any of the belligerents; but as matters stand we have made the written record in so many unsettled questions of grave controversy that every thoughtful man must dread the reckoning."[18]

Theodore Roosevelt was Shaw's choice for the presidency even though their views, if Shaw's postelection confession to Wilson may be believed, were not altogether harmonious. How then could he have advocated Roosevelt's candidacy at such a critical moment? There is no precise answer, for Shaw never made clear exactly how their views diverged. But something may be surmised. It seems likely, judging from the frequent criticism Shaw aimed at the hysteria of the press, that he felt Roosevelt was too pugnacious in his rhetoric. But if so, Shaw obviously did not regard Roosevelt's verbal bellicosity—his apparent readiness to go to war—as a barrier to his fitness for the presidency. Roosevelt had two superior qualifications: he was absolutely correct on the preparedness

[17] Ibid., pp. 394-401.
[18] Ibid., p. 522, LIV (1916), 472; Shaw to Judson, May 3, 1916, Shaw to Houston, July 21, 1916, Shaw to Charles Evans Hughes, Feb. 5, 1930, all in Shaw MSS.

issue, and he had the ability to formulate an honorable policy and then sustain it. In office he would undoubtedly act with restraint, as he once had; and he would again be able to draw on the counsel of Elihu Root, the statesman Shaw most admired.[19]

Shaw recognized that the Republican leadership still resented Roosevelt's past apostasy, but he nevertheless believed Roosevelt could secure the nominations of both the Progressive and Republican parties. As he saw it an upsurge of bipartisan feeling would make Roosevelt's preconvention candidacy into a force the political establishment—the Republican Old Guard—would have to recognize. Given the backing of only a few such Republican leaders, Roosevelt could gain the GOP nomination and, with the Progressive endorsement also in hand, would give Wilson his most formidable challenge in November. Things of course did not go according to Shaw's scenario: Roosevelt rejected the Progressive nomination and none was forthcoming from the GOP. Nevertheless Shaw accepted the outcome. While he expressed dissatisfaction with the Old Guard, he felt that Republican nominee Charles Evans Hughes was a commendable candidate for the presidency, one whom he intended to support.[20]

Disappointed by Wilson's victory, Shaw continued to indicate how greater firmness on Wilson's part might have averted the precarious diplomatic situation that had emerged by early 1917. But once the United States declared war in April 1917, Shaw accepted the country's belligerent status as a fact and supported the war effort. He applauded the democratic idealism that was central to Wilson's war message,[21] although he personally felt that security represented America's basic interest in entering World War I. His presence at a private dinner where Herbert Hoover recounted the peril in which un-

[19] Shaw to Wilson, Dec. 1, 1916, Wilson MSS; *American Review of Reviews*, LIII (1916), 274-75, 298.

[20] Ibid., pp. 523-26, 644-50, LIV (1916), 4-13, 473; Shaw to Judson, May 8, 1916, Shaw to Roosevelt, Nov. 27, 1916, Shaw to Lunn, Dec. 29, 1916, all in Shaw MSS.

[21] Shaw to Wilson, Apr. 27, 1917, Wilson MSS; *American Review of Reviews*, LV (1917), 452.

restricted submarine warfare had placed England made Shaw realize that the Allies were confronted with defeat unless American intervention was forthcoming. As he explained in an editorial: The United States "could never have lived safely in the same world with a completely triumphant Germany."[22]

Shaw had definite views on how to prosecute the war. In the sense that the United States had steadily supplied England with credit, food, and munitions, he reasoned, we were already a partner in the war effort and could make our most effective contribution to it by continuing to act as a storehouse for the Allies. In addition the United States should vigorously move to keep transatlantic supply routes open by expediting the construction of merchant vessels and by dispatching the appropriate naval units to counteract the submarine menace.[23]

Despite the alarm caused by Russia's military disintegration, Shaw rejected the idea of recruiting large expeditionary forces. Indeed, as late as the opening months of 1918, Shaw was positive that the "English and French combined are from two to three times as strong as the Germans will ever be on the Western Front."[24] While the dispatch of some U.S. Marines would be useful as a stimulus to Allied morale, the presence of American army divisions in France would be redundant. Their recruitment would actually hurt the war effort by diverting manpower from the essential tasks of raising food, operating factories, and constructing ships.[25] Moreover, as his correspondence indicates, Shaw was worried that the formation and deployment of substantial ground forces would jeopardize America's long-range interests. Certain that a German victory represented an unacceptable threat to American security, Shaw

[22] Shaw to Lunn, Dec. 18, 1928, Shaw MSS; *American Review of Reviews*, LV (1917), 565. He felt security had a lot more to do with our declaration of war than the government was willing to let on. See Shaw to Laura Williams, Mar. 24, 1917, Shaw MSS.

[23] Shaw to Wilson, Jan. 25, 1918, Wilson MSS; *American Review of Reviews*, LV (1917), 458.

[24] Shaw to Josephus Daniels, Feb. 21, 1918, Shaw MSS.

[25] Shaw to Wilson, Dec. 8, 1917, Jan. 25, July 18, 1918, all in Wilson MSS; Shaw to R. Fulton Cutting, May 18, 1917, Shaw to Roosevelt, Jan. 29, 1918, Shaw to Albert Cummins, Jan. 31, 1918, all in Shaw MSS; *American Review of Reviews*, LVII (1918), 242.

was also suspicious of the Allies. He feared that they intended to dupe the United States into bleeding itself on European battlefields while husbanding their own strength in order to undertake a land-grabbing spree once hostilities had ceased.[26]

Although backing the idea of a draft, Shaw dissented from the way it was being administered. Its proper use was to check inflation and to insure American productivity by allocating manpower to farms, factories, and shipyards. Draftees could still receive enough military training in their spare time to enable them to take their part in a reserve force. Wilson was not to blame for the misuse of the draft, for at worst he had only listened to unsound advice which had urged the formation of large ground forces. The fault belonged instead to various desk generals who had frustrated the proper functioning of the law by putting millions of conscripts into uniform, training them inadequately in poorly constructed cantonments, and ordering them overseas where they were not needed.[27] Shaw argued that this was folly. "You cannot fight whales in the North Sea," he said of the policy our army leaders were pursuing, "by massing great herds of buffalos in the Yellowstone Park." Generals who really wanted to help the war effort "should enlist in the Navy and fight submarines."[28]

Shaw contended that the navy should receive military priority. An effective fleet was needed for several reasons: to assure a flow of matériel across the Atlantic, perhaps to allow an attack upon the Black Sea flank of the Central Powers, and to buttress America's postwar diplomacy.[29]

In the spring of 1918 Shaw finally admitted that he might have been wrong about the army,[30] but the numerous indict-

---

[26] Shaw to Beveridge, July 2, Aug. 11, 1917, Shaw to Amos Parker Wilder, Oct. 5, 1917, all in Shaw MSS.

[27] Shaw to Newton Baker (not sent), Dec. 26, 1917, Shaw to Lunn, Jan. 3, 1918, Shaw to Roosevelt, Jan. 29, 1918, Shaw to Daniels, Feb. 21, 1918, all in Shaw MSS; *American Review of Reviews*, LV (1917), 458, LVI (1917), 17, LVII (1918), 124-25.

[28] Ibid., p. 242; Shaw to Daniels, Feb. 21, 1918, Shaw MSS.

[29] Shaw to Daniels, Jan. 31, Feb. 21, 1918, Shaw to Charles Barton, Feb. 20, 1918, all in Shaw MSS; *American Review of Reviews*, LVII (1918), 236-37, 242.

[30] Shaw to Wilson, Apr. 20, 1918, Wilson MSS; *American Review of Reviews*, LVII (1918), 452-54.

ments he had already made of its leaders convinced at least a few readers that he was disloyal. Shaw was aware that he might be accused of undermining the war effort,[31] but he correctly recognized that his primary journalistic responsibility was to describe the situation as he saw it, not as others wanted it depicted. Shaw put it this way: "He would be a very unpatriotic American citizen who had trained himself all his life to think about public affairs and should then deem it right to acquiesce and keep silent in the face of a mistaken policy."[32] Yet when his analysis of the war was officially questioned, Shaw reacted not with a staunch plea for the freedom of the press, but with what can most charitably be described as circumspection.

His troubles revolved around an incident that pitted him and his partner, Charles Lanier, in a dispute with the Committee on Public Information, America's wartime propaganda bureau. Shaw's initial involvement with the CPI was occasioned by a rebuke forthcoming from Colonel Ernest Chambers, Canada's director of press censorship. Apparently Chambers objected to something Shaw had written in the *Review* about the annexationist secret treaties that the various Allied powers had negotiated prior to America's entry into the war. Shaw wrote to CPI director, George Creel, who was acting as intermediary, to explain his position: he had not intended to criticize the Allies but had simply mentioned the treaties as background for a general discussion of the war. In any case he considered himself so completely identified with the anti-imperialist outlook of British Liberalism that he felt free to participate occasionally in England's "family quarrels."[33]

The episode was only a prelude to a more serious controversy in which Shaw and Creel were again involved. Added to the cast were Lanier, Guy Stanton Ford of the CPI, and Claude

---

[31] Shaw to Baxter Taylor, Mar. 12, 1918, Shaw to the Rev. Frederick J. Stanley, Mar. 30, 1918, both in Shaw MSS.

[32] Shaw to Daniels, Feb. 21, 1918, Shaw MSS.

[33] William Stewart Wallace, comp., *The Macmillan Dictionary of Canadian Biography*, 3rd ed. rev. and enl. (London: Macmillan, 1963), p. 128; Shaw to Creel, Apr. 8, 1918, Shaw MSS.

Van Tyne of the National Security League, a private organization originally formed to advocate preparedness and which
now was trying to spur the American people into greater efforts
in behalf of the war. Shaw, as it happened, had been named
to its advisory committee shortly before the trouble began.
The problem originated when Shaw, acting on a suggestion
from Lanier, agreed to have the Review of Reviews Company
publish a book about the World War. Its format, which has
been described as a "catechism of war information," and parts
of the material were borrowed from a feature that had been
appearing in *Stead's Review,* the Australian offshoot of William
T. Stead's old *Review of Reviews.* Lanier handled the details
of publication while Shaw persuaded Creel to write an introduction for the book which was released under the title *Two
Thousand Questions and Answers About the War.*[34]

Virtually everyone connected with the project was soon
embarrassed, Creel the most acutely; for as it turned out,
America's propaganda czar had unwittingly prepared an introduction for a book whose patriotic intent was suspect. Ford,
a well-known historian who was currently serving as director
of the CPI's Division of Civic and Educational Cooperation,
informed Creel that he regarded *Two Thousand Questions* as
a "pacifist half pro-German affair" and notified Shaw that he
could "hardly regard with equanimity the extensive distribution of this book." The supposedly objectionable passages,
explained Shaw, happened to be ones that were reprinted from
Stead's Review and were not at all pro-German; they merely
represented the views of British Liberalism. (This, of course,
was precisely what he had said in apologizing for the editorials
that had been questioned in Ottawa.) In an attempt to placate
Creel and Ford, Shaw promised that the book would be revised
before another printing was undertaken and even asked the
latter to suggest someone qualified to supervise the revision.[35]

[34] George T. Blakey, *Historians on the Homefront: American Propagandists
for the Great War* ([Lexington]: University Press of Kentucky, 1970), pp. 26-28,
89-93.

[35] Ibid., pp. 22-24; Ford to Creel, June 25, 1918, Ford to Shaw, July 3, 1918,
both quoted in ibid., pp. 90-91; Creel to Shaw, June 26, 1918, Shaw MSS. Lanier

But when the incident appeared nearly over, it was revived and made controversial by the intervention of Van Tyne, a distinguished historian at the University of Michigan who was doubling during the war as a propagandist for the National Security League. Known for an irascible temperament and acid vocabulary, Van Tyne released to the press a stinging indictment that labelled *Two Thousand Questions* a "masterpiece of pro-German propaganda." Assailing the book for its propagation of numerous examples of "disloyal and subtly pernicious" information, he censured the Review of Reviews Company for publishing it and Creel for preparing the introduction.[36]

Just as the controversy was at its worst—with arguments pro and con being aired in the press and even in Congress—Shaw was in England as the guest of the British Ministry of Information! Along with several newspaper reporters and such other prominent editors as Mark Sullivan of *Collier's* and Ellery Sedgwick of the *Atlantic Monthly,* Shaw left New York on August 24, 1918, on a ship sailing as part of a troop convoy destined for Liverpool.[37]

Shaw found the trip a tonic. Although his itinerary would be crowded from the moment the group landed in England, it offered a respite from his editorial duties which the war had made more demanding than ever. Since the trip was designed to familiarize influential journalists with war activities in England, the schedule Shaw followed was packed with luncheons, dinners, visits to industrial and military facilities, and

---

blamed the misunderstanding on his conception of the book. Anticipating that the war might be over by the time it was published, he viewed *Two Thousand Questions* not as a propaganda medium but as a forum for an honest discussion of the war. Lanier to Shaw, June 28, 1918, Shaw MSS.

36 Blakey, *Historians on the Homefront,* pp. 11, 63-64; Van Tyne NSL publicity release, reprinted in U.S., *Congressional Record,* 65th Cong., 2d sess., pp. 10380-81, quoted in ibid., p. 93.

37 The information in this and the following two paragraphs on Shaw's trip to Europe is found in the following sources: in his article, "In England and France, at the Climax," *American Review of Reviews,* LVIII (1918), 607-18, and in two diaries filed in the Shaw MSS. These are entitled "Diary kept by Albert Shaw on a visit to Europe, England and Scotland, 1918" and "Diary kept by Albert Shaw during visit to the front in France, 1918."

meetings with such dignitaries as King George V, Prime Minister David Lloyd George, and the American admirals William Sims and Hugh Rodman. Shaw himself spoke on several occasions and listened to numerous other speeches including one (Van Tyne would have been pleased to know) on German "beastliness." On September 27 Shaw left England for France in order to visit the front where he witnessed an artillery barrage and a memorable aerial encounter. He was also able to enjoy some time in Paris with his elder son, Albert, Jr., who was then stationed nearby, taking advanced artillery training with his American unit. After returning briefly to England, Shaw's party arrived back in New York in late October.

As he was en route home, Shaw learned that the war was virtually over when a duly authorized subordinate of Lloyd George showed the touring journalists details of the pending armistice agreement. Shaw fully realized, however, that stopping the shooting was only a preliminary step to the even more important one of creating a harmonious and stable postwar world. Like Wilson, whose lead on world affairs he now followed, Shaw had been interested in the theory of world organization at least as far back as his days at Johns Hopkins when he had been enrolled in Herbert Baxter Adams's course in international law. However, it seems likely that Warren Kuehl's description of Wilson's attitudes toward internationalism prior to 1914 best summarizes Shaw's own views on the subject: "His casual remarks reveal him as one of those many generalists of the prewar era who believed in a federation without devoting much thought to it."[38]

Circumstances now required that Shaw pay much attention to the details of peace-making, the debate over the League of Nations, and the place of the United States in the postwar world. Despite some reservations he had over Wilson's failure to appoint a distinguished Republican like Root or Hughes to the American peace delegation, Shaw earnestly supported

---

[38] Warren F. Kuehl, *Seeking World Order: The United States and International Organization to 1920* (Nashville: Vanderbilt University Press, 1969), p. 224.

the president's plans for achieving world security. He even enjoined Republican politicians not to turn the Versailles negotiations and the league question into partisan issues and made it plain that he regarded the League of Nations as the sine qua non of international stability. "There is nothing," Shaw wrote in April 1919, "that the United States professes to desire for herself and her neighbors that will not be the better safeguarded if world peace is maintained by a League of Nations. What we might seem to contribute to the League would be given back to us in double measure."[39]

Yet for the second time in five years he started to find fault with Wilson's handling of international questions. While he disliked Henry Cabot Lodge and did not think the Massachusetts senator's controversial reservations were necessary—since some were unwise and some already implied in the Constitution—he began asking gently why Wilson could not accept the better ones or at least agree to a compromise of some sort. In any event Shaw thought that the debate over the League of Nations was constructive in that it gave people an opportunity to consider the issues. He still expected the Senate to ratify the Versailles settlement.[40]

Then, in the summer of 1920, after becoming increasingly disturbed by Wilson's adamant opposition to compromise, Shaw called for a reassessment of the league's necessity. He now blamed Wilson for making the question of the league into a partisan issue, and while he initially seemed to expect that Republican presidential candidate Warren G. Harding would support American membership in the league in the likely event of his election, Shaw soon began insisting that it would be a mistake to join the League of Nations without further study.[41]

There were several reasons behind Shaw's growing coolness

<hr/>

[39] *American Review of Reviews*, LIX (1919), 10, 117-19, 344, 458-59.

[40] Ibid., LX (1919), 15, 240, 556-57, 563, LXI (1920), 117; Shaw to Will H. Hays, Dec. 6, 1919, Shaw to Millard Snider, Apr. 7, 1920, Shaw to John Sibley, June 15, 1943; all in Shaw MSS.

[41] *American Review of Reviews*, LXI (1920), 348-50, 566-70, LXII (1920), 117-18, 235, 342-44; Shaw to Harding, Sept. 23, 1920, Shaw MSS.

toward the league: anger about Wilson's refusal to compromise, partisanship (for the deadlock did result in the politiza-
tion of the league issue), and primarily a reappraisal of the
international situation. From the time discussion began on
whether to establish the League of Nations, Shaw made it
apparent that he considered the question of American interests
a central part of the debate. Shaw himself made persuasive
arguments for the case that our interests were safest in a just
and secure world, precisely what the league was meant to
promote. But once the euphoria of the immediate postwar
period had passed and the league actually began to function,
Shaw became disillusioned with it. He declared in an editorial:
"The League of Nations, as constructed at Paris, is a beautiful
creation in many respects; but, in practical application to the
out-of-door world, this League is not at all what it purports
to be."[42]

At the heart of this statement was Shaw's realization that
the war had caused social and economic dislocations as well
as military imbalances throughout a vast area extending from
central Europe to eastern Asia. To someone like Shaw whose
awareness of national interests was keen—yet naive, for he
habitually regarded American commitments as benevolent—
the situation seemed to invite years of disequilibrium. Cynical
even during the war years about the motives of the leading
Allied powers, he now posed the question whether they
regarded the league as Wilson had or merely as a vehicle to
consolidate the military and territorial advantages they had
derived from their triumph in the world war. Was the league
really a federation of nations, Shaw asked rhetorically, or one
of victors?[43]

Shaw concluded from this assessment of the situation that
it was not, after all, in the best interests of the United States
to accept membership in the league. Instead he suggested that
the new Republican administration could participate most

[42] *American Review of Reviews*, LXII (1920), 569.
[43] Ibid., LX (1919), 552, LXI (1920), 567, LXII (1920), 234, 340-44, 564, 567-68,
LXIII (1921), 20; Shaw to Beveridge, Oct. 1, 1923, Beveridge MSS.

intelligently in international affairs by promoting trade, by working for disarmament, and by advocating a world court, goals which he supported in the *Review*.[44]

[44] *American Review of Reviews*, LXIII (1921), 13, 348-50, 460-61, 564, LXIV (1921), 5-6, 12; Shaw to Harding, June 25, 1921, Shaw to Raymond Fosdick, Mar. 6, 1924, both in Shaw MSS; Kuehl, *Seeking World Order*, p. 302.

10

Guardian of American Values, 1916-1937

In the midst of the 1916 campaign, Congress, pressed by President Wilson to avert a threatened nationwide rail strike, enacted the Adamson Act, a law providing for a mandatory eight-hour day on America's railroads. In establishing maximum hours of labor the bill embodied one of the basic Progressive goals, yet Shaw reacted harshly to the news of its passage. "The arrogance was on the side of the railroad brotherhoods," he charged. "They made certain sweeping demands, refused to arbitrate them, and declared that they would paralyze commerce by stopping every wheel between the Atlantic and Pacific Coast on all railroads." "The war madness in Europe," he added in a revealing passage, "has aroused the spirit of restlessness and turbulence throughout the world. Our labor troubles in this country are but an echo of that disposition to appeal to force rather than to reason."[1]

Shaw's rejection of this last of Wilson's prewar reforms signalled a turning point in his treatment of domestic issues, for earlier in 1916, even after he had broken with Wilson over foreign affairs, he had still hailed the passage of the rural credits and child labor acts, claiming as he had done with previous Wilsonian reforms that they marked the fruition of Bull Moose objectives. Moreover it had been only four years since Shaw had been named to the arbitral board in the 1912 railroad dispute, an appointment which testified to his reputation for balanced judgment on labor-management questions. But, starting with his denunciation of the Adamson Act, Shaw began compiling a far different record, one marked by hostility to organized labor and unfeigned admiration for big business. It enabled him for the first time since Theodore Roosevelt's retirement from the presidency to claim substantial accord with Republican doctrine.[2]

His aboutface on economic issues was not adventitious, for he typically viewed such questions from the perspective of the national interest and not from any fixed point on the radical-conservative continuum. It was not the mere possession of economic power that he decried, but the abuse of it, the temptation to place class spirit above the national good. Like others of the nationalist wing of progressivism, Shaw had been quick to criticize the arrogance of business leaders during the period when the great trusts had been emerging even as he admired the productivity of large-scale enterprise. Conversely he had often commented favorably about organized labor while regarding it not as a permanent good but as a useful response to the shortsightedness of certain industrialists. Events during and immediately after the war persuaded him that conditions had changed.

Shaw's increasingly favorable attitude toward business became evident in his discussions of taxation and the rights of private enterprise. The question of taxation became controversial in 1917 when Congress began debate on how to finance American participation in the world war. Enactment of a bill was complicated by the fact that there were two sharply opposed views to be considered. Both cut across party lines. The conservative conceded the necessity for a modest increase in income tax rates but argued that borrowing and consumption taxes should be the mainstays of war finance. The progressive insisted on using taxation to achieve social reform and called for the employment of steeply graduated income, inheritance, and excess profits taxes.[3]

The resulting law, the War Revenue Act of 1917, represented a triumph for progressives, for it imposed an excess profits tax whose rates were graduated from 20 to 60 percent, an estate

[1] Link, *Wilson and the Progressive Era,* pp. 235-40; *American Review of Reviews,* LIV (1916), 362, 365-66.

[2] Ibid., pp. 140-41.

[3] Sidney Ratner, *American Taxation: Its History as a Social Force in Democracy* (New York: Norton, 1942), pp. 372-76, 382-83.

tax whose maximum level was 25 percent, and an income tax
of unprecedented bite. The last, remarked political economist
E. R. A. Seligman, was the first tax in the history of the world
"to take as much as two thirds of a man's income."[4]

Habitually orthodox on most matters on taxation—the significant exception being his advocacy of a levy on utility
franchises—Shaw disliked an income tax as a matter of principle
despite its legitimization by the sixteenth amendment to the
Constitution. But cognizant of the fact that waging war, even
on the scale he recommended, would require enormous
revenues, he grudgingly accepted high taxation as a necessity
and confined his arguments to particular aspects of the bill
as he followed its errant course through Congress. He reserved
most of his comment for the excess profits tax, to his way of
thinking the most objectionable part of the bill. A blanket
tax on profits, he warned, would handicap the war effort by
undermining business incentive to operate at maximum levels
of output. The advocates of such a tax had acted under a
delusion, for contrary to their beliefs war did not ordinarily
mean swollen profits. It was true that there were often large
book profits, but "in thousands of individual instances"
dividends were foregone so that profits could be reinvested in
capital expansion. To minimize the harm caused business a
distinction should be made between the normal level of profits
and war-induced gains. It was proper to tax the latter heavily.[5]

For a time it seemed as if the type of tax Shaw favored
would be enacted, but Robert LaFollette and others whom
Shaw had already dismissed as "aggressive radicals" for their
role in inflating the income tax rates blocked its passage. A
compromise measure that Shaw considered awkward and unfair
in that it taxed not only war profits per se but to an extent
normal profits as well was at last agreed upon.[6]

Another provision of the bill that Shaw disliked called for
a substantial increase (to be applied in stages) in the rates on

4 Ibid., pp. 376-81; Seligman quoted in ibid., p. 376.
5 American Review of Reviews, LVI (1917), 23, 357.
6 Ibid., LV (1917), 473, LVI (1917), 467; Ratner, American Taxation, pp.
377-78.

second-class mail. In his opinion this clause had no place in a bill that was otherwise concerned with taxation and was likely to be counterproductive anyhow since the periodicals which would be most affected by the rise in fees generated much business for the Post Office at the rates they were currently charged.[7]

The return of peace and the election in 1920 of a Republican administration which opposed progressive taxation at last freed Shaw to undertake a crusade for tax reduction. He continued to attack the excess profits tax and also began insisting that income taxes be slashed as well. An editorial headlined "Clearing the Way for Business" revealed his sentiments with clarity. "In short," he declared in endorsing the revenue plans submitted by Secretary of the Treasury Andrew Mellon, "taxation should be held down severely as regards the total amount of the nation's gross income that the Government lays its hands upon. . . . The excess-profits taxes, and the unduly high surtaxes on large incomes have defeated their own ends. They have interfered most seriously with the expansion of business and the full utilization of labor."[8]

Shaw paralleled his pleas for a reduction of taxation with arguments calling for greater freedom for business. During the war Shaw had endorsed as a justifiable way of mobilizing America's productive forces the far-reaching measures that were instituted to control the economy,[9] but immediately thereafter he began arguing that business had served America well throughout the war and deserved to be released from unreasonable restraints. The emergence of a new public-spirited type of businessman, imbued with what Shaw referred to as a "deepened sense of social responsibility," impressed him deeply. Shaw now lauded free enterprise and assailed the threats to it that the labor movement seemed to be posing in the aftermath of the war.[10]

[7] *American Review of Reviews,* LV (1917), 582, LVI (1917), 468.
[8] Ibid., LXIV (1921), 339-40.
[9] Ibid., LVIII (1918), 234, 570; Shaw to W. Z. Ripley, Apr. 25, 1917, Shaw MSS.
[10] *American Review of Reviews,* LX (1919), 5.

The Plumb Plan, a union-sponsored measure that advocated governmental purchase of all railroad lines in the United States, especially troubled him. Since the government had already taken control of the railroads during a wartime transportation crisis, the question that prevailed at the war's end was whether to return them to private management or to nationalize them altogether as the brotherhoods demanded. Shaw attempted to show that the Plumb Plan did not fit in with the established tradition of private management and government oversight and that in its details the proposal was impractical, filled with absurdities. Furthermore the aggressiveness with which the railroad brotherhoods argued their cause was a grave portent, for they were now in a position to "declare a general strike, paralyze all industry, and reduce great cities to starvation."[11]

Worried that labor's new militancy indicated a recrudescence of the class spirit that business had been spreading before the war, Shaw also viewed with alarm the many strikes that took place throughout 1919 and 1920. Whether discussing the Boston police strike, the soft coal strike that made John L. Lewis famous, or a New York printers strike which forced him and his key staff members into exile in Chicago where they temporarily published the *Review,* Shaw emphasized the theme that labor should beware "the temptations that come with the sense of power."[12] Privately he wondered whether unionism had outlived its usefulness, while in print he linked labor excesses with un-Americanism and "Sovietism."[13]

Shaw's inclusion in his editorials of these twin specters was more than just the cheap device it appeared to be, for there is much evidence to show that the war and the mood of unrest it fostered revived Shaw's latent fear of disorder and caused him to defend American institutions with a stridency like

11 Ibid., pp. 230-36, 568; Shaw to Will H. Hays, Dec. 6, 1919, Shaw MSS.

12 *American Review of Reviews,* LX (1919), 229-31, 455-60, 465, LXI (1920), 460. On the printers strike see Shaw to J. F. Taintor, Oct. 27, 1919, Howard Florance to C. W. A. Veditz, Nov. 11, 1919, Florance to Shaw, Nov. 19, 20, 1919, all in Shaw MSS.

13 Shaw to Herbert Magoun, Mar. 22, 1920, Shaw MSS; *American Review of Reviews,* LX (1919), 565, LXI (1920), 13, LXVI (1922), 228-29.

that he had exhibited in the troubled 1890s. The examples are numerous. He again espoused immigration restriction with much of the fervor he had shown a generation before. He denounced the Klan, but not without appending an occasional qualification.[14] He was positive that Sacco and Vanzetti were guilty of murder just as charged and that the issue that they had been convicted more on the basis of their anarchistic philosophy than on reliable evidence was a red herring intended to excite the gullible. The real anarchists were the picketers who demonstrated in their behalf.[15] He also regarded Mussolini rather favorably. "It is easy to criticize a revolution of this type," he wrote of Italian Fascism, "but Italy may well be congratulated upon its escape from the clutches of a revolution of the Moscow type. It had to be one thing or the other; and the Italians were lucky in their successful choice of solvency and work. The future will give plenty of opportunity for the vagaries and eccentricities of the many people who, for one reason or another, dislike the discipline of Fascism, which deals so roughly with fools."[16]

Shaw was preaching a double standard. As he wrote off Italian liberty, Shaw worried throughout the 1920s that the American way of life was being endangered by the federal bureaucracy. Both free enterprise and America's hallowed individualism seemed to be at stake. Taxes were excessively high and resulted in an unjustifiable invasion of privacy; the number of federal officials had proliferated beyond reason; the independent regulatory commissions had become so many "Frankensteins." "What some people call 'liberalism,'" Shaw instructed Charles Evans Hughes in a letter that called attention to the threat posed by the bureaucratic establishment,

14 Ibid., LXVII (1923), 14-15, LXIX (1924), 349-50, LXX (1924), 122-25.

15 Ibid., LXXVI (1927), 135, 227-32; Shaw to William Starr Myers, Sept. 27, 1927, Shaw to A. Lawrence Lowell, Oct. 4, 1927, Shaw to Felix Frankfurter, Oct. 4, Nov. 29, 1927, all in Shaw MSS.

16 *Review of Reviews*, LXXXI (Jan. 1930), 36. Other indications of Shaw's approval of Mussolini's regime are seen in *American Review of Reviews*, LXIX (1924), 469, and LXXIII (1926), 351. For the attitudes, favorable and otherwise, of American intellectuals toward Italian Fascism, see John P. Diggins, *Mussolini and Fascism: The View from America* (Princeton: Princeton University Press, 1972), 42-73, 204-61, 444-95.

"would not be in the interests of the people, but exactly the reverse."[17] Those who advocated placing curbs on Wall Street during the speculative fever of 1929 were wrong, argued Shaw. Speculation was bad, to be sure, but the government had given it indirect encouragement through the capital gains tax; things would take care of themselves.[18]

Shaw was aware that his position on these and related issues might cast doubt on his fealty to progressivism, for in the New Nationalist approach to reform bureaucracy had played a vital role. But as he told William Allen White in 1931, he felt that he had long since "earned the right to be called a Republican Progressive." He insisted that he still was one.[19] Many former Bull Moosers had again become loyal Republicans and, said Shaw, without betraying their convictions; in fact, most Republicans were now progressive. The issues that had split Old Guard and Progressive in 1912 had disappeared years ago. Those who acknowledged this represented the true spirit of progressivism which meant the capacity to recognize change. Reform was still necessary—for instance, government regulation of the recklessly competitive crude oil industry was appropriate—yet it was folly to berate business as though it were still the age of the robber barons.[20] Business, he argued even during the depression, had become "institutionalized" (as he had predicted it would in his *Average Man* essays) and exemplified "success based upon scientific improvement and admirable public service."[21]

Politicians like Robert LaFollette, George Norris, and Smith W. Brookhart received Shaw's contempt for their failure to recognize this. With the exception of LaFollette who bolted

17 *American Review of Reviews*, LXXI (1925), 346, 566-67, LXXVI (1927), 354; *Review of Reviews*, LXXIX (May 1929), 36; Shaw to Hughes, Feb. 5, 1930, Shaw to Paul Shoup, Jan. 27, 1931, Shaw to Harlean James, Jan. 15, 1932, Shaw to William Dyche, Jan. 16, 1932, all in Shaw MSS.
18 *Review of Reviews*, LXXIX (May 1929), 34-35, LXXX (Aug. 1929), 30, and (Dec.), 38-40; *Review of Reviews and World's Work*, LXXXVI (Dec. 1932), 23.
19 Shaw to White, Mar. 20, 1931, Shaw MSS.
20 *American Review of Reviews*, LXI (1920), 573-74, LXVII (1923), 236, LXXI (1925), 7, 228; *Review of Reviews*, LXXVIII (May 1929), 36, LXXXIII (Mar. 1931), 32, and (Apr.), 34.
21 Shaw to James, Jan. 15, 1932, Shaw MSS.

in 1924 to lead a new third-party movement, they masqueraded as Republicans while repeatedly breaking party ranks to ride off on personal hobbies. Norris's claim to the label *progressive* struck Shaw as ridiculous, for the Nebraskan's advocacy of a federally operated hydroelectric project at Muscle Shoals, Alabama, typified the irresponsibility Shaw loathed. Norris had not only countered the policies of three successive Republican administrations, all of which wanted the location to be developed by private capital,[22] but his arguments for government operation of power and other facilities at Muscle Shoals relied upon vague fulminations against something he called the "Power Trust" and had no "sane or practical grasp."[23]

At an earlier date in his career Shaw might have agreed with someone like Norris or at least have acknowledged that any differences between their views represented but an honest divergence of opinion. Populists and Coxeyites, he had once asserted, were not heretics but only misguided former neighbors of his. But since then he had become increasingly self-righteous and intolerant of dissent, perhaps growing somewhat crotchety as he aged, and consequently was almost unable to write dispassionately about those whose views he disapproved of. Norris was guilty on several counts. He was antediluvian in his distrust of private enterprise and visionary in his espousal of ideas tainted by sovietism. He was a meddler as well. Rather than concern himself with the Tennessee River, on which Muscle Shoals was located, he should confine his thinking to plans for developing the Platte Valley of his own Nebraska. Southerners had sound theories and should be allowed to formulate their own plans for the development of Muscle Shoals.[24]

22 *American Review of Reviews*, LXX (1924), 9, LXXI (1925), 244, LXXII (1926), 17; *Review of Reviews*, LXXXI (Feb. 1930), 40, LXXXIII (Mar. 1931), 30; Shaw to Walter Head, Feb. 3, 1931, Shaw to Bruce Barton, Mar. 29, 1931, both in Shaw MSS.

23 Shaw to White, Mar. 20, 1931, Shaw MSS. See also Shaw to Thomas W. Martin, Feb. 25, 1931, Shaw to Owen D. Young, Mar. 21, 1931, both in Shaw MSS.

24 *Review of Reviews*, LXXXIII (Feb. 1931), 35 and (Apr. 1931), 36; Shaw, "Owen D. Young as a Public Servant," ibid. (Feb. 1931), 42-45, and "The Unsolved Problem of Muscle Shoals," ibid. (Apr. 1931), 49-53. See also Shaw, "Control

Despite Shaw's contempt for Norris the two actually had in common a sincere concern for the plight of rural America. Planning to write a book on farming for a series edited by President Kenyon Butterfield of the State Agricultural College of Massachusetts, Shaw displayed a sentimental attachment to farming that derived from memories of his youth in Ohio and Iowa.[25] He saw in agriculture the underpinning of America's basic institutions, "the principal stronghold of the doctrines of private property, democratic equality, and the family unit."[26]

Shaw did not allow this nostalgic vision of farming to obscure the commercial aspect of agriculture. Fully aware that farmers all over the United States faced economic hardships (as he did on his dairy farm), Shaw believed that the difficulty was most acute in the great one-crop regions of the South and Middle Border where overproduction had become a chronic problem. Much could be done to improve the situation if the type of trained intelligence that had successfully been applied to the rehabilitation of American cities in the previous generation could now be applied to the problems facing rural America. Farmers could do a lot to help themselves simply by developing a professional outlook and studying soil conservation and crop rotation, accounting methods, and marketing techniques. Government also had to become involved. Local agencies could provide good roads and the latest in consolidated rural schools; state governments could endeavor to promote crop restriction by working with farm cooperatives, while the federal government could provide not only credit facilities, as it was already doing, but also encouragement in the form of higher prices.[27]

A plan to boost prices had already come before the nation

---

of Power," *Proceedings of the Academy of Political Science*, XIV (May 1930), 3-10, for a refreshingly genial statement of the problem.

[25] Shaw to Kenyon Butterfield, Sept. 12, 1923, Shaw to Edward Healey, Apr. 17, 1924, both in Shaw MSS.

[26] *American Review of Reviews*, LXVII (1923), 236.

[27] Shaw Memorandum for Albert Shaw, Jr., Nov. 17, 1923, Shaw MSS; *American Review of Reviews*, LXVIII (1923), 119-20, 236, 245; *Review of Reviews*, LXXXII (Sept. 1930), 26-27; Shaw, "Better Economic Organization of Agriculture," *Proceedings of the Academy of Political Science*, XII (1926), 503-11.

in 1924 in the form of the McNary-Haugen bill, the purpose of which was to raise the prices of several basic farm commodities to a so-called ratio or parity level. Three years later it passed Congress only to be vetoed by President Coolidge. In 1928 a version modified to meet his objections received a second veto. Although Coolidge's objections were based in part on the fear of the enlarged bureaucracy that implementation of the McNary-Haugen plan would have necessitated, Shaw thought that the president was mistaken in vetoing the bills. In this case the end justified the means, Shaw believed. Since a prosperous agricultural community was essential to maintaining the American way of life, he reasoned, and since governmental policies designed to stimulate production of the basic crops during the wartime emergency had resulted in aggravating the long run ills of farming, the federal government had a unique responsibility to aid the American farmer. Whatever its liabilities, McNary-Haugenism was worth a try.[28]

Shaw favored Frank Lowden for the presidency in 1928, thinking that the former Illinois governor was most likely to take action in behalf of the farmer. Yet he easily acquiesced in Hoover's nomination and strongly supported his candidacy against that of Al Smith, who, he thought, was too much the product of the Tammany system of politics to be an effective president.[29]

Shaw's skepticism about Hoover quickly yielded to admiration for the way he behaved under the adversity of the depression. He not only recommended measures like a system of mortgage banks and the Reconstruction Finance Corporation to shore up business that seemed eminently sensible to Shaw, but the president also had the moral integrity to reject the various panaceas that threatened to unbalance the budget and harass private enterprise.[30]

28 *American Review of Reviews,* LXIX (1924), 460, LXXV (1927), 14, 240-41, 350-51, LXXVII (1928), 453; Shaw to Frank O. Lowden, Apr. 23, 1927, Shaw MSS.
29 *American Review of Reviews,* LXXVII (1928), 460, LXXVIII (1928), 119-24, 130-31, 241; Shaw to Samuel C. Mitchell, Jan. 18, 1928, Shaw to Gov. John Hammill, July 21, 1928, both in Shaw MSS.
30 *Review of Reviews,* LXXXI (Jan. 1930), 29, 37, and (Apr.), 34, LXXXIV

At seventy-five years of age Albert Shaw was like a good many other venerable progressives in that he emphasized the nostalgic when discussing the depression. In so doing, he all but repudiated the ideas on cities he had developed forty years before in favor of a still earlier vision of the wholesome life. The image he held was of Paddy's Run or of Grinnell, or of some felicitous combination of the two. Over the long run, he suggested, the decentralization of industry would do much to stabilize the economy by getting men away from the artificiality of cities and into settings where they could more readily provide for themselves in hard times. Patience seemed the best prescription for the current depression. "Mollicoddling by social doctrinaires and misguided philanthropists" would only make things worse, but if the public remained calm and abided by traditional virtues like spunk and self-reliance, conditions would improve; business crashes were self-limiting. As Shaw quaintly stated it, "success to the lad who scorns to rely upon a job-giver, a trade-union, or a loud-talking propagandist of economic revolution!"[31]

The election of 1932, Shaw believed, would be critical in determining the course of the depression. The important thing was to sustain the confidence of business leaders. The Republicans, he thought, were sure to renominate Hoover, whose election would be just the thing to reassure businessmen as to the continued soundness of federal policy. But the Democrats represented an uncertain factor. They would do well to nominate either banker Melvin Traylor or General Electric president Owen Young. Both represented the public-spirited type of entrepreneur whose contributions to the wartime mobilization effort he admired so much. Newton Baker, Wilson's former secretary of war, would also be a good choice,[32]

(Nov. 1931), 32, LXXXV (Jan. 1932), 20, (Apr.), 13-14, (May), 12, and (June), 11-12, LXXXVI (Aug. 1932), 18-19.

31 Ibid. (July 1932), 10; Otis L. Graham, Jr., *An Encore for Reform: The Old Progressives and the New Deal* (New York: Oxford University Press, 1967), pp. 71-72.

32 Shaw, "Owen D. Young," *American Review of Reviews*, LXXXIII (Feb. 1931), 42-45; L. W. Burnham, "Melvin Traylor," ibid., LXXXV (Mar. 1932), 25-27, 58-59; *Review of Reviews and World's Work*, LXXXVI (Oct. 1932), 13, 17; Shaw to

but there was a chance that the nomination might go to New York governor Franklin D. Roosevelt. While Hoover could readily defeat him, the mere candidacy of this "shallow and smooth-tongued demagogue" who had mishandled the power, taxation, and other issues that had arisen during his governorship of New York would disturb business. Besides there was always the possibility that the "prejudiced and ignorant" electorate would end up voting him into the presidency.[33]

Shaw's initial optimism about Hoover's bid for a second term soon yielded to the realization that 1932 would be a Democratic year. Although he would have preferred to see a Democrat other than F.D.R. profit from the public's inclination to repudiate the party in power, Shaw made an effort to reexamine his qualifications for the presidency. Corresponding with Louis Howe about a sketch of F.D.R. that was being prepared for the *Review*, the editor suggested that in two or three instances parallels might be made between the careers of the two Roosevelts, Franklin and Theodore. And in retrospect Shaw even concluded that the decisiveness of F.D.R.'s victory was fortunate; it was best that he take office with a substantial popular mandate. Alert to the need for national unity in the bleak early months of 1933, Shaw resolved to support Roosevelt editorially, for criticism of him at this point would be divisive and would impair his ability to withstand the demands of those who advocated inflation and other mischievous nostrums.[34]

Roosevelt's first months in office surpassed Shaw's expectations. Not only did he adroitly handle the banking crisis and protect the Treasury from monetary "fanaticism" and from

Martin Davey, Feb. 12, 1932, Shaw to Patrick J. Hurley, July 29, 1932, both in Shaw MSS.

[33] Shaw to George White, June 1, 1932, Shaw to Gen. James C. Harbord, June 3, 1932, both in Shaw MSS. On the issues of Roosevelt's governorship see *Review of Reviews*, LXXXII (Oct. 1930), 42-43, LXXXIII (May 1931), 29, LXXXIV (Dec. 1931), 32, LXXXV (Feb. 1932), 23; Shaw to Walter Head, Nov. 8, 1930, Shaw to H. C. Hopson, Sept. 30, 1931, both in Shaw MSS.

[34] Shaw to Josephus Daniels, July 5, 1932, Shaw to Howe, July 13, 1932, Shaw to A. H. Ferguson, Oct. 4, 1932, Shaw to Lucy Shaw Stephenson, Nov. 11, 1932, Shaw to Wilbur C. Hall, Nov. 23, 1932, Shaw to Sen. L. J. Dickinson, Sept. 18, 1933, Shaw to James, Nov. 27, 1933, all in Shaw MSS.

the onslaughts of the "impudent" veterans and bureaucrats lobbies,[35] but his administration launched an impressive program of reconstruction. The NIRA which modified the outmoded Sherman Anti-Trust Act by authorizing firms in the same industry to make agreements aimed at controlling wasteful competition seemed "almost overwhelming in its possibilities for good."[36] The AAA had merit, for it offered a plan that might arrest the decline of rural culture.[37] Even the TVA (despite its connection with the Muscle Shoals project) appeared to hold "fascinating" potential.[38]

Enthusiastic as his vocabulary was, Shaw's endorsement of the emerging New Deal was at heart fragile, for its spirit and techniques were alien to him as to many of his one-time associates in reform. Those former progressives—Roosevelt in New York and Gifford Pinchot in Pennsylvania—who held public office in the 1930s or who were or had been involved in social work were inclined to adjust their conceptions of reform in response to the crisis of the depression.[39] But those like Shaw whose contact with social problems was largely limited to the observer's role tended to be more rigid in their outlook and, as Otis Graham has remarked, were apt to measure the New Deal against "the intellectual and moral standards of their own triumphant era before World War I."[40]

Although Shaw still thought of himself as a reformer, he could accept neither the tempo nor the direction of reform in the 1930s. He insisted that change be orderly, that it be based upon meticulous study of the pertinent data, that it promote the national welfare rather than that of any special interest, and that it take place within the framework of the American

[35] Shaw to Frederick Koker, Nov. 28, 1933, Shaw MSS; *Review of Reviews and World's Work*, LXXXVII (Apr. 1933), 14, and (May), 7-10, and (June), 15, LXXXVIII (Sept. 1933), 14. Shaw was also pleased to see the dry lobby rebuffed, for he had never been too keen about national prohibition and recognized that it had failed to win popular acceptance. The government could use the revenue from the excise on liquor. Ibid., LXXXIX (Jan. 1934), 44-45.

[36] Ibid., LXXXVIII (July 1933), 14, and (Oct.), 12.

[37] Ibid., (Sept.), 11.

[38] Shaw to George Fort Milton, May 26, 1933, Shaw MSS.

[39] Graham, *Encore for Reform*, pp. 57-69.

[40] Ibid., p. 66.

heritage of individualism and capitalism. His response to a reader who had complained of the *Review*'s conservatism was typical: "We believe ourselves perfectly open to new ideas, but also we hope that we are not unmindful of the history of this and other countries."[41]

Shaw supported the New Deal until the spring of 1934, but his correspondence and an occasional remark in the *Review* reveal that he had begun to have misgivings about it some months beforehand. Encouraged by New Deal policies, labor had become dangerously militant; certain bureaucrats were behaving with undue zeal; at times events in the capital seemed puzzling. Shaw's confession to a friend that he thought he could learn more about the New Deal by reading the *New York Times* than by visiting Washington anticipated his ultimate sense of bewilderment and estrangement.[42]

By April 1934 he no longer felt obliged to mute his antagonism toward the New Deal. "Last year it was necessary to follow the White House lead," he explained to an acquaintance some months later. "[But] I am not thinking it my duty to uphold any longer the policies of the so-called 'New Deal' and the Brain Trust."[43] Save for a brief editorial truce that Shaw observed in the aftermath of Roosevelt's overwhelming re-election in 1936, he belabored New Deal policies until financial difficulties forced him to retire from publishing in 1937 when he donated the *Review*'s short-lived successor, the *Digest*, to some young associates.

Initially Shaw concentrated his ire on misguided administrators like Hugh Johnson and James Farley, on interest groups which manipulated the government for their own ends, and on programs that did not work out as he had hoped. He grew disillusioned with the NRA and TVA (and later the AAA) and inevitably came to despise the relief system for its pro-

---

41 Shaw to Martin Wilson, Nov. 21, 1933, Shaw MSS.

42 Shaw to L. J. Hackney, June 3, 1933, Shaw to Frederic Delano, Aug. 15, 1933, Shaw to Roger Babson, Aug. 28, 1933, all in Shaw MSS; *Review of Reviews and World's Work*, LXXXVIII (Oct. 1933), 14, and (Nov.), 11-13, and (Dec.), 16.

43 Ibid., LXXXIX (Apr. 1934), 44, and (May), 42-43, and (June), 9; Shaw to Hurley, Aug. 30, 1934, Shaw MSS.

fligacy and stifling of self-initiative.[44] If funding were terminated, he observed in an unusually bitter statement,
"Several million lazy fellows, who have been refusing to work
because they preferred to draw relief money, would have to
take care of themselves on the 'root-hog-or-die' principle."[45]

With the enactment in 1935 of new measures like the
Wagner and Social Security Acts, which he deemed paternal-
istic, Shaw became increasingly disturbed by what seemed to
be the leftward direction of the New Deal, and he made
Roosevelt a frequent target, aiming at him the type of barb that
was common in Liberty League manifestoes. Shaw's anguish
at the trend of events was nowhere more apparent than in a
letter to Herbert Hoover, whom he now considered a friend
and confided in accordingly. Shaw wrote:

I would be rather pleased if you would read my parallel [in the
December *Review of Reviews*] between Haroun al-Raschid and
F.D.R. in his capacity as twentieth-century Caliph. This strange
assumption of personal government on the part of a man elected
to perform the duties of the presidency is to my mind a more
astonishing thing than Hitlerism in Germany. It could not be
tolerated, but for the use of money in sums beyond human
comprehension to deaden the principles of more than half of the
total American electorate.

It is going to be hard to awaken the conscience of a bribed and
corrupted nation. I wish I could face the future a little more
cheerfully. Drunken sailors are expected to sober up when out at
sea. We, as a nation in contrast, while far out at sea find our
Ship of State run by a crew of Bedlamites.[46]

[44] *Review of Reviews and World's Work*, XC (Aug. 1934), 9, 13, 50, and
(Sept.), 20, and (Oct.), 24-26, and (Nov.), 21-23, and (Dec.), 17; *Review of
Reviews*, XCI (Feb. 1935), 15.

[45] Ibid. (May 1935), 20. Although he disliked federal dispensation of relief,
Shaw respected Harry Hopkins, also a Grinnell alumnus, and usually exonerated
him of guilt in the misuse of funds. The culprit was Postmaster General Farley
who, he believed, calculatingly used government largesse to purchase votes for
the Democratic party.

[46] *Review of Reviews*, XCII (Aug. 1935), 16, and (Sept.), 18, and (Dec.), 13,
XCIII (Jan. 1936), 15, and (Feb.), 17; Shaw to Hoover, Nov. 25, 1935, Shaw
MSS; George Wolfskill, *The Revolt of the Conservatives: A History of the
American Liberty League, 1934-1940* (Boston: Houghton Mifflin, 1962), pp.
102-142.

For all its vitriol Shaw's criticism of the New Deal was not without certain insights. Though somewhat overdrawn and colored by the yeoman mystique, his analysis of the farm program was shrewd. Shaw had originally held high hopes for it, feeling as he had for many years that the viability of agriculture needed to be restored. In practice, however, the AAA in its various stages failed to achieve the desired results. In Shaw's view its drafting and administration had been shaped by the demands of wheat producers from the belt of states bounded by Nebraska on the north and Texas on the south. The key AAA policies of acreage reduction and compensatory benefit payments had made these "barons" wealthy but had failed to do much for the "real" farmers who lived east of the Missouri River. Shaw believed that it was impossible to administer a centralized agricultural program that would be equitable for all. The prevailing regulations had helped Kansas wheat producers while harming their counterparts in Pennsylvania. And even if one were to justify a restrictive policy in the case of wheat, it was inappropriate for cotton (which could not afford to lose its overseas markets) and, as Shaw's own farming experience testified, for dairying.[47]

By the time Shaw retired in 1937, the impetus of the New Deal had been spent. It was therefore fitting that his editorial valedictory discussed the New Deal as a phase in America's constitutional history. Appropriately subdued in tone, the editorial took as its point of departure the approaching sesquicentennial of the Constitutional Convention. The drafting of the Constitution had been a monumental event, but behind it lay the long experience of the colonies and local communities in developing instruments of republican government. Recent events had brought the federal government as never before into the daily lives of the people, diverting to its use immense sums of money. Roosevelt's goal of a more abundant life for

[47] *Review of Reviews and World's Work,* LXXXVIII (Sept. 1933), 11, and (Oct.), 14-15, LXXXIX (Mar. 1934), 15. XC (July 1934), 52; *Review of Reviews,* XCI (Apr. 1935), 18, XCII (Oct. 1935), 17, XCIII (Mar. 1936), 25; *Digest,* I (Sept. 18, 1937), 12-13, and (Sept. 25), 12-13; Shaw to (Mr.) Boyle, Nov. 4, 1933, Shaw to Hall, July 2, 1934, both in Shaw MSS.

Americans was unexceptionable but his methods of achieving it misguided; it was unlikely that good times could be conferred by the federal bureaucracy.[48]

Progress, observed Shaw, originated with individuals of character and initiative and with their fellow citizens who were prepared to cooperate in the spirit of neighborliness. Although the people had the right to employ their agencies of government as they wished, the American tradition was one of "federative balance." State and local institutions of government were best equipped to supplement individual resourcefulness in the fight against social ills. The federal role in it should remain confined to the few tasks it could best perform. "Let us celebrate the Constitution as a plan of government," Shaw concluded in a restorationist vein, "but also let us not forget that it rests upon the much older and equally permanent plans and principles of the state governments, and of the local communities which form the constituent parts of each one of our forty-eight commonwealths."[49]

[48] *Digest,* I (Oct. 23, 1937), 12-14.
[49] Ibid., p. 14.

11

A Sabbatical at Last, 1937-1947

The demise of Shaw's magazine was not a sudden or, as an obituary might have put it, unexpected event, but simply the passing of an elderly invalid. The end had been almost two decades in arriving, for soon after the conclusion of the first world war, the *Review of Reviews* passed into the declining stages of what can be termed a magazine's life cycle. This cycle, as Theodore Peterson has shown, includes several phases: the conception by the periodical's editor of a new approach—"The Big Idea," a struggle for survival during the early years, success and with it a hardening of the "Idea" into a formula, loss of contact with its constituency, petty experimentation with the contents, a desperate groping for some means of salvation, and finally failure.[1]

Since the decline of the *Review* coincided with Shaw's increasingly vociferous conservatism, the question inevitably arises whether a causal sequence existed between the erosion of the periodical's circulation and its editorial policy. Probably not. In the absence of information which by its nature would be almost impossible to obtain, it could just as well be argued that Shaw's orthodoxy cemented the loyalty of enough readers to keep the *Review* afloat at a time when long-term changes within the periodical industry were sapping its vitality. It was these changes, and management's uncertain response to them, that made the demise of the *Review* inevitable. In modern American life there was to be a place either for the small-circulation opinion magazines or for the new lavishly financed mass magazines. The fundamental problem of the *Review of Reviews* was that it fitted into neither category.

Evidence that the *Review* had reached its geriatric years

came in the early 1920s with the loss of the circulation that had been gained during the war. A promotional campaign initiated in 1923 by Albert Shaw, Jr., who had joined the *Review*'s business staff four years previously, briefly stabilized conditions. But an irreversible slide soon set in, and by 1926 circulation had fallen to the 150,000 mark, or about where it had been in 1900. The volume of advertising was declining apace. With the *Literary Digest* still doing well and the new and sprightly *Time* generating widespread appeal, the weeklies with their advantage in immediacy now had all the better of things.[2]

The gravity of matters was made evident in early 1928 when Charles Lanier decided to sell the sizeable share of the American *Review* that he had acquired from the Stead estate in 1913. Although the timing of his decision was influenced by illness, financial considerations undoubtedly played a part in his thinking, for Lanier had recognized as early as 1926 that "the very life of the magazine" was in jeopardy and requested in vain that he be authorized to hire and fire and to implement plans he had made for revitalizing the *Review*.[3] Business had deteriorated since then, the year 1927 resulting in the first of a long series of annual deficits on the *Review*'s balance sheets. Even though Lanier had evidently become a source of dissension, his wish to sell precipitated a crisis. It meant that Shaw would either have to join him in selling, chance the uncertainty inherent in getting a new partner in the unlikely event an outsider wished to buy into the *Review*, or else—as he decided to do—purchase Lanier's share of the business for a steep $225,000. Shaw was reluctant to undertake the greater financial and managerial responsibilities that Lanier's retirement meant, but blaming his erstwhile partner for the *Review*'s difficulties, he predicted that things would now improve.[4]

---

1 Peterson, *Magazines in the Twentieth Century*, pp. 68, 119, 145, 156, 174-76; Clay S. Felker, "Life Cycles in the Age of Magazines," *Antioch Review*, XXIX (Spring 1969), 20-27.

2 Albert Shaw, Jr., to author, Mar. 18, 30, 1969; Mott, *American Magazines*, IV, 574-75, 663, V, 293-307.

3 Lanier to Shaw, Dec. 4, 1926, Shaw to Frank Simonds, Jan. 31, 1928, Shaw to John C. Fisher, Feb. 17, 1928, Shaw to Mary and John C. Fisher, June 17, 1929, all in Shaw MSS.

The *Review*, however, remained in trouble, and with the first issue of 1929 changes were instituted designed to give it the verve and the enhanced appeal to advertisers that Lanier had said it needed. First, a larger page size was adopted to allow for a handsomer format with bolder print and a more appealing use of illustrations. The larger page, which conformed with that used by many other periodicals, also had the advantage of offering a convenience and an economy to those advertisers who purchased space in more than one magazine. Second, the *Review* also—and quite belatedly because of Shaw's objections—began interspersing advertisements and text in an effort to make the former more noticeable. There were also changes in content. Some minor features were deleted, while "Leading Articles" received an overhauling, the number of reviews being slashed and the department subsumed into a new and more attractively presented section called "News and Opinion."[5]

With the onset of the depression, the situation became even grimmer. Almost one-third of the already dwindling amount of advertising space was lost just in the depression's first year, though thanks to an increase in rates in late 1929 the initial decline in gross revenue was only a deceptively modest 10 percent.[6] The situation, however, was indeed serious, for the magazine was already losing money. For instance, in 1929 with a gross advertising revenue of almost $350,000 the *Review* was operating at a deficit of more than $100,000. And this in what has been described as "a lush year for magazines generally." Within two years the gross advertising income had fallen by

---

[4] Memorandum to Father from Albert Shaw, Jr. (undated but probably 1931), Shaw to George Allen, Feb. 20, 1928, Shaw to Mary and John C. Fisher, June 17, 1929, Shaw to Sir Henry Lunn, June 28, 1928, Jan. 8, 1932, Howard Florance to Brown Bros. Harriman & Co., July 6, 1931, all in Shaw MSS.

[5] Shaw to Francis H. Sisson, Nov. 19, 1920, Florance to Shaw, Oct. 22, 1928, Feb. 28, 1929, *Review of Reviews* to Alfred Frankenstein, Oct. 30, 1928, *Review of Reviews* to William McAndrew, Nov. 3, 1928, all in Shaw MSS; Albert Shaw, Jr., to author, Mar. 18, 30, 1969; Peterson, *Magazines in the Twentieth Century*, pp. 34-35.

[6] Magazine Publishers Association to author, Feb. 24, Mar. 3, 1969; Albert Shaw, Jr., to author, Mar. 18, 1969; Memorandum to Father from Albert Shaw, Jr. (1931), Shaw MSS.

more than half, and, to compound the difficulty, Shaw's other publication, the fiction-oriented *Golden Book Magazine,* was in similar straits.[7]

The collapse of the *Review*'s circulation coincided with a trend toward more sophisticated advertising techniques which might have prejudiced its survival even had sales remained stable. During and since the first world war, the advertising industry had grown and had become increasingly rationalized. National advertising was now controlled by large agencies which had become concerned with market research and which wanted to know not only how well a periodical sold but who bought it. Because of this "what had been popular magazines now became 'mass media.' "[8] Albert Shaw, Jr., who had succeeded Lanier as business manager and now seemed central in formulating policy, spelled out the problem for his father. Periodicals of specialized or mass constituencies were the preferred advertising medium. The *Review* was neither, its primary appeal being to people with less than $10,000 annual income, or as he explained it, to "the scholar, the college president, and the high-school student." This type of constituency had always comprised a large share of the *Review's* traditional one and was something Albert Shaw had once valued. But to appeal to this group was "to get off the track," pointed out his son, who suggested that they direct the *Review* toward business executives.[9]

Shaw revealed his awareness of the *Review*'s desperate need for corporate advertising in a series of letters, by turn poignant and indignant, that he sent to business leaders like Henry Ford and railroader Paul Shoup. Although virtually every one of these letters stressed the point that it was to the businessman's advantage to help sustain the *Review* as a bulwark of conservatism in a time of depression and disintegrating standards,[10]

---

7 Peterson, *Magazines in the Twentieth Century*, p. 151. A sketch of the *Golden Book,* which the Shaws published from 1925 to 1935, is in Mott, *American Magazines,* V, 116-24.

8 Greene, *America's Heroes*, pp. 288-89.

9 Shaw to Walter Head, June 25, 1930, Memorandum to Father from Albert Shaw, Jr. (1931), both in Shaw MSS.

10 Shaw to Allen, Feb. 20, 1928, Nov. 17, 1931, Shaw to Gen. Charles H.

they did not mean that he was willing to sacrifice the integrity of his "Progress" editorials to business expediency. He was just calling attention to a well-established fact.

To compensate for the continued dearth of advertising revenue a policy of strict retrenchment was initiated in 1932. Pared to sixty-four pages of text and advertising—less than one-fourth the size it had attained in its most prosperous years, the *Review* now featured an abbreviated "Progress," caricatures, and some contributed articles. These were much diminished in length, for the writers' fees that had once amounted to upwards of a thousand dollars monthly had become an intolerable burden.[11] Although Shaw usually opposed substantial change or accepted it only with reluctance, the new policy had his approval. He thought it might even prove a blessing in disguise. "I do not believe in the impertinence of *Time*," he instructed an associate, "but at least they understand that the public wants the thing stated brightly and very briefly."[12]

There were additional changes, too numerous to detail, for throughout its final decade the *Review* was tinkered with in a spate of experimentation typical of a dying magazine. Departments were added, dropped, sometimes lengthened, more often shortened, and shifted about in kaleidoscopic confusion. However appropriate each move seemed, such incessant change was almost sure to be self-defeating; it had the effect of announcing that the *Review* was in trouble.[13]

Sherrill, Nov. 28, 1930, Shaw to Ford, Dec. 5, 1930, Shaw to Shoup, Jan. 27, 1931, Aug. 17, 1932, Shaw to Owen Young, Mar. 21, 1931, all in Shaw MSS. Peterson, *Magazines in the Twentieth Century*, pp. 20-43, makes some interesting observations on the subtleties of the relationship between periodical publishers and advertisers.

[11] Shaw to Simonds, Jan. 13, 1931, Jan. 7, 1932, Shaw to Henry Morgenthau, Jr., July 7, 1932, Florance to Charles F. Thwing, Apr. 27, 1932, all in Shaw MSS. Letters mentioning the handsome fees once paid to writers are scattered throughout the Shaw MSS. Among them are: *Review of Reviews* to William Hard, Judson Welliver, and Alfred Zimmern, all on Feb. 24, 1927, *Review of Reviews* to Agnes Laut and Frank Simonds, both on Jan. 26, 1928.

[12] Shaw to Florance, Aug. 3, 1932, *Review of Reviews* to P. W. Wilson, July 6, 1933, both in Shaw MSS.

[13] Florance to Thwing, Apr. 27, 1932, Florance to Norman Mick, Jan. 26, 1933, both in Shaw MSS; Peterson, *Magazines in the Twentieth Century*, p. 175.

The acquisition of *World's Work* in 1932 marked another futile attempt to arrest the *Review*'s slide. It too had financial problems, its publishers, Shaw remarked, bringing it "voluntarily into my office [where it] gently expired in my son's arms."[14] The Shaws could have it, provided they assumed the liability of its subscription list. They had no intention of incorporating any of *World's Work*'s features into the *Review*, but the chance to eliminate a rival, albeit an old and valued one, and at the same time to increase the circulation of the *Review* seemed too good to reject. Still their decision to accept the offer was a gamble, for it confronted them with a dilemma inherent in the modern periodical industry. One way to increased advertising was through increased circulation, but if the depression continued, a weary old publication like the *Review of Reviews* would be unlikely to attract enough new advertising dollars to pay for the greater costs of production and distribution that more subscribers meant.[15]

Conditions generally remained bleak, but five years later in a stratagem plotted by Albert Shaw, Jr., who felt that they had "to go weekly" to survive in a field where *Time* (with *Newsweek* now imitating it) was establishing the pace, the *Review of Reviews* acquired its other venerable rival, the *Literary Digest*. In terms of circulation the latter still seemed reasonably healthy with more than half a million customers per issue, but its readership had begun falling several years beforehand, while in percentages its decline in advertising revenue had been even more precipitous than the *Review*'s. Its notoriously inept electoral poll in 1936 merely confirmed a slide that was already well underway; it too had fallen victim to its own traditions.[16]

Shaw, who was almost eighty at the time, and no longer able

14 Shaw to Daniel Willard, Nov. 29, 1932, Shaw MSS.

15 Florance to Simonds, July 25, 1932, *Review of Reviews* to E. E. Free, July 28, 1932, Shaw to Charles L. Pack, Aug. 11, 1932, Charles Brodek to Albert Shaw, Jr., Dec. 29, 1935, all in Shaw MSS; interview with Albert Shaw, Jr., Dec. 29, 1969; Peterson, *Magazines in the Twentieth Century*, p. 77.

16 Magazine Publishers Association to author, Mar. 3, 1969; Albert Shaw, Jr., to author, Mar. 18, 1969; *Time*, XXIX (June 28, 1937), 40; Albert Shaw, Jr., to Shaw, Feb. 12, 1937, Shaw MSS.

to put in more than an occasional appearance at his Manhattan office, was dubious about the merger but let his son and the younger editors put it through since the others felt so strongly about it. Although Shaw was listed as editor of the resulting hybrid—the *Digest,* the primary responsibility for it rested with Albert Shaw, Jr., and managing editors Howard Florance and David Page. Shaw's younger son, Roger, who for several years had analyzed international affairs for the *Review,* was named foreign editor. Shaw insisted that the spirit of the *Digest* was that of the *Review.* The casual reader would have been more impressed by its resemblance to the *Literary Digest,* for it retained the latter's weekly publishing schedule and much of its departmentalization. From the *Review* it borrowed Shaw's editorial column, now just one or two pages long, and a section on periodicals.[17]

The new arrangement never had an opportunity to succeed. Soon after the merger had been agreed upon Shaw came down with a case of pneumonia that made it increasingly difficult for him to continue his editorial writing. Then came the crushing blow—the cancellation of automobile advertising. The bedridden Shaw had ample time to consider what action to take and on consultation with his sons decided to quit the periodical business. With his own losses having mounted to over $750,000 in the preceding decade, he thought it best not to test Albert Shaw Jr.'s calculation that it would take an additional $1,000,000 to put the magazine on a solid footing. At the end of October 1937 he thus gave the *Digest* to Page and some other young editors on the staff who shortly reclaimed for it the name of *Literary Digest* in a futile effort to save a distinguished publication. *Time,* fittingly, wound up purchasing the rights to the title.[18]

17 Shaw to Albert Shaw, Jr., Apr. 5, 1937, Shaw to Albert Beveridge, Jr., June 22, 1937, Shaw to Nellie Hall, Nov. 15, 1937, all in Shaw MSS; Albert Shaw, Jr., to author, Mar. 18, 1969.

18 For legal reasons the transfer of the *Digest* to Page and his associates took the form of a business transaction in which Shaw sold his interest in the magazine for the token sum of $1.00. Roger Shaw remained with the *Digest* as foreign editor. Albert Shaw, Jr., to author, Mar. 18, 1969; Shaw to Hall, Nov. 15, 1937, Shaw to Will Noyes, Feb. 2, 1938, both in Shaw MSS; Peterson,

Although a combination of circumstances operative in the periodical industry as a whole was accountable for the *Review*'s demise, Shaw's reluctance to change must bear considerable responsibility for it. Symptoms of the periodical's illness had become evident by the early 1920s, and while one can readily appreciate his feelings on the subject, the fact is that he postponed treatment of them for almost a decade. The modifications that were finally made in 1929 improved the magazine's appearance, but that was about all. The depression hurt by cutting still more into the already dwindling sales and by virtually wiping out advertising. The depression need not have been fatal, however. For instance, in its own youth, when it had had the reputation of an imaginative and upcoming publication, the *Review* had been able to weather the hard times of the 1890s. And to use a more pertinent example, some magazines—notably *Time*—gained in both circulation and advertising during the 1930s. The responsibility, therefore, goes back to management, to Albert Shaw especially. Even though his active role in it began diminishing after he reached his seventies, new policy was not implemented without his approbation. The knowledge that the *Review* was his "baby" was sufficient to stifle initiative. When the original formula proved wanting, and when the Shaws could not or would not devise any fundamentally new approach, or vest an imaginative outsider with authority to inaugurate meaningful change as Albert Shaw, Jr., once suggested, the *Review* acquired the reputation of a loser. All that was left was merger, and as one irreverent commentator put it, "the *Review of Reviews* and the tottering *Literary Digest* staggered into each other's arms and over the brink."[19]

Once the painful but compelling decision had been made to leave the enterprise whose destiny he had guided for almost half a century, Albert Shaw proclaimed, perhaps too insistently,

---

Magazines in the Twentieth Century, p. 152; Robert T. Elson, *Time Inc.: The Intimate History of a Publishing Enterprise, 1923-1941* (New York: Atheneum, 1968), pp. 5, 153-55, 340.

[19] Quoted in Mott, *American Magazines*, IV, 664.

that he looked forward to retirement as a sabbatical that would allow him to proceed with several long-deferred writing projects. But the intended sabbatical had to be postponed, for various problems, including the debilitating aftermath of his illness and an annoying law suit intervened, making the first months of his retirement into what Shaw himself called a "nightmare."[20]

Undoubtedly Shaw's greatest source of consolation during this bleak period and through the remainder of his life was his second wife, the former Virginia McCall, whom he married in 1933, not quite two years after the death through heart failure of Bessie Bacon Shaw, his wife for thirty-eight years. Previously employed as her future husband's secretary, the new Mrs. Shaw was only twenty-two at the time of her marriage but a mature and cultured woman. She was devoted to her husband and fitted harmoniously into his life. Throughout their marriage their circumstances were comfortable. Although he had lost much of his fortune on his business and in the depressed stock market of the 1930s, Shaw retained a substantial portfolio of securities, which were handled for him by his elder son. The income from them, supplemented by profits from the farm, if any, and from a newly established realty firm which he owned jointly with his sons, enabled Shaw to maintain his residence in Hastings, to summer as usual in the Adirondacks, to winter in Florida, and even to make a final trip to Europe on the eve of World War II.[21]

It took a good two years for Shaw to recover his strength and cheerfulness and to feel like making any sustained effort to write. But once he did so, he began work in earnest. He had numerous projects in mind, and, although he had started some of them while still active professionally, they added up

[20] Shaw to George Gray Barnard, Dec. 10, 1936, Shaw to Hall, Nov. 15, 1937, Shaw to Brodek, Oct. 5, 1939, all in Shaw MSS.

[21] *New York Times*, May 5, 1933; Richard T. Ely to Shaw, May 5, 1933, Shaw to Albert Beveridge, Jr., June 22, 1937, Shaw to Albert Shaw, Jr., Apr. 5, 1937, Mar. 30, May 8, 1939, Albert Shaw, Jr., to Shaw, Aug. 31, 1939, Feb. 15, 1943, Shaw to Hamilton Holt, Nov. 11, 1939, Virginia Shaw to Shaw, Oct. 19, 1945, all in Shaw MSS; interview with Albert Shaw, Jr., Sept. 3, 1964.

to a good deal of work. The subjects were varied: a history of Ireland, biographies of Wilson and T. R., memoirs of his youth, an account of American foreign policy. Shaw was still able to express himself felicitously, but the projects, only the last of which was published, were burdened with numerous personal asides and large amounts of extraneous material. The biographies remained fragments, and so the result of Shaw's efforts was disappointing.[22]

The one manuscript of the group to be published, *International Bearings of American Policy,* was written during World War II and, at Shaw's request, published by the Johns Hopkins Press. Its publication by this particular press was fitting, for it was at the Johns Hopkins some sixty years before that Shaw had first looked into the subject of internationalism. And the Baltimore institution had long been host to the now prestigious Albert Shaw Lectures on Diplomatic History, a series of visiting lectureships endowed by Shaw at the suggestion of Herbert Baxter Adams.[23]

Studded with Shaw's recollections and with quotations from his earlier writings, *International Bearings* was episodic in structure and treated many topics in a benign manner: imperialism (Shaw dissented from Julius Pratt's description of him as one of "the expansionists of 1898"), the diplomacy of the first world war, the League of Nations, the outlook for the postwar world. Shaw adhered to his previous judgments in some instances but also tried to refurbish Wilson's reputation as a diplomatist and to reassert his own internationalism which had flagged during the 1930s. Proud of his association with Wilson, Shaw made no attempt to be analytical but contented himself with indicating how America's quintessential ideals, as expounded by Wilson, still offered the world the best hope

22 Shaw to Lyman Powell, July 10, 1935, Shaw to Owen Lattimore, Dec. 23, 1938, Shaw to John C. French, July 4, 1943, Shaw to John Sibley, July 8, 1943, all in Shaw MSS. Citations for those manuscripts that proved useful in this study have been given in the notes to chapters one and seven.

23 Albert Shaw, *International Bearings of American Policy* (Baltimore: Johns Hopkins Press, 1943). Shaw offered to reimburse the publisher for any unmet expenses. Shaw to H. B. Adams, Jan. 5, 21, 1899, Shaw to Isaiah Bowman, Dec. 30, 1942, July 19, 1943, all in Shaw MSS.

for achieving lasting peace and security. Once again he championed the League of Nations, or at least a rejuvenated version
of it, and going beyond the position he had assumed in 1919
offered a somewhat visionary plan for creating a new international agency that would preclude the renewal of naval rivalries
and would keep the seas free for use by the commerce of all
nations.[24]

The book's reception was mixed. Sales were slow, but, save
for one critic who tellingly chided that it could have been
written in 1910—1920 at the latest, the reviewers were gentle.
Shaw took encouragement from their amiability to sound out
its publishers about preparing a second edition. If advertised
properly, he said, it was bound to sell well; at the least many
copies would be purchased by his numerous fans who had
faithfully followed his editorials and were still anxious to share
his opinion of events.[25]

Although nothing seems to have come from Shaw's query,
he remained optimistic about his writing. To the very end
of his life, relates Albert Shaw, Jr., he was talking of new
projects. But death came to Shaw before any of them could
materialize. On June 25, 1947, less than a month short of his
ninetieth birthday, he passed away in a New York City hospital
and was interred two days later in the Sleepy Hollow Cemetery
in North Tarrytown, New York.[26] Appropriately, his final
resting place was near the city where he had made his reputation but in the countryside where he felt more at home.

Shaw was born before the Civil War and lived long enough
to feel apprehension about the emerging cold war.[27] During his

[24] Shaw, *International Bearings of American Policy*, pp. 5-8, 57-75, 390-91, 401,
420, 431, 452, 464; Shaw to Sibley, July 8, 1943, Shaw MSS.
[25] For the favorable reviews see: *New York Times*, Sept. 24, 1944; Frank
Maloy Anderson, review of *International Bearings, American Historical Review*,
XLIX (July 1944), 744-45; William Starr Myers, review of *International Bearings*,
American Political Science Review, XXXVIII (July 1944), 557-58; the critical
review appeared in the (London) *Times Literary Supplement*, June 3, 1944;
Johns Hopkins Press to Shaw, July 9, 1945, Shaw to C. W. Dittus, July 13,
1945, both in Shaw MSS.
[26] Interview with Albert Shaw, Jr., Sept. 3, 1964; *New York Times*, June 26,
28, 1947.
[27] Shaw to John Kingsbury, Sept. 13, 1946, Shaw MSS.

lifetime the United States had changed from a predominantly rural nation to an overwhelmingly urban nation. Shaw's
own career illustrated in microcosm the process of transition
that had taken place: starting in journalism in bucolic Grinnell, he moved first to Minneapolis, a bustling regional center,
and finally to New York City, the hub of events as Herbert
Baxter Adams had counseled him over half a century before.
Once established in New York he became a self-made million-
aire and an editor of national and even international reputation.

The magnitude and rapidity of change in the five decades
that followed the Civil War, accompanied as it was by agrarian
upheaval, industrial strife, and political and moral corruption
in the cities, made Shaw uneasy, but throughout this period he
retained his faith in the ultimate triumph of righteous progress.
In it he was sustained by his belief in the precepts of Christianity and in principled Republicanism, and he was guided by
his scholar's certainty that the techniques of research would
enable man to diagnose society's various ailments and to pre-
scribe proper remedies for them.[28] Above all his strong sense
of nationalism, shaped during his youth and young manhood
in the Midwest at a time when vigorous patriotism was in the
air, taught him that America's fundamental institutions were
sound and should be preserved.

The thesis of Shaw's *Political Problems of American Development* underscores his concern with the national well-being:
"the struggle of the American people to realize national unity
upon the basis of a homogeneous and well-conditioned democracy."[29] Certain words and phrases in it say much about
Shaw. *Struggle* divulges his notion that social difficulties could
be overcome; *national unity* tells of his insistence that labor
unions and trusts be subordinated to the national interest as
the South had been; *homogeneous* betrays his veneration of
Anglo-Saxon mores and his relegation of colored people at home
and abroad to an inferior status; *well-conditioned democracy*

---

[28] Shaw to Thwing, May 10, 1937, Shaw MSS.
[29] Shaw, *Political Problems*, p. v.

shows his commitment to political reform. "The state, then, is our highest form of corporate life," he later explained:

It authorizes and regulates other forms of association, and is, in short, the corporation of corporations—the clearinghouse of all normal forms of activity. It sanctions and regulates the most important forms of private relationship, namely, those of the family. It defines and protects personal liberty in its various forms. It supports the institution of private property, limiting it according to the demands of the social welfare. It makes rules under which it administers justice. It provides for its own perpetuation through the training of the young, the encouragement of agriculture and industry, the establishment of wholesome conditions, whether physical or moral. It takes care that there shall continue to be high standards of national life and character. It ministers directly to the advancement of science and art, and it fosters the exercise of public spirit, philanthropy, private thrift and industry, and those virtues without the existence of which society decays and the state itself must disintegrate.[30]

This infatuation with the health of the nation shaped Shaw's outlook on reform. Aloof during most of his adult life from meaningful contact with the disadvantaged, as he aged he seems to have lost something of the warm concern for human beings that was most obvious in his thinking at the time he was involved in municipal reform. Even then he had relatively little direct knowledge of the poor and foreign-born and could be quite callous in his attitude toward them. As his interest in urban affairs waned, he took an increased concern in the poor of the South but the annual junket he made to that region could only have provided him with an artificial glimpse of human deprivation. Increasingly he regarded reform more as a way of maintaining the well-being of the nation than that of individuals. He essentially wished to preserve the values of rural and small-town America in an urban-industrial setting, yet the fact remains that during his progressive years he was able to accommodate change. He accepted the inevitability of

30 Ibid., pp. 13-14.

big business, prophesied the continued growth of cities, fore-told the replacement of independent entrepreneurs by the managerial class, and argued that government should function as an instrument of social management.

His commitment to reform, however, culminated in 1912. Although he did approve of Wilson's domestic achievements, Shaw's nationalism led him to disagree with Wilson's major foreign policy decisions and he quickly deserted the Progressive party to rejoin the GOP. It became apparent to Shaw that by 1920 industry was approximating his notions of order, efficiency, and public-spiritedness far more than either government or the unions. Accordingly he became a partisan of big business and a critic of organized labor and of the federal bureaucracy. And because the New Deal, displaying many of Tammany's familiar excesses on a nationwide scale, appeared to be assaulting the ideals and the heritage he cherished, he ended his career feeling revulsion for the direction in which society was moving and dismay at the existence of the regulatory state he had once defended.

Even before he abandoned the path of reform during World War I, Shaw had revealed himself to be safely orthodox on many of the issues that had been debated during the previous two decades: on the gold standard, the income tax, and to a lesser extent the protective tariff. Does this mean that he was inhibited in his public views by his dependence on the patronage of others? On readers and especially advertisers, as even Lincoln Steffens discovered when he acquired proprietorship in a periodical?[31] Or did his growing wealth and prestigious social connections have something to do with the views he held and the way he expressed them? After all his career as a reformer terminated about the time he made his first million.

The answer to these questions must take into account two things. First, it would be unreasonable to think that his rising professional and social status, if not the number of dollars he had accumulated at any given moment, had nothing to do with his outlook on things. Certainly his association with college

31 Steffens, *Autobiography*, pp. 575-76.

presidents, bankers, board chairmen and others of a similarly established position placed him in conservative surroundings. But to rely on answers such as these is to overlook what seems to be the more critical factor of his psychological and intellectual orientation. The evidence shows that Shaw strongly believed in the virtues of moderation. He disdained muckraking, Stead's jarring approach to reform, and the controversial Iowa College professor George D. Herron, an ardent social gospeler of the 1890s whom he dismissed as an "agitator."[32] Or recall how timidly he reacted to the reprimands of Chambers and Ford during World War I. In his own writings—even in the 1880s and 90s when he was doing his most original work—he consistently accented the moderate and traditional aspects of the subjects he discussed. Some of this caution might have been due to concern for his own reputation, but the impression remains that he simply felt circumspection was a virtue in itself. Moreover the antipathy he displayed was directed not toward capitalism but toward its excesses. All the same his views did seem sufficiently controversial in the context of the times for his detractors to charge him with radicalism.

The story of Shaw's internationalism, like that of his progressivism, takes several sharp turns. He had a long-standing faith in the need for an association of nations but at the same time suspected the motives of the countries without whose support it could have no meaningful existence. He championed Wilson's League throughout 1919 only to reverse himself on it the following year. Overcome by disillusionment in the 1930s, he flirted with isolationism in his determination that the United States should remain out of the impending war. The examples are several. He finally repudiated the American presence in the Philippines, not because the policy had been immoral to begin with, but because he now believed Great Britain had duped us into pursuing a course of involvement in the Far East that was solely to her advantage. He supported the neutrality measures. And though the evidence here is only tentative, he probably opposed the various policies designed

---

[32] Shaw to George A. Gates, Dec. 31, 1894, Shaw MSS.

to assist the Allies that the United States pursued between September 1939 and December 1941. He seems to have feared that they would prolong what would otherwise be a short war.[33]

After the attack on Pearl Harbor, Shaw accepted the war as his country's war but misjudged it, as he had World War I, by feeling that it could be won without a significant commitment of American ground combat forces. Similarly he unrealistically hoped politics could be set aside in 1944 to allow a national unity ticket—headed by Cordell Hull, or Georgia's Senator Walter George, or by J. William Fulbright of Arkansas—to run uncontested for the presidency.[34] Only when he renewed his endorsement of a world association in the 1940s did he return to his own best ideals of internationalism.

A reformer when he was an imperialist and a reactionary at the same time he was antiimperialistic, a sturdy individualist who deplored the materialist excesses of individualism, a businessman who criticized big business when he was successful and lauded it while he was failing. These are some of the dualities that abound in Shaw's behavior and thought. Had he not outlived most of his friends from public life by twenty or more years, his own life would have seemed more consistent. But then it would not illustrate the complexities of progressivism as well as it does or reveal the tenacity with which he clung to the concept of the national welfare and the other ideals he had formed in his youth and early adulthood. This inner steadfastness furnishes the key to resolving at least some of his inconsistencies: that the times had changed more than had Albert Shaw who remained a self-appointed—and disappointed—keeper of the American creed.

[33] *Review of Reviews*, XCIII (Mar. 1936), 28, and (May 1936), 19, XCV (Mar. 1937), 17; Shaw, "Our Own Business," *Digest*, I (Oct. 2, 1937), 12-13; Shaw to Brodek, Oct. 28, 1939, Shaw MSS.

[34] Shaw to Jack McCall, Dec. 19, 1941, Shaw to Sibley, Nov. 3, 1944, both in Shaw MSS; interview with Albert Shaw, Jr., Sept. 3, 1964.

Appendix

Circulation Data for the *Review of Reviews**

Year of Ayer	Data	Year of Ayer	Data
1891	none given	1915	175,000
1892	60,000	1916	196,000
1893	(one vol.) 88,000	1917	223,162
1894		1918	242,305
1895	90,000	1919	219,419
1896	90,833	1920	207,786
1897	90,833	1921	172,552
1898	90,833	1922	223,870
1899	106,000	1923	205,263
1900	127,375	1924	150,795
1901	150,000	1925	195,556
1902	178,200	1926	171,197
1903	178,200	1927	164,371
1904	178,200	1928	160,669
1905	178,200	1929	170,037
1906	178,200	1930	178,012
1907	204,625	1931	160,005
1908	204,625	1932	167,265
1909	200,000	1933	none given
1910	200,000	1934	130,016
1911	200,000	1935	122,845
1912	200,000	1936	124,464
1913	175,000	1937	138,587
1914	175,000		

* The statistics are from *N. W. Ayer & Son's American Newspaper Annual* and its successor publications. Beginning with the 1917 issue the figures for the *Review* were those sworn to the Audit Bureau of Circulations. From 1897 on, the date of issue of the Ayer volumes lagged one year behind the date of the statistics. Thus, for instance, the figures given in the 1900 volume of the *American Newspaper Annual* represented the *Review*'s average monthly circulation for the preceding year, 1899. These figures were secured by averaging the total sales for

several months. Each ABC report was founded on a computation of circulation during a period of at least three months. Although the statistics are not precise, the trend they indicate seems to be reliable. Ayer's 1938 issue showed the 1937 circulation of the *Digest*, headed by David P. Page who had succeeded Albert Shaw as editor prior to its folding, as 464,030. On the surface of it, this is substantial—except that three years earlier the circulation of its predecessor, the *Literary Digest*, had been over one million weekly, and in 1931 a million and a half.

Bibliography

Rather than list the many works that were of use in the preparation of this biography, I shall simply refer the reader to the notes where I have cited the most helpful secondary materials. I shall use the following pages to describe the organization of the Shaw Manuscripts, to indicate the other manuscript collections that were consulted, and to list chronologically the substantial corpus of Shaw's own writings. I have omitted from this list all Shaw's editorials, thousands in number if each were to be individually mentioned, and have undoubtedly overlooked some miscellaneous publications as well; but otherwise every effort has been made to make the list as complete as possible.

A. *Manuscripts*

Since the Papers of Albert Shaw at the New York Public Library are voluminous and since they constitute the most important body of sources for this study, a word about their organization seems in order. Despite the bulk of the Shaw collection, they are not overly difficult to use due to a detailed catalogue and a sensible arrangement. The copies of the principal letters Shaw sent—together with those which his assistants wrote to him when he was away from the office—date from 1891 until 1934, and are filed chronologically in bound letterpress copy books, each of which is indexed. Most incoming letters are kept in one of two places: the alphabetically arranged Personalities and Groups file which contains Shaw's correspondence with his Ohio and Grinnell friends, and with such men as Richard T. Ely, Newton Hawley, Jesse Macy, and others to whom Shaw was fairly close or who were of some prominence; and the General Correspondence, a collection of papers filed by year and broken down by the alphabet according to the surname of the sender. Some letters sent by Shaw are also included in the Personalities and Groups segment. Special groupings of his extensive correspondence with Albert Beveridge, Theodore Roosevelt, and William T. Stead are available. Other segments of the Shaw Papers are mainly topical and easy to spot: the Diaries, Farm, Financial, General Education Board, manuscripts of speeches and articles, Scrapbooks, the unpublished works from Shaw's last years, and so on.

Relatively little systematic material is available on the years before 1891 and on the operation and finances of the *Review of Reviews*. The period before 1891 is covered by letters in the Personalities and Groups file and can be supplemented with a collection of letters between Albert Shaw and his mother in the possession of Albert Shaw, Jr. Financial data for the *Review* are available until 1904 only. Manuscripts used collaterally are:

Adams, Herbert Baxter. MSS, Johns Hopkins University Library.
Beveridge, Albert J. MSS, Library of Congress.
Bryce, James. MSS, Bodleian Library, Oxford University.
Butler, Nicholas Murray. MSS, Low Library, Columbia University.
Carnegie, Andrew. MSS, Library of Congress.
Ely, Richard T. MSS, State Historical Society of Wisconsin.
Folwell, William Watts. MSS, Minnesota Historical Society.
Gilman, Daniel Coit. MSS, Johns Hopkins University Library.
Jameson, John Franklin. MSS, Library of Congress.
Ogden, Robert Curtis. MSS, Library of Congress.
Press Club of Minneapolis. Minutes, 1882-92, Minneapolis Public Library.
Roosevelt, Theodore. MSS, Library of Congress.
Seminary of Historical and Political Science, The. Minutes, 1879-92, Johns Hopkins University Library.
Southern Education Board. MSS, Southern Historical Collection, University of North Carolina Library.
Taft, William Howard. MSS, Library of Congress.
Thwing, Charles F. MSS, Case Western Reserve University Library.
Wilson, Woodrow. MSS, Library of Congress.

B. *Writings of Albert Shaw Exclusive of Editorials*

1. Letters from Europe to the *Minneapolis Tribune* in chronological order, 1888-1889.

"The Lights in London Town," July 1, 1888; "Take a Wise Man's Advice," July 8; "Two Styles of Government," July 15; "An English Election Study," July 22; "A Liberal Leader," July 29; "A Glance at Ireland," August 5; "Irish Blue Coats," August 12; "Enjoy Being Robbed," September 2; "Tariff in America," September 16; "All About Ulster," September 23; "Survived Ridicule," September 30; "Is Well Governed," October 21; "Can All Keep Clean," October 28; "More of Glasgow," November 4; "Some Scotch Towns," November 11; "English Elections," November 25; "The Property Vote," December 2; "Dr. Shaw in London," December 9; "A Peoples' Palace," December 16; "Dr. Shaw in Paris," January 6, 1889; "Christmas in Paris," January 20; "Painting the Town," January 27; "After the Election," February 24; "Peeps at Paris Life," March 4; "Germany of Today," April 1; "A View of Vienna," April 14.

2.   Articles, Books, Published Speeches, and Reviews, 1882-1947.

"Local Government in America," *Fortnightly Review,* n.s. XXXII (October 1882), 485-95.

"Local Government in Illinois," *Johns Hopkins University Studies in Historical and Political Science,* ser. I, no. 3, Baltimore: Johns Hopkins University, 1883.

"The Growth of Internationalism," *International Review,* XIV (April 1883), 267-83.

Icaria: A Chapter in the History of Communism. New York & London: G. P. Putnam's Sons, 1884.

"Our Working Constitution" (review), *Dial,* V (March 1885), 291-94.

"New Studies in Political and Social Science" (review), *Dial,* VI (July 1885), 72-74.

"Recent Economic Works" (review), *Dial,* VI (December 1885), 210-13.

"The Economics of Distribution" (review), *Dial,* VII (June 1886), 37-40.

"Seven Books for Citizens" (review), *Dial,* VII (November 1886), 149-52.

"Cooperation in the Northwest," *Johns Hopkins University Studies in Historical and Political Science,* ser. VI, nos. 4-6. Baltimore: N. Murray, 1888.

Cooperation in a Western City, Publications of the American Economic Association. Baltimore: John Murphy & Company, 1886.

"The American State and the American Man," *Contemporary Review*, LI (May 1887), 695-712.

"Political and Economic Literature from the Universities" (review), *Dial*, VIII (July 1887), 61-64.

"Flour-Making in the United States," *Chautauquan*, VIII (October 1887), 16-20.

"The Scandinavians in the United States," *Chautauquan*, VIII (December 1887), 169-72.

"Life in the Amana Colony," *Chautauquan*, VIII (February 1888), 300-302.

"Social Remedies" (review), *Dial*, VIII (February 1888), 242-45.

"The American Tariff," *Contemporary Review*, LIV (November 1888), 683-94.

"In Praise of British Municipalities—An Interview with an American Observer," *Pall Mall Gazette*, November 24, 27, 1888.

The National Revenues: A Collection of Papers by American Economists. Chicago: A. C. McClurg & Company, 1888. [Editor.]

"Municipal Socialism in Scotland," *Juridical Review*, I (January 1889), 33-53.

"Americanizing the French Republic," *Pall Mall Gazette*, February 14, 1889.

"European Town Life," *Chautauquan*, IX (June 1889), 519-22.

"Municipal Government in Great Britain," *Political Science Quarterly*, IV (June 1889), 197-229.

"The American State Legislatures," *Contemporary Review*, LVI (October 1889), 555-73.

"The French Constitution," *Chautauquan*, n.s. I (November 1889), 185-89.

"Glasgow: A Municipal Study," *Century Magazine*, n.s. XVII (March 1890), 721-36.

"Belgium and the Belgians," *Atlantic Monthly*, LXV (April 1890), 481-96.

"Rising Bulgaria," *Chautauquan*, n.s. II (April 1890), 37-42.

"The Servian Kingdom," *Chautauquan*, n.s. II (May 1890), 161-65.

"The Greeks of To-day," *Chautauquan*, n.s. II (June 1890), 303-7.

"London Polytechnics and People's Palaces," *Century Magazine*, n.s. XVIII (June 1890), 162-82.

"How London Is Governed," *Century Magazine*, n.s. XIX (November 1890), 132-47.

"Budapest: The Minneapolis of Europe," *Northwestern Miller,* XXX (holiday number, Christmas, 1890), 5-7.

"Constantinople and the Waning Turks," *Chautauquan,* n.s. IV (May 1891), 157-59.

"Hungary's Progress and Position," *Chautauquan,* n.s. IV (June 1891), 292-95.

"Paris, The Typical Modern City," *Century Magazine,* n.s. XX (July 1891), 449-66.

"Parochial versus Public Schools: A Significant Incident," *Christian Union,* XLIV (September 1891), 485-86.

"The Opportunity for a New Magazine," *Westward Ho!* I (November 1891), 3-9.

"A Model Working-Girls' Club," *Scribner's Magazine,* XI (February 1892), 169-77.

"A Year of General Booth's Work," *Forum,* XII (February 1892), 762-71.

"Budapest. The Rise of a New Metropolis," *Century Magazine,* n.s. XXII (June 1892), 163-79.

"An American View of Home Rule and Federation," *Contemporary Review,* LXII (September 1892), 305-18.

"The Great Northwest," in Hamilton Mabie and Marshall Bright, eds., *The Memorial Story of America.* Philadelphia: John C. Winston Company, 1892.

"Hamburg's New Sanitary Impulse," *Atlantic Monthly,* LXXIII (June 1894), 787-96.

"The Government of German Cities," *Century Magazine,* n.s. XXVI (June 1894), 296-305.

"What German Cities Do for Their Citizens. A Study of Municipal House-Keeping," *Century Magazine,* n.s. XXVI (July 1894), 380-88.

"The Dispensary System in South Carolina," *Outlook,* LII (July 13, 1895), 75.

Municipal Government in Continental Europe. New York: Century Company, 1895.

Municipal Government in Great Britain. New York: Century Company, 1895.

"The Higher Life of New York City," *Outlook,* LIII (January 25, 1896), 132-39.

"Empire-Building in South Africa," *Cosmopolitan,* XX (March 1896), 472-80.

"Notes on City Government in St. Louis," *Century Magazine,* n.s. XXX (June 1896), 253-64.

"The Public Schools and the Catholic Schools in New York," *Catholic World* (reprinted from the *New York Journal*), LXIV (October 1896), 138-39.

"The Essential Structure of the Greater New York Charter," *Independent,* XLIX (March 11, 1897), 303-4.

"The History of the Last Quarter-Century in the United States, 1870-1895" (review), *American Historical Review,* II (April 1897), 561-65.

"Advantages of Municipal Ownership," *Independent,* XLIX (May 6, 1897), 569-70.

"The Municipal Problem and Greater New York," *Atlantic Monthly,* LXXIX (June 1897), 733-48.

"Is England's Trade at Last Passing from Her," *New York Herald,* December 26, 1897.

"The Story of Gladstone's Life" (review), *Book Reviews,* V (December 1897), 145-49.

Introduction to Baron Pierre de Coubertin, *The Evolution of France Under the Third Republic.* New York: Thomas Y. Crowell & Company, 1897.

"The United States," in Frederick Whelen, ed., *Politics in 1896.* London: Grant Richards, 1897.

"Co-operation and the Individual Man," *Savings and Loan Review,* XVIII (September 1898), 21-23.

"The Trans-Mississippians and Their Fair at Omaha," *Century Magazine,* n.s. XXXIV (October 1898), 836-52.

"De Tocqueville: The New Edition of His 'Democracy in America'" (review), *New York Times, Saturday Supplement,* December 10, 1898.

"The City in the United States. The Proper Scope of Its Activities," in Clinton Rogers Woodruff, ed., *Proceedings of the Indianapolis Conference for Good City Government and Fourth Annual Meeting of the National Municipal League . . . 1898.* Philadelphia: National Municipal League, 1898.

"Businesslike Information About Cuba" (review), *Book Buyer,* XVII (January 1899), 584-88.

Introduction to "Governments of the World To-Day," *Chicago Record,* February 1, 1899.

"Open Letter—Concerning Corn and the Trans-Mississippi Farmer,"
  Century Magazine, n.s. XXXV (February 1899), 635-36.
Introduction to Lyman Pierson Powell, ed., *Historic Towns of the
  Middle States.* New York: G. P. Putnam's Sons, 1899.
Life of Colonel George E. Waring. New York: Patriotic League,
  1899.
"Education in America" (review), *Outlook,* LXV (August 4, 1900),
  836-39.
"The Campaign Issues: From a Republican Standpoint," *Outlook,*
  LXVI (October 13, 20, 1900), 397-403, 441-49.
"The American Presidential Election," *Contemporary Review,*
  LXXVIII (November 1900), 609-32.
"The University's True Assets," in *The Hullabaloo.* Baltimore:
  Published by the Class of 1900, Johns Hopkins University, 1900.
"The Real Value of the Exposition," *Cosmopolitan,* XXXI (Sep-
  tember 1901), 463-72.
"The New President of the United States," *Contemporary Review,*
  LXXX (November 1901), 609-33.
"The Outlook for the Average Man, in a Non-Competitive Society,"
  University Record of University of Chicago, VI (April 1902),
  369-83.
"Speech of Albert Shaw, Ph.D.," *Columbia University Quarterly,*
  IV (Installation Supplement, June 1902), 78-84.
"Education Means Everything," in *Proceedings of the Fifth Con-
  ference for Education in the South . . . 1902.* Knoxville:
  Published by the Southern Education Board, 1902.
"The President and The Trusts," *Century Magazine,* n.s. XLIII
  (January 1903), 381-87.
"Making A Choice of a Profession: Journalism," *Cosmopolitan,*
  XXXV (June 1903), 155-60.
"The American Presidential Election," *Contemporary Review,*
  LXXXVI (August 1904), 264-80.
The Business Career in Its Public Relations, Barbara Weinstock
  Lectures on the Morals of Trade. San Francisco: Paul Elder
  and Company, 1904.
"Relations of Municipal Administration," in Howard J. Rogers,
  ed., *Congress of Arts and Sciences Universal Exposition, St.
  Louis, 1904.* 8 vols. Boston and New York: Houghton
  Mifflin and Company, 1905-1907. (See vol. VII.)

"Shandon Centennial," *Ohio Archaeological and Historical Quarterly*, XIV (January 1905), 1-11.

"Problems of Our Economic Life," *Vanderbilt University Quarterly*, VI (July 1906), 151-75.

"Our Legacy From a Century of Pioneers," *South Atlantic Quarterly*, V (October 1906), 311-32.

"Presidential Address" (Third Annual Meeting of the American Political Science Association), *American Political Science Review*, I (February 1907), 177-86.

Political Problems of American Development, Columbia University Lectures. New York: Columbia University Press, 1907.

The Outlook for the Average Man. New York: Macmillan Company, 1907.

"The Opportunity of the Publicist in Relation to Efforts for Social Betterment," in Alexander Johnson, ed., *Proceedings of the National Conference of Charities and Correction . . . 1909.* Fort Wayne, Ind.: Press of Fort Wayne Printing Co., n.d.

A Cartoon History of Roosevelt's Career. New York: Review of Reviews Company, 1910.

"Cooperation as a Means of Reducing the Cost of Living," *Annals of the American Academy of Political and Social Science*, XLVIII (July 1913), 225-37.

"Progress and the Academic Spirit," *Johns Hopkins University Circular,* no. 257 (July 1913), 4-19.

"Knowledge in the Guidance of Communities," *University of Cincinnati Record,* IX (October 1913), 3-16.

"Problems of the Constitutional Convention," *Proceedings of the Academy of Political Science in the City of New York,* V (October 1914), 39-53.

"Jefferson's Doctrines under New Tests," in Clark S. Northup, William C. Lane, John C. Schwab, eds., *Representative Phi Beta Kappa Orations.* Boston and New York: Houghton Mifflin Company, 1915.

"Treaty Thraldom and Release," in Lindsay Russell, ed., *America to Japan.* New York: G. P. Putnam's Sons, 1915.

"A Student at Johns Hopkins," in *Elgin Ralston Lovell Gould: A Memorial.* New York: Privately printed, 1916.

"Problems of the Common Defense," *Proceedings of the Academy of Political Science in the City of New York,* VI (July 1916), 5-11.

"The Monroe Doctrine and the Evolution of Democracy," *Proceedings of the Academy of Political Science in the City of New York*, VII (July 1917), 471-78.

"Resident Aliens and Treaty Obligations" (discussion), *Proceedings of the Academy of Political Science in the City of New York*, VII (July 1917), 585-88.

President Wilson's State Papers and Addresses. New York: Review of Reviews Company, 1917. [Editor.]

"The Government as Employer" (discussion), *Proceedings of the Academy of Political Science in the City of New York*, VIII (July 1918), 114-17.

"The Demobilization of Labor in War Industries and in Military Service," *Proceedings of the Academy of Political Science in the City of New York*, VIII (February 1919), 261-68.

"The Larger Commonwealth of a Civilized World," *The League of Nations Magazine*, V (February 1919), 86-89.

"Dr. Van Hise as Economic Statesman," in *Memorial Service in honor of Charles Richard Van Hise at the University of Wisconsin, April 29, 1919*. [Madison]: n.p., 1919.

"Meeting New Tests of Rural and Urban Life," *High School Quarterly*, VIII (July 1920), 237-39.

"Balancing Rural and Urban Development," *World Agriculture*, I (January 1921), 81-82.

"National Economy and New Expenditure," *Proceedings of the Academy of Political Science in the City of New York*, IX (July 1921), 482-85.

"Industrial Relations in Governmental Employment," *Proceedings of the Academy of Political Science in the City of New York*, IX (January 1922), 679-86.

"How Railroads Adapt Themselves to National Conditions," *Proceedings of the Academy of Political Science in the City of New York*, X (July 1922), 97-100.

"Individualism in a New Social Epoch," *Phi Beta Kappa Key*, V (October 1922), 5-27.

"Agricultural Policies," *Proceedings of the Academy of Political Science in the City of New York*, X (January 1924), 539-42.

"Walter Hines Page—Memorial Address," *North Carolina Historical Review*, I (January 1924), 3-25.

The Messages and Papers of Woodrow Wilson. 2 vols. New York: Review of Reviews Corporation, 1924. [Editor.]

Introduction to Harlean James, *Land Planning in the United States for the City, State and Nation*, Land Economics Series. New York: Macmillan Company, 1926.

"The University in the Democratic Era," in *Proceedings of the Semi-Centennial of Vanderbilt, October 15 to 18, 1925*. Nashville: Vanderbilt University, 1925.

"The Philosophical Mind Dominates," *William and Mary College Quarterly*, 2d ser. VI (July 1926), 208-28.

"Scholarship under Tests of Change," *Princeton Alumni Weekly*, XXVI (April 28, May 5, 1926), 757-59, 798-99.

"Better Economic Organization of Agriculture," *Proceedings of the Academy of Political Science in the City of New York*, XII (January 1927), 503-11

Introduction to John Nolen, *New Towns for Old: Achievements in Civic Improvement in Some American Small Towns and Neighborhoods*. Boston: Marshall Jones Company, 1927.

"The Human Element in American Relations," *Annals of the American Academy of Political and Social Science*, CXXXVIII (July 1928), 54-56.

Abraham Lincoln: A Cartoon History. 2 vols. New York: Review of Reviews Corporation, 1929.

"Control of Power," *Proceedings of the Academy of Political Science*, XIV (May 1930), 3-10.

"William Allen White," *Golden Book Magazine*, XI (April 1930), 94.

"This Man Holmes," *Golden Book Magazine*, XII (August 1930), 96-97.

"The Fox-hunting Virginian, George Washington," *Golden Book Magazine*, XIII (February 1931), 34-35.

"Jesse Macy, A Tribute," Introduction to Katherine Macy Noyes, ed., *Jesse Macy: An Autobiography*. Baltimore and Springfield, Ill.: C. C. Thomas, 1933.

"The Versatile William Morris," *Golden Book Magazine*, XX (August 1934), 168-70.

International Bearings of American Policy. Baltimore: Johns Hopkins Press, 1943.

Introduction to Charles S. Macfarland, *Lyman Pierson Powell, Pathfinder in Education and Religion*. New York: Philosophical Library, 1947.

3. Articles in the *Review of Reviews,* 1891-1937.

In the *Review of Reviews* (American edition),
April 1891-June 1897

"Profit-Sharing in the Pillsbury Mills," IV (September 1891), 172-74 (not signed).

"Some Statistical Undertakings at Washington," IV (December 1891), 519-24.

"The 'Polytechnic' and Its Chicago Excursion," V (February 1892), 61-66.

"Municipal Problems of New York and London," V (April 1892), 282-308.

"Conventions and Summer Gatherings of 1892," V (May 1892), 411-24.

"A Greek Play on the Prairies," VI (September 1892), 174-77 (not signed).

"Two Great Americans: George William Curtis and John G. Whittier," VI (October 1892), 280-86 (not signed).

"Physical Culture at Wellesley," VI (December 1892), 545-49.

"American Millionaires and Their Public Gifts," VII (February 1893), 48-60 (not signed).

"Our Fifteen New Forest Reservations," VIII (July 1893), 63-66.

"Leland Stanford: Some Notes on the Career of a Successful Man," VIII (August 1893), 155-68.

"The Gothenburg System of Liquor Traffic," VIII (November 1893), 548-54 (not signed).

"Carter Harrison, of Chicago," VIII (December 1893), 663-66 (not signed).

"Relief for the Unemployed in American Cities," IX (January 1894), 29-37.

"National Budgets—American and European," IX (February 1894), 160-61 (not signed).

"Relief Measures in American Cities," IX (February 1894), 179-91.

"Negro Progress on the Tuskegee Plan," IX (April 1894), 436-43.

"Some Notes on Bermuda and Its Affairs," IX (May 1894), 563-72.

"The Nation's New Library at Washington," IX (June 1894), 674-77.

"The Rescue of Virginia's Historic Shrines," IX (June 1894), 680-81.

"William V. Allen: Populist," X (July 1894), 30-42.

"Toronto as a Municipal Object Lesson," X (August 1894), 165-73.

"The New Hawaiian Constitution," X (September 1894), 284-87.
"The Re-establishment of Olympic Games," X (December 1894), 643-46.
"Mr. Bryce's New Chapters on Current American Questions" (review), XI (January 1895), 60-64.
"The Electric Street Railways of Budapest," XI (March 1895), 287-89 (not signed).
"John Clark Ridpath: A Typical Man of the Ohio Valley and the Old Northwest," XI (March 1895), 294-96 (not signed).
"Our 'Civic Renaissance,'" XI (April 1895), 415-27.
"College Oratory in the West," XI (June 1895), 665-69 (not signed).
"Recent Progress of Italian Cities," XII (November 1895), 553-65.
"South Carolina's New Constitution," XIII (January 1896), 66-71.
"Murat Halstead, Journalist," XIII (April 1896), 439-43.
"Vacation Camps and Boys' Republics," XIII (May 1896), 572-76.
"The Rosewaters and the *Bee,* of Omaha," XIII (June 1896), 709-10 (not signed).
"John Brown in the Adirondacks," XIV (September 1896), 311-17.
"Model Lodging Houses for New York," XV (January 1897), 59-61 (not signed).
"A Plea for the Protection of Useful Men," XV (February 1897), 192-94 (not signed).
"The New Administration at Washington," XV (April 1897), 413-34.

In the *American Monthly Review of Reviews,*
July 1897-July 1907

"Local History and the 'Civic Renaissance' in New York," XVI (October 1897), 446-49 (not signed).
"Some American Novels and Novelists" (review), XVI (December 1897), 753-59.
"The Hispano-American Crisis in Caricature," XVII (April 1898), 412-16 (not signed).
"Baron Pierre de Coubertin," XVII (April 1898), 435-38.
"Bismarck Behind the Scenes, as Shown in Dr. Moritz Busch's 'Secret Pages'" (review), XVIII (October 1898), 483-86.
"The Army and Navy 'Y.M.C.A.,'" XVIII (November 1898), 529-37.
"Col. George E. Waring, Jr.," XVIII (December 1898), 682-85.
"President Faure: A Sketch," XIX (March 1899), 293-98 (not signed).

"Our Delegation to the Hague," XIX (May 1899), 545-57.

"The New San Francisco Charter," XIX (May 1899), 569-75.

"The School City—A Method of Pupil Self-Government," XX (December 1899), 673-86.

"Guy V. Henry—A Knightly American," XX (December 1899), 702-5 (not signed).

"A Professor's Freedom of Speech," XX (December 1899), 713-16 (not signed).

"The Educational Opportunity at Berea," XXI (March 1900), 311-12 (not signed).

" 'Learning By Doing' at Hampton," XXI (April 1900), 417-32.

"Paris and the Exposition of 1900," XXI (June 1900), 679-88.

"A Hundred Years of the District of Columbia," XXII (December 1900), 675-86.

"The Career of Henry Villard," XXIII (January 1901), 59-60.

"The Electors and the Coming Election," XXIII (January 1901), 66-71.

"Abraham Lincoln in Contemporary Caricature," XXII (February 1901), 156-66 (not signed).

"Japanese Immigration," XXIII (February 1901), 207-8 (not signed).

"The Career of William M. Evarts," XXIII (April 1901), 435-40.

"Frederic Harrison in America," XXIII (May 1901), 558-59 (not signed).

"Preserving the Hudson Palisades," XXIV (July 1901), 49-56 (not signed).

"Theodore Roosevelt," XXIV (October 1901), 435-40 (not signed).

"A Successful Farm Colony in the Irrigation Country," XXVI (November 1902), 561-66.

"A Great Citizen of Georgia," XXXIII (February 1906), 174-76.

"What Hampton Means by 'Education,' " XXXIV (September 1906), 305-14.

"McIver of North Carolina," XXXIV (October 1906), 422-23.

In the *American Review of Reviews,*
August 1907-December 1928

"A Great American Editor," XXXIX (February 1909), 169-70.

"Dr. Edward Everett Hale," XL (July 1909), 79-81.

"An Engineer and His Lifework," XL (August 1909), 175-76.

"College Reform—and Football," XL (December 1909), 724-29.

"Woodrow Wilson and the New Jersey Governorship," XLII
(November 1910), 555-62 (not signed).
"A National Lesson from Adams County," XLIII (February 1911),
171-80.
"Robert Lanier, Skilled Craftsman," XLV (May 1912), 552-54 (not
signed).
"William T. Stead," XLV (June 1912), 689-95.
"Roosevelt and the Third Term," XLV (June 1912), 699-704 (not
signed).
"President Wilson's Cabinet," XLVII (April 1913), 423-40.
"The Taking of Vera Cruz and What Followed," XLIX (June 1914),
666-73 (not signed).
"An Ogden Memorial," LII (November 1915), 603-6.
"Our Foremost War Writer," LIII (April 1916), 424-25.
"The War Against Alcohol," LVII (January 1918), 66-67.
"In England and France, At the Climax," LVIII (December 1918),
607-18.
"Theodore Roosevelt," LIX (February 1919), 156-60.
"A Teacher and Leader," LIX (May 1919), 480-82.
"A University's Recognition of Leadership," LX (August 1919),
188-92.
"Beveridge's 'Marshall'" (review), LXI (January 1920), 81-82.
"The Court of Industrial Relations," LXI (March 1920), 294.
"'Justice and the Poor'" (review), LXI (March 1920), 301-2.
"The Public Forum," LXI (May 1920), 521-25.
"Pennsylvania's Plans for School Consolidation," LXII (August
1920), 185-87.
"Porto Ricans as Citizens," LXIII (May 1921), 483-91.
"The Stead Memorial in New York," LXIV (August 1921), 146.
"From New York to Idaho," LXIV (August 1921), 177-82.
"The Tariff-Making Process," LXIV (September 1921), 287-91.
"California's Farm Colonies," LXIV (October 1921), 397-404.
"James Bryce, As We Knew Him in America," LXV (March 1922),
277-84.
"Henry Stead of Australia," LXV (March 1922), 304-5.
"Records of Northwestern Pioneering," LXV (April 1922), 419-24.
"The Farm and Country Movement, in Various Reports" (review),
LXV (May 1922), 559-60.
"Mr. Page and His Letters from London" (review), LXVI (Novem-
ber 1922), 510-12.

hysical Treatment for Mental Disorders," LXVI (December 1922), 625-36.

"Secretary Lane's Letters" (review), LXVI (December 1922), 641-42.

"Mr. Wilson's Records of the Peace Conference" (review), LXVII (January 1923), 81-84.

"The Reminiscences of Oscar S. Straus" (review), LXVII (January 1923), 84-85.

"Nine Eastern Governors and Their Programs," LXVII (February 1923), 163-70.

"Nine Governors of the Middle West," LXVII (March 1923), 275-86.

"George E. Roberts," LXVII (April 1923), 394-400.

"Woodrow Wilson's Leadership," LXIX (March 1924), 260-67.

"Touring in Great Britain," LXX (October 1924), 372-80.

"France Re-Visited," LXX (December 1924), 598-610.

"Martha Berry and Her Patriotic Work," LXXI (June 1925), 593-97.

"William Jennings Bryan," LXXII (September 1925), 259-63.

"How Florida Is Getting On," LXXV (May 1927), 519-28.

"Albert J. Beveridge," LXXV (June 1927), 609-11.

"Walter C. Head: Citizen," LXXVII (March 1928), 276-78 (not signed).

"The Founder of An American Family," LXXVII (April 1928), 379-82 (not signed).

"Highlights in the Presidential Campaign," LXXVIII (November 1928), 491-93 (not signed).

In the *Review of Reviews*
January 1929-August 1932

"Lincoln: 70 Years Ago," LXXXI (February 1930), 64-69.

"Owen D. Young as a Public Servant," LXXXIII (February 1931), 42-45.

"The Report on Prohibition," LXXXIII (March 1931), 42-45.

"The Unsolved Problem of Muscle Shoals," LXXXIII (April 1931), 49-53.

"Research in Law and Justice," LXXXIII (May 1931), 36-43.

"America's Stake in Its Railroads," LXXXIV (July 1931), 42-46.

"The Conference for Better Homes," LXXXIV (December 1931), 41-43.

"Mr. Edison's Views of Life and Work," LXXXV (January 1932), 30-31.

"Will Hays: A Ten-Year Record," LXXXV (March 1932), 30-31.
"Roger Babson Reflects," LXXXV (May 1932), 23-25.
"Mr. Hoover as President," LXXXVI (July 1932), 24-29.

In the *Review of Reviews and World's Work,*
September 1932-December 1934

"Private Leisure and Public Service," LXXXVI (October 1932), 25-26.
"Civic Progress Under Stress of Hard Times," LXXXVI (November 1932), 36-41.
"Highways and Railroads," LXXXVII (February 1933), 39-40.
"Executives in the 'New Deal,' " LXXXVII (April 1933), 23-30.

In the *Review of Reviews,*
January 1935-July 1937

"Business Leadership at Its Best," XCI (June 1935), 29-34, 66.
"Who Shall Control Our Children?" XCII (August 1935), 38-43.
"Virginia Offers an Example," XCII (September 1935), 42-44, 64.
"Planning the New U.S.A.," XCII (October 1935), 36-39, 55.
"Strangling Our Railroads," XCIII (May 1936), 59-65.
"Harvard and the Nation," XCIV (November 1936), 54-58.
"Pan America's Past," XCIV (December 1936), 58-62.
"Congress: How Can the Mechanism Be Improved?" XCV (January 1937), 52-55 (not signed).
"Who Elected Roosevelt?" XCV (February 1937), 44-45.
"If You Go To England," XCV (March 1937), 55-59.
"Politics and the Supreme Court," XCV (May 1937), 34-35.

In the *Digest,*
July 17, 1937-October 23, 1937

"Ever Normal Granary," I (September 18, 1937), 12-13.
"Subsidy for Health," I (September 25, 1937), 12-13.
"Our Own Business," I (October 2, 1937), 12-13.
"Third-Term Reticence," I (October 9, 1937), 12.
"For Control of New York," I (October 16, 1937), 12.
"America's Bill of Rights," I (October 23, 1937), 12-14.

Index

DATE DUE

GAYLORD

PRINTED IN U.S.A.